China's Role in Reducing Carbon Emissions

T0330615

China, a still developing economy comprising a fifth of the world's population, will play a key role in the global movement towards reducing carbon emissions. The aims of the Paris Agreement may stand or fall with China, both for its own contribution and the example it will set the developing world.

China's Role in Reducing Carbon Emissions discusses the prospects for China achieving radical reductions in carbon emissions, within the context of the current economic and political landscape. With a particular focus on technologies such as such as wind power, solar power and electric vehicles, Toke examines how China is transitioning to a state of stable energy consumption via a service-based economy and heavy investment in non-fossil energy sources. The book concludes that China may be set to reduce its carbon emissions by approximately two-thirds by 2050.

This book is a valuable resource for students and scholars of climate change, sustainable development, political science and energy, as well as energy professionals seeking to understand the implications of recent developments in China.

David Toke is Reader in Energy Politics at the University of Aberdeen's Department of Politics and International Relations. He is Co-ordinator of the MSc Programme in Energy Politics and Law.

China's Role in Reducing Carbon Emissions

The Stabilisation of Energy Consumption and the Deployment of Renewable Energy

David Toke

LONDON AND NEW YORK

First published 2017 by Routledge

2 Park Square, Milton Park, Abingdon, Oxfordshire OX14 4RN
711 Third Avenue, New York, NY 10017

Routledge is an imprint of the Taylor & Francis Group, an informa business

First issued in paperback 2018

British Library Cataloguing in Publication Data
A catalogue record for this book is available from the British Library

Library of Congress Cataloging in Publication Data
Names: Toke, David., author.
Title: China's role in reducing carbon emissions : the stabilisation of energy
consumption and the deployment of renewable energy / David Toke.
Description: Abingdon, Oxon ; New York, NY : Routledge, 2017.
Identifiers: LCCN 2016050412 | ISBN 9781138244412 (hb) |
ISBN 9781315276946 (ebook)
Subjects: LCSH: Carbon dioxide mitigation–Government policy–China. |
Renewable energy sources–China. | Energy consumption–China.
Classification: LCC TD885.5.C3 T645 2017 | DDC 363.738/7460951–dc23
LC record available at https://lccn.loc.gov/2016050412

ISBN: 978-1-138-24441-2 (hbk)
ISBN: 978-0-367-03044-5 (pbk)

Typeset in Goudy
by Wearset Ltd, Boldon, Tyne and Wear

Contents

Illustrations

Figures

Tables

Acknowledgements

I wish to acknowledge the help of Lauri Myllyvirta, Greenpeace's Coal and Pollution expert covering China and of Kaare Sandholt, who is a Program Coordinator at the China National Renewable Energy Centre, for pointing me in the direction of some strategic issues. I thank Jingchao Zhang and Ye Jiandong of Tsinghua University for organising a seminar in July 2015 which was very helpful. I thank Christian Ploberger, David Elliott and Jonathon Porritt for giving me some feedback on earlier drafts of parts of the book. I thank the three (anonymous) reviewers commissioned by Routledge for their comments on an earlier draft of this book. I thank my wife, Yvonne, for formatting charts in this book and also for proofreading chapters. I also wish to thank Matt Prescott for some initial suggestions in the early stages of research for the book.

1   Introduction

China has sometimes been cursed by Western environmentalists for its apparently manic charge towards dirty industrialisation. However, a different scenario is also possible – that China might actually make a lot of the running in saving the planet from what seems to many to be the most difficult global problem of our time, that of climate change.

I am not the first to see that this is a possibility. Jonathan Watts, in a book published in 2010, wrote of how Chinese modernisation was leading to a convergence between China and the West in consumption:

> This brings with it a temptation to assume that as in Europe Japan, South Korea and Taiwan, a rise in incomes will inevitably bring an improvement in the environment. Under this optimistic scenario, the world's biggest population is now clambering over the hump of the dirtiest, most wasteful phase of economic development. Once China manages to overcome that obstacle, our species can breathe easy. The heavy lifting will have been done. Other developing nations will be able to follow.[1]

On the other hand Watts warns about the dangers of increasing consumption, something that he fears may derail the optimistic scenario.[2]

I focus on looking at whether China can seriously reduce its energy related problems, specifically its carbon emissions. I look at this through the lens of ecological modernisation. Watts talks of convergence between the West and China, but in theoretical terms this could mean a convergence in the approach to ecological protection via ecological modernisation, a theory which has been used to understand management of ecological problems in Europe.

The theory behind ecological modernisation (EM) is examined in Chapter 2, but a key part of that theory is that economic development can be combined with the task of environmental protection. EM, as far as I am concerned, is a framework for understanding in political terms how ecological protection is occurring. In the instance of climate change, if EM is to work then there will have to be radical reductions in carbon emissions at the same time as continuing economic development.

My use of EM here, essentially, involves first, analysing some core features of EM as has been applied to Europe. I will then analyse the extent to which these are present in the case of China and reduction of carbon emissions. I can then make some comments about how Chinese policy might move forward from here to increase the possibilities for radical reductions in carbon emissions. I argue that reduction or stabilisation in at least some types of pollution in Europe is partly associated with relatively modest rates of economic growth and a shift from industrial to service industries, the latter of which have lower energy intensities. In fact, China is showing signs of moving also in this direction, and thus achieving this core condition of EM. It is also focussed on ramping up installation of low carbon, particularly renewable energy, technologies. This technological focus is another core condition of EM.

However, a question remains about how wedded China is to other aspects of EM, including the involvement of environmental NGOs in decision making, the role of local government in making decisions that affect energy and also the implementation of policies through decentralised and market based economic means. Consideration of these aspects involves a discussion of how far China's 'top-down' methods of implementing environmental policies are achieving optimal outcomes.

As is often said, China is the largest carbon emitter in the world today, although, as I discuss in Chapter 4, this characterisation may be misleading. Indeed, my argument in this book suggests it is plausible to argue that China's carbon emissions will be dramatically lower in 2050 than was the case in 2015. To meet the minimum target reached at Paris of less than 2 degrees warming above pre-industrial levels, the world would need to reduce net carbon emissions to zero by the end of the twenty-first century, with reductions starting preferably by 2020. If the world has a chance of achieving this, let alone the preferred target of keeping temperature rises to below 1.5 degrees above pre-industrial levels, then China must start reducing emissions now. A reduction of emissions from China of at least a half and preferably two-thirds or more by 2050 compared to 2015 levels needs to be achieved.[3][4] The arguments in this book suggest that this is possible. That is not to say that all of China's environmental problems will go away – indeed some may be more difficult to solve than meeting radical targets for reduction of carbon emissions. However, a caveat is that China's strategy needs to move farther in the direction of a strong version of a 'Eurocentric' notion of ecological modernisation if this is to be the actual outcome.

Popular pressures mean that the Government has little choice but to adopt policies that will simultaneously reduce local air pollution and with it reduce the global pollution that generates climate change. The people demand these changes as a top priority. Some effective progress is being made through recent trends in moderation of growth in energy demand and in deploying renewable energy in particular. However, many changes need to be made. The economic system is in many respects economically uncompetitive and local government officials have been attacked for being partial to local polluting industry rather following the wishes of their ordinary citizens. Yet the pressures for ecological improvement are very strong.

My (ecological modernisation) argument about change in China revolves a lot about technological change. But I will be dismayed if this is characterised as some sort of prediction of a grand techno-fix solution – for that is to repeat much of the simplistic misunderstanding of the relationship between environmentalism and technology that seems to infect discussion of how environmental problems are addressed in practice. The great technological changes necessary depend on intense and consistent public pressure for change, particularly in terms of pressure from civil society in making government and business adopt policies and practices that lead to green energy technical solutions. Often the change is about ordinary people making decisions to choose more sustainable technology (albeit encouraged by regulation or incentives) – this includes choices about buying more energy-efficient products, making their homes more energy efficient, putting solar panels on their roofs, perhaps (especially in the future) buying electric cars. It can mean supporting community energy projects. Most frequently it will involve supporting campaigns by pressure groups to lobby government to make it easier for sustainable energy to be implemented.

The opposition often drawn between 'behavioural' and 'technological' change as a means of advancing ecological objectives is a very false one. In order to achieve technological change you have to have behavioural change in the sense that people must demand change, and support specific technological changes through both the political process and the market. This is the essence of ecological modernisation itself. It is wrong to parody EM as some top-down imposition of technology, and this is discussed further in the next chapter. However, suffice it to say here, China is embarking on an (as yet far from complete) EM-style process, or at least it has to do so. Regardless of such arguments, I deploy EM as a device to evaluate what is happening in China. EM practices are themselves open to criticism, so my use of EM as an analytical device should not be confused to saying what 'should' happen.

One aspect of the discussions about China that certainly does dismay me is a tendency to divert discussion away from the changes going on in China that are encouraging green energy because in some way this might give succour to the Chinese Communist Government. I notice that Ben Chu, in an otherwise insightful text on China, attacks people who draw attention, for example, to the quickened production of wind turbines and solar panels.[5] There are immense environmental problems in China. However, I do not think it helps the cause of democracy to ignore such progress as is being made for fear that it will interfere with the propaganda battle against the authoritarianism of the Chinese system of government.

As is argued progress is starting to be made in some important areas partly because it is the only plausible way that China can develop its economy in the future. Most importantly, because it is the growing will of the Chinese people that pollution should be made into a top, if not the top priority of our day.

At the end of the day we have to study what is happening in China with regard to energy outcomes and the impact on carbon emissions. It is vital to our future to understand what is happening in the largest country on Earth. This is much, much, more important than worrying about whether the conclusions are on message in the great superpower rivalry stakes. Besides which, if it is the case that China might turn the corner (and thus lead the world, in view of its size, towards a more sustainable future) this probably has little to do with the system of government. It says a lot about the will and capabilities of the Chinese people themselves.

In the next chapter, Chapter 2, I outline the nature and relevance of ecological modernisation (EM) theory. To summarise EM, we can say, using a text drawn from a previous book I wrote:[6] 'essentially, the idea of EM is that it combines economic development and environmental protection as a way of conducting good business; as Neil Carter puts it:[I]n short, business can profit by protecting the environment'.[7] EM's central theme is that consumers demand higher quality, environmentally sustainable, goods and services and business responds to this pressure, so increasing economic development. This produces a 'positive sum' solution whereby economic development is increased, rather than decreased by environmental protection and where policy, according to Maarten Hajer 'conceptualises environmental pollution as a matter of inefficiency, while operating within the boundaries of cost-effectiveness and administrative efficiency'.[8] EM demands a holistic response by industry to environmental problems, that is policies must be considered for their total environmental impact, rather than environmental policy being limited, as Albert Weale says, to one-off 'end of pipe' responses.[9]

This, as is discussed is essentially a 'Eurocentric' theory. However, far from making it less relevant to China, the point argued in this book is that in order for China to even move off the starting blocks in pursuit of radical carbon reductions it has to first achieve the core aspects of ecological modernisation. Such core aspects of EM include: modest economic growth levels in a predominantly service-oriented economy; mobilising green technologies to tackle environmental problems; environmental governance and agreement about technological means; and 'smart' market based means of promoting green technological solutions pursued in a competitive economic environment. The details of these aspects are set out in the next chapter.

However, changes in governance are still needed if China can achieve the 'core' conditions of ecological modernisation (EM) that are a pre-requisite for radical cuts in carbon emissions. This is the conclusion that we come to by comparing the core conditions of EM with what exists in China today.

Certainly, at present, EM strategies have not yet succeeded in achieving radical cuts in carbon emissions, but recent trends see a levelling out of carbon emissions from China, a surprise in itself. I argue that China is moving away from being a development economy and towards being a more Eurocentric type of economy that is susceptible to EM strategies. However, the remains of what I call top-down 'productionist' policies which impel government agencies to promote increasingly loss making energy intensive infrastructural and heavy industry need to be abandoned.

The Chinese Government has set in motion a very large and rapid transformation in the energy sector with a great emphasis on renewable energy. That having been said, the emphasis on top-down strategies needs to give way to more decentralised economic and political ones. EM is concerned with government setting macro-level regulations, incentives and institutional structures. In contrast to this, in China today local government tends to usurp the 'invisible hand' of the market in deciding business objectives. This leads to a lack of competition and inefficiency, an outcome that make some part of the renewable energy, including Chinese wind power manufacturing, relatively uncompetitive abroad. On the other hand China's solar pv industry is strong precisely because it began in the international market and had to be competitive. In political terms, the primacy currently given to economic over environmental objectives needs to be changed by greater power being given to local environmental groups and ordinary people to ensure the adoption of green strategies.

I outline the economic and political background in Chapter 3. This discusses how the over-productionist development model, which has led to superficial high economic growth rates, is grinding to a halt. I argue that the system has been unsustainable not only in ecological terms, but also in economic terms. The economy has slowed and is suffering increasing debts. Attempts by the government to stave off unemployment by keeping unprofitable heavy industry going is a process that itself reduces economic growth. However, regardless of this the economy is now rebalancing in favour of a much more service-based economy. I reproduce arguments which suggest that China's future economic growth will be much lower than in the past, largely because it will be largely based on services. This is a pattern that has already been observed in other countries which have followed a developmentalist path before finding that this could not be carried on. This change to slower growth based more on a service oriented economy has enormous implications for China's future levels of energy consumption, which will stabilise.

Chapter 4 considers the implications of lower economic growth, the transition to a more service-based economy and determined policies to reduce pollution from industry. This chapter examines how the era of big increases in energy and coal consumption is at an end. Carbon emissions seem to be at a point at which they start declining, and the likelihood is that carbon emissions will decline substantially as time goes on. Moderate economic growth and a much more service-based economy are inevitably associated, in the medium if not the short term, with a stabilised level of energy consumption. Service activities are several times less energy intensive compared to the manufacturing output upon which the Chinese growth has been based. I look at how official, government, energy projections have generally greatly overestimated future levels of energy consumption, and suggest this is the case also in China for the future. I look at some indicators for energy consumption, compared with Europe and the USA, and conclude that key determinants of energy consumption are likely to be close to European patterns which are much lower than those of the USA. Determined policies to ensure energy efficiency are emerging and will entrench these trends.

Chapter 5 looks at the pollution problem in China, and how governance structures are geared to deal with this and reduce carbon emissions. The chapter looks at some critical pollution problems, including particularly the issue of air pollution. Movements to curb pollution are examined, as are the challenges and opportunities facing civil society groups in trying to achieve anti-pollution objectives. The different ways that popular pressure has mounted on the Government to take action to curb air pollution is discussed. A range of environmental groups and activists have increased their activity, from insiders to outsiders organising demonstrations, and a range of tactics are used. A new Chinese middle class has emerged which sees anti-pollution measures as more of a priority whereas previously economic development took precedence. I look at governance and pollution, and examine how China's 'authoritarian' environmentalism may fail to achieve sustainable outcomes. The governance structures are such that productionist priorities remain embedded at a local level, often leaving pollution unchecked and are only being overcome through slow attrition.

Chapter 6 focuses on the supply side and looks in particular at the main means of fuel switching, and likely outcomes, to reduce carbon emissions. The main means of reducing carbon emissions are examined. China has overtaken the West in terms of deployment of non-fossil generation both in volume and also in per capita measures. Renewable energy is now being installed at the same rate, on a per capita basis, as the EU and the USA, albeit in much larger total volumes in China. Considerable amounts of nuclear power and hydroelectricity plant are being deployed – much more than in the USA and EU, although it is projected that deployment of these latter two technologies in China will slow because of environmental concerns. Nuclear power is likely to become more expensive as regulatory oversight increases and hydroelectricity schemes are likely to encounter greater resistance than in the past.

On the other hand wind power and solar pv are becoming cheaper and their deployment is likely to speed up as a result. China is the largest producer of wind turbines and solar pv in the world, although it is much more competitive in the world in solar pv sales than sales of wind turbines. China began the solar pv industry as an export endeavour so had to be competitive whilst the Chinese wind industry is cosseted by self-reinforcing monopolies. Reforms are needed in China to make the electricity industry more competitive and also so that it can absorb much greater quantities of renewable energy. Electric vehicle (EV) and battery storage technology contributions are reviewed. EVs and batteries will form a crucial part of the energy system in the future, and advances in both reinforce each other. It is plausible that by 2050, energy-related carbon emissions from China will be reduced by two-thirds compared to 2015. This target is reached in the context of achieving the 'high penetration' scenarios projected by the Chinese Renewable National Energy Centre (CNREC). The main threat to this strategy is whether the Chinese Government is persuaded by pro-coal interests to reduce development of renewable energy in order to shore up its profitability.

The concluding chapter, Chapter 7, puts the evidence in the context of ecological modernisation theory, and finds that while China is moving towards some 'core' EM objectives and methods, including moving away from a 'productionist' economy and towards a more service oriented one, and also in prioritising technological means of achieving carbon abatement through renewable energy deployment, it is still lacking progress on other aspects. This includes making the energy economy based on more competitive market based means and also in improving environmental governance to tip the balance more in favour of environmental NGOs and less towards the interests of polluting industries.

The material from this book has been drawn mainly from academic papers and books, public policy reports, reports published by a range of governmental and non-governmental agencies and groups, and articles in newspapers and magazines. Some material has been drawn from a limited number of interviews, and also some material was drawn from interchange with a series of speakers at a seminar organised to help me write this book at Tsinghua University.

Notes

1 Watts, Jonathan (2010) *When a Billion Chinese Jump*, London: Faber and Faber, p. 385
2 Ibid., pp. 390–391
3 Intergovernmental Panel on Climate Change Synthesis Report,(2014) *Climate Change Synthesis Report – Summary for Policymakers'*, p. 9, available online at www.ipcc.ch/pdf/assessment-report/ar5/syr/AR5_SYR_FINAL_SPM.pdf
4 Unsigned (2016) 'China', *Climate Action Tracker*, available online at http://climate actiontracker.org/countries/china.html
5 Chu, B. (2013) *Chinese Whispers*, London: Phoenix, p. 180
6 Toke, D. (2011) *Ecological Modernisation and Renewable Energy*, London: Palgrave, pp. 1–2
7 Carter, N. (2001) *The Politics of the Environment*, Cambridge: Cambridge University Press, p. 226
8 Hajer, M. (1995) *The Politics of Environmental Discourse*, Oxford: Oxford University Press, p. 33
9 Weale, A. (1992) *The New Politics of Pollution*, Manchester: Manchester University Press

2 An ecological modernisation theory for China and carbon reduction

The aim of this chapter is to map out how the theory of ecological modernisation can be deployed to analyse China's role in reducing carbon emissions from energy sources. In the process there will be some reflection of what the case of China reveals about the workings of ecological modernisation itself.

It is very important to apply EM to China, first as a means of mapping out the extent to which China may, at one level, be said to be following the EM path, and at another, as a form of feedback on EM itself to see which emphases can be applied to developing countries. We can attempt to deploy EM analysis of the conditions necessary for sustainable ecological protection to happen in the case of carbon reduction by applying EM. We have to ask, (1) 'What are the essential features of EM? and (2) 'To what extent do these conditions apply to China, and if they do not completely at present what changes may need to occur?'.

I will set the scene to answer these questions by mapping out some key characteristics and debates about EM that are relevant to the study of EM and China, before moving on to look at some important contributions to the discussion of the relationship of EM to China itself. Having reflected on these discussions I can then map out my own approach to EM and China, which, as I shall argue, involves assessing the extent to which China is meeting the standards of an admittedly Eurocentric version of EM.

My approach is an analytical one in that I set out to discuss how ecological modernisation processes are occurring and the extent to which they can be said to be occurring in China. When I am discussing the core features of 'Eurocentric' EM I am analysing what is practice, and I separate this from making normative statements, i.e. of what should happen, such as the need to strengthen EM practice to achieve the Paris targets. Then, after considering the results of this I can design an analytical tool that expresses in a reasonably specific form how EM operates, with an eye to designing this format so that it can be used to analyse progress in a particular case study. This template can then be deployed in the case of China's role in reducing carbon emissions. We can then assess how far and in what respects China is so far achieving EM criteria and what issues need to be addressed to ensure that they meet minimum EM criteria. Hence, I will be able to draw some guidelines about how China might tackle its carbon reduction programme, and also reflect on some lessons for EM itself.

What is ecological modernisation?

For the purposes of this study I take Ecological modernisation (EM) as an academic theoretical approach to understand how ecological change and environmental protection is achieved in modern industrial states. As Hajer has pointed out, a key aspect of EM is 'the fundamental assumption that economic growth and the resolution of the ecological problems can, in principle, be reconciled'.[1] According to a range of scholars, this can be achieved through governance structures which prioritise environmental protection, and negotiations between government, industry and environmental interest groups to bring forward the application of the advanced technological means to resolve environmental problems which have been given priority by the body politic.[2] Janicke emphasises a 'consensus oriented policy model that focuses the central state on strategic tasks and transfers detailed regulations more strongly to decentralised actors'.[3] This includes 'smart' regulation' that brings forward ecologically necessary technological change.[4] This involves the 'complementarity ... of market-based and regulatory instruments'.[5]

Janicke explains that such techniques face opposition in the shape of polluting industries who lose out,

> [s]ince industrial restructuring is inextricably connected with ecological modernisation, 'ecological industrial policy' should make the restructuring process socially and economically acceptable. It can promote diversification in product types or provide social cushioning, retraining, and conversion of the work force.[6]

Overall EM strategies are centrally involved with the promotion of market based, globalised, competition:

> The capitalist logic of technological modernisation and the competition for innovation in combination with the market potential of global environmental needs: marketable technological solutions for environmental problems offer a broad spectrum of "win-win solutions.[7]

Others, such as Spagaaren, have directed attention towards the ways in which consumption patterns can be explicitly diverted into more ecologically sustainable directions. Consumer awareness of ecologically sustainable forms of consumption and a desire to pursue greener 'lifestyle choices' encourages such trends.[8]

This focus on consumption is of vital importance to understanding EM processes, but in one crucial aspect it may be wanting, in that it does not do enough to discuss how consumption patterns differ in European style economies compared to ones that are still developing. This is very important from an ecological point of view since it may be the different types of developmental and post-developmental consumption patterns that are responsible for the apparent decoupling of economic growth from carbon emissions observable in the West. Because this aspect tends to be under-emphasised in EM literature to date I shall spend a little time unpacking this dimension of consumption patterns.

As developing economies grow, eventually they pass a certain point where the proportion of gross domestic product (GDP) consisting of manufacturing begins to fall off rapidly compared to services which (relatively) take their place. Production of, and employment in, manufacturing will decline as a proportion of GDP whilst the proportion of services rises steadily.[9] Associated with this is a relative decline in rates of economic development.

There is a straightforward set of explanations for this phenomenon. Developing economies strive to build infrastructures such as road and rail networks and utilities such as electricity grids and distribution networks. However, once such networks have been instituted work on the infrastructural assets declines to what is needed for maintenance and incremental improvement. To a large extent one could say the same for what could be called 'domestic infrastructure' such as fridges and TV sets. Once every household has got them, the rate of manufacturing of such products will stagnate. The demand for some products, notably cars, will still increase. There is also likely to be less emphasis on export driven manufacturing. Economic growth rates will generally decline and employment and economic activity will shift to services.

I will explain and expand on the ramifications of such change for the economy and for energy consumption in the case of China in Chapters 3 and 4. However, in essence the point that is crucial in this discussion about EM theory is that not only does GDP growth tend to moderate, but such growth as there is tends to be bound up in services. The combination of such changes (moderate growth levels and higher proportion of GDP on services) will generally repress pollution levels compared with high growth manufacturing oriented developmental economies. This may apply especially to the issue of carbon emissions, and underpins the apparent decoupling of economic growth from carbon emissions in Western European economies.

Of course there is a critique of the possibilities that EM contains the means to solve the climate change problem, involving as it does achievement of objectives as set out in the 2015 Paris Agreement on Climate Change. For example, York and Rosen have argued that there are doubts about EM's claim to promote resource efficiency. This may be insufficient to cancel out the pull for more resource consumption in the wake of industrial growth rates.[10] This is particularly the case in the circumstance of carbon reduction which needs to be rapid if climate change objectives are to be achieved. On the other hand, if carbon emissions can be stabilised then this opens up a more plausible argument that non-fossil fuels can substitute for coal, oil and natural gas leading to decarbonisation of the economy.

A key criticism of EM is that it has been based on the experience of Western economies, and thus may have limited relevance to newly industrialising nations,[11] including, most of all, China. In fact EM theorists have attempted to 'move away from EMT's initially Eurocentric formulation'.[12] This has often involved absorption of sociological theorists. Indeed greater understanding of sociological trends and issues of reflexivity in governance have been achieved. However, a lot may be lost in terms of analysing practice if some attention is not focussed on the simple initial proposition that EM can produce environmental improvement in the context of continuing economic development.

EM applied to developing countries

In order to draw up a theory that can be suitable for the analysis of China it is useful to look at some existing work applying EM to developing countries. In the debate around how EM may or may not apply to developing countries we can, broadly, observe two types of approaches. Essentially one approach says that EM is simply not applicable to developing countries whilst the other approach, what I would call a 'selective' approach, maintains that EM applies in at least some ways.

First, there is the approach which emphasises some aspects of EM whilst explicitly or implicitly de-emphasising others and work by Sonnenfield and Rock may fall into this category.[13] They sketch out some theory for EM regarding what he calls 'late industrialism'. Initial concern for rapid industrialisation in an export-led growth strategy obscures the growing deleterious environmental impacts of such a strategy – unlike 'Eurocentric' EM industrial pollution such as acid emissions or deposition of toxic heavy metals may actually be increasing. However, 'substantial evidence, much of it assembled by EMT (ecological modernisation theorists)' suggested that the 'global-local linkages attending export-oriented industrial development strategies have also had positive environmental effects on firms and industries in emerging economic … as a consequence of product and process regulations in Northern markets'.[14] This can be extended to China in the example of renewable energy. Markets for renewable energy have been developed in the West, and so enabled wind and solar pv technologies to be developed to such an extent that they are relatively cheap to deploy in China itself.

Sonnenfield, in an EM centred study of pulp and paper manufacturing in Malaysia, Thailand and Indonesia, stresses the importance, for EM, using Janicke's words 'that a reduction in the resource input of production will lead to a reduction in the amount of emissions and waste and also the cost of production'.[15] He argues that EM not only promotes environmental improvements in Western economies but also 'NICs (newly industrialising countries) … have the advantage of being able to use the advantage of being able to use the latest, cleaner technologies from the onset of large-scale modern manufacturing' Indeed, this links up with how China is able to marshal renewable energy technologies to be major contributors to its energy production capabilities.[16] However, Sonnenfield also says, in another notion that chimes with criticisms of China's recent rush to industrialisation (including its rapid increase in production of carbon dioxide emissions), that

[t]he biggest problem for the applicability of ecological modernisation theory in NICs – and by extension for ecological modernisation – may be in the area of dematerialisation. The cases examined here suggest that production is supermaterialising in the South, even if arguably dematerialising in the North.[17]

Langhelle articulates the second general view of EM in developing countries which says that sustainable development is a more appropriate template for developing countries compared to EM. Langhelle argues that such contradictions show up some of the problems of trying to analyse NICs using EM, and she argues that sustainable development is not only quite distinct from EM, but also more appropriate for understanding environmental politics in NICs. There, so her argument runs, the key issues are avoiding environmental overload in the context of development whilst at the same time assuring that development is equitable both in income distribution and the avoidance of environmental degradation.

Of course, both approaches to analysis of environmental issues in developing countries – selective EM and sustainable development – have their merits, but they also have some important shortcomings. The 'selective' approach has merit insofar as it can use EM templates to analyse how environmental policies are managed and implemented in developing countries, but it does not offer convincing pathways through which key challenges such as climate change can be tackled and overcome. Meanwhile, the alternative 'sustainable development' approach has merits in that it highlights issues such as equity not tackled by EM, and focuses on the problems of development, but it fails to analyse how it is that societies are transformed into ones where EM becomes applicable.

This shortcoming, however, may have more to do with the analytical gaps left by EM theory than problems with sustainable development theory itself. As discussed earlier, an implicit but as yet poorly analysed feature of EM (amongst EM theorists) applying to the Western European political economies is the restructuring of the economies towards services rather than infrastructural development. This is something that has occurred in Europe. The follow-on effect of this change decouples economic growth from increases in carbon emissions. This change makes it easier to conceive of a radical reduction in carbon emissions of those (Western) economies compared to developing countries where carbon emissions have been rising substantially in recent years.

Of course, a radical reduction in carbon emissions does not automatically follow, but the shift to a more service-oriented economy seems to be a precondition for such reductions. The understanding that such a gap in understanding exists have very great relevance to analysing the relationship of EM to China since, as will be argued later in the book, China may be undergoing precisely the restructuring of the economy away from development and towards the sort of service economy familiar in the West.

Some theorists point to the possibility of different trends within EM itself. Christoff identifies a distinction between 'weak' and 'strong' EM whereby the former is more concerned with narrow technical considerations driven by 'corporate' concerns, the latter being more akin to sustainable development incorporating more international concerns. Longer term ecological impacts are valued more highly when making economic decisions compared to 'weak' EM. The strong EM version also involves a heavy emphasis on 'bottom-up' pressures to meet local demands for sustainability and also an emphasis on decentralised solutions in general.[18,19] Hajer talks about a difference in styles of governance between 'top-down' technocratic' EM concerned solely with delivery, through decision-making limited to policy elites, of the relevant technological changes and more 'deliberative' EM involving the active involvement of a varied type of NGOs in negotiation and contestation over environmental issues.[20]

EM as applied to China

Here our particular focus is to set out an EM perspective that can help us understand China and assess possibilities for radical carbon reduction. In order to judge these issues, we can start by examining some attempts to analyse Chinese environmental policy using ecological modernisation. They can be said to belong to the 'selective' mode of EM approaches to EM which emphasises some aspects of EM theory rather than others.

Chinese authorities have themselves published analyses which adopt the notion of ecological modernisation to describe their policies and industrial pathway, and they seem to conform to this notion of a development-inspired technological path. According to Zhang, *et al.*: 'This Chinese interpretation of ecological modernisation is … primarily limited to the technological economic dimensions of sustainable development, without entering too much into relations with equity, equality, citizen empowerment and the like'.[21]

A crucial contribution on the relevance of EM to China comes from one of the leading EM authors, Mol. He has argued that too much focus, in EM theory, has been placed on the 'growing compatibility between environmental protection and economic growth' and also a perceived emphasis on technology as a solution. Rather he argues that '[t]he basic premise of ecological modernisation theory is the centripetal movement of ecological interests, ideas and considerations within the social practices and institutional developments of modern societies'.[22]

Mol argues that the mechanisms of EM in China 'may differ from the situation in Western Europe'.[23] Mol recognises that environmental improvements in China have only been partial, but he places emphasis on a growth in environmental regulations and institutions, including such innovations as Environmental Protection Bureaux (EPBs), and also decentralisation in markets and decision-making. In fact, Mol's own research indicates that such reasoning may be tentative given his acknowledgement of limitations on the activities of environmental NGOs, and the still developing nature of markets and environmental information. Nevertheless, he suggests that '[i]f OECD innovations in environmental governance can be captured by the concept of ecological modernisation, then China's environmental reforms can be labelled as a variant, or different style, of ecological modernisation'.[24]

A different perspective on the role of ecological modernisation in China is provided by Chen, who utilises what he calls a 'hybrid' model of developmental state and ecological modernisation to conceptualise China's renewable energy policy.[25] He emphasises the contribution of EM in the technology dimension of adopting renewable energy as a means of countering pollution problems. He describes the Chinese system as a developmentalist one, involving top-down measures from the Chinese state to ensure deployment of renewable energy. He says that a conflict between EM and 'Near East' (including Chinese) political economies is about the 'compressed' space of civil society. He appears to de-emphasise the role of participative environmental governance in EM. In the case of China, he says, the relationship between state and society and economy is much more hierarchical than in the case of European style ecological modernisation and 'the state's involvement has been extensive enough for the pilot agency to have sufficient political support to execute particular industrial policies, whilst the space allocated to civil society is compressed in exchange for rapid economic performance'.[26] He supports such a characterisation by pointing to 'the continuing strict control over citizens' participation in environmentally sensitive problems, and rigid monitoring of institutionalised groups and societies, not to mention the close censorship of public opinion on massive environmental incidents via the internet and the medias'.[27]

Chen's description of the development state, with which he identifies China as being a 'Near Eastern' example (with many similar characteristics as Japan), He says, using the term 'pilot agency' to mean government agencies:

> In developmental states, the pilot agency regularly announces the development plan and goals, laying out the outline of the programme. The private sector then adjusts its operations based on the programme. The government decides which successful enterprises will be given further support, for example, subsidies, and whether underperforming businesses will receive some degree of penalty.[28]

Although, in common with other analysts, Chen sees the Chinese system as decentralised to the extent that 'local officials are facilitators in fostering local industry in the transition process',[29] he argues that this is underpinned by a coherent, organised system of monitoring and control by the central government to ensure that the renewable energy programme is implemented according to the wishes of the central government. Local government officials themselves are given incentives and penalties according to the extent to which they have achieved central targets. Chen contrasts this centralised hierarchical system with the more 'bottom-up', 'participatory' approach pursued in the West.[30] The Chinese 'authoritarian' system can, he argues, produce at least as good as results as can be seen in the West in terms of effective systems for the deployment of renewable energy.[31]

It may be that this (top-down 'authoritarian') system can work in producing volumetric outputs, but I shall go on in later chapters to assess just how and in what ways this system can be effective in producing outcomes involving the efficient reduction of carbon emissions. It is also relevant to do this in the context of looking at work on the effectiveness of China's top-down system in achieving environmental improvements. However, for the moment it is pertinent to say that studies utilising EM theory which have looked at the Chinese system of environmental regulation suggest that it is not working well.[32,33]

A further approach by Knutsen and Ou makes some insightful analysis of the efforts by the Chinese steel industry to respond to what is called ecological modernisation (EM) for technological reform, and criticises the outcomes as being unsatisfactory in various respects.[34] Energy efficiency techniques, for example, are not being incorporated as well as they might be. However, the implicit assumption here is that the Chinese system, as constituted, is an EM system, as opposed to one just called that by government documents. As argued in later chapters, there are various ways in which the industrial structure and economic and political governance may be at variance with EM that has been described in, say, Europe. For example, industries such as steel may be in a position that is more protected than most. This in itself seems to demand any attempt to analyse the relevance and outcomes in China using EM to make an explicitly independent specification of what EM constitutes. Analysts using EM to evaluate outcomes in China should specify what they mean by EM; that is, independently of claims made in government documents about ascribing to an EM strategy.

A point I want to make here is that different analysts seem to apply EM to China using different emphases. Mol downplays the importance of technological issues and also of the relationship of economic growth to environmental outcomes in favour of looking at development of EM styles in environmental governance. On the other hand Chen is sceptical about claims to EM in environmental governance while focussing on the state's role in promoting green technological change as an instance of EM. Kundsen and Ou seem to take their cue from the references to EM made in Government documents and discuss the shortcomings of this alleged EM strategy. All these approaches have merits in that they use EM to analyse aspects of Chinese political ecological economy and industry, but they conflict in some key aspects, and in any case they may not use EM fully to help us understand China's ability to embark on a radical carbon reduction path.

My task, in this work, is to use EM to develop a notion of how China is in, and where it is not in, a position to engage in a programme of radical reduction in carbon emissions. EM as practiced so far in Western Europe is not a sure-fire way of following this path (yet), but at least it gives us a notion of where it can start in a better position than the 'supermaterialist' tendencies observed in developing countries. In short, we should simply start off with a discussion of the essentials of EM and then see how far China matches up to them. We should not assume that what is happening in China is EM because some or other aspect of the Chinese industrial or regulatory system seems to have EM characteristics or because some government documents say an EM approach is being used. Rather we need to analyse the extent to which current trajectory of Chinese ecological politics and economy match up to EM as practiced in Europe and then see what changes may make them more compatible with this so-called 'Eurocentric' EM.

We begin this by setting out some clear notions of some essential aspects of EM as practised in Europe, and then we look at the extent to which there is evidence for this in China at present, or possibilities for it to emerge in the near future. There does, after all, seem to be at least a measure of consensus about what constitutes EM in a European context, as discussed earlier. If we define EM as constituting some essentials of what can be seen in Western European conditions, then at least we have a measure of agreement about the nature of EM. However, there is another strong argument for using a European template for assessing progress towards EM in China, and that is because there has been a decrease in various types of pollution, including air pollution, in Europe. For example sulphur dioxide emissions have been declining in Europe, whilst increasing in Asia, albeit with hope of stabilisation in China.[35] In such cases there can be said to be progress in decoupling economic growth from levels in air pollution. Of course, pressure from scientists and environmental NGOs often, if not usually, continually raises the bar for what is an acceptable level of pollution, and so in this sense EM becomes a moveable feast of environmental targets and objectives. As Blühdorn puts it,

> These refinement processes … [of ecological modernisation] … do not take the whole of modern society any closer to an objectively definable and fixed state of sustainability, but they are part of a dynamic and multi-dimensional process which involves several competing ideas about what is (ecologically) necessary, and which both the ecological goal posts as well as the means of achieving them are permanently being reviewed.[36]

Even in the case of carbon emissions there is evidence that there is a decoupling of economic growth from growth in carbon emissions in Europe, even though this may be but a start to the process of dealing with climate change. This is on the basis of a high level of emissions of course. However, the point to ask about the progress of EM in China is whether China's level of emissions can be at least stabilised and then radically reduced, as may be possible within a European context under conditions of a 'strong' EM approach. In the EU, with relatively stable or falling levels of carbon emissions there is the possibility of radical reductions in emissions with ramped up programmes of energy conservation and deployment of non-fossil energy sources. Is it equally plausible to assume the plausibility of such a pathway in the case of China?

It is the case that in European countries in the twenty-first century such as Germany, UK, France Italy, The Netherlands, Denmark, Switzerland and Spain, energy consumption has broadly stabilised. Carbon emissions have been substantially reduced in these countries as renewable energy has been intro-duced.[37] It is certainly the case that research into 'embedded' carbon in imported products makes Western countries' carbon emissions higher than just the domestic energy consumption figures would imply. However, data, for example on the UK's total carbon responsibility over time, has still suggested that trends since the start of the century indicate a fall in carbon emissions.[38]

The future possibility is that if energy consumption can be at least stabilised or preferably reduced further, then low carbon energy technologies may be able to increasingly substitute for and displace fossil fuels. So, in essence, then for these reasons, it might be advisable, for analytical reasons, to utilise the Euro-pean EM stereotype as a means of analysing the state of China's progress towards adopting EM practices.

Hence it may be useful to flesh out here some basic characteristics of Euro-pean EM, then, so that we can see whether they are present in China. This may help us understand the way that carbon emissions and economic growth may be decoupled in China.

Some basic characteristics of 'Eurocentric' EM

In setting out this basic template, I do so with an eye, of course, on Chinese conditions to the extent that some distinctions between EM theory and Chinese practice can be drawn out at the start. This will help pose questions that can be addressed in the empirical analysis that follows in succeeding chapters.

Leading on from earlier discussions about the nature of EM and also how analysts discuss the relationship of EM to ecology in developing contrives, and especially China, it is possible to draw up a relevant list of core elements of EM as seen in Western Europe. This is not to say that there is no possibility of EM innovation in China or elsewhere, nor that what is happening in Europe is necessarily better than what is happening or can happen in China. However, this is to say that in order to evaluate the possibilities for ecological transition (and particularly the case of carbon abatement) in China, then a comparison between European EM with what is happening in China is a fruitful one. It can help us evaluate possibilities for transition in China – and of course shed light on where Europe needs to put more effort as well. The aim of this list as dis-cussed below is to focus on parts of EM theory that can be investigated in the empirical studies in this book. It represents an effort to boil down EM theory to a tool that is useful for analysing progress in a particular country of a particular ecological problem. It is assumed, in drawing this up, that the tool will be applied to analyse China's role in reducing carbon emissions. Hence the core essentials discussed below are invented as a tool with specific bearing on the climate change abatement strategy. I have selected those aspects which can be effectively used to discriminate and analyse any differences and similarities between China and 'Eurocentric' EM.

Of course, there are various aspects of EM theory that one could add to the tool. One that is prominent is 'the polluter pays principle', but I find it difficult to discriminate clearly in practice between different cases (e.g. China and Europe) using this notion. For instance, in the case of carbon pricing, as discussed in this chapter, the EU's efforts are still relatively weak and undoubtedly need to be strengthened. The point of this list of core EM concepts is that these are notions that are relatively straightforward to compare between Western European practice and what is happening in China (and changes over time in this comparison).

Moreover, there is an issue of interpretation concerning the 'polluter pays principle' on the subject of 'who' the polluter is. In the instances of exported products, is it the country that manufactures the products or is it the country that imports them? Conventionally, in current public policy terms, it is normally the manufacturer that is assumed to be the polluter in terms of the carbon 'embedded' in the product during its manufacture. This may, as discussed in Chapter 4, exaggerate China's carbon footprint in comparison to those of importing countries (e.g. Europe) since China is a net exporter of goods that are actually used in other countries. However, EM practice is to use policy instruments to minimise carbon emissions at the point of use (burning) of fossil fuels, a practice which I assume in this book. So I will go along with this convention and assume that on the one hand it is China's responsibility to reduce emissions used in manufacture of products on its soil – but also in the converse that its carbon footprint will decline as the amount of carbon-intensive exports is reduced.

Modest economic growth levels in a predominantly service-oriented economy

One crucial reason why many European states have been reducing carbon emissions, or at least stabilising them, is because these states have modest rates of economic growth, whereby relatively lower energy intensive services predominate in the economy. This tends to produce relatively weak upward pressure on growth of energy supplies. So an issue becomes whether there are possibilities for China to moderate its rates of economic growth and transition to a more service-oriented economy. I am not going to specify a precise numerical value for 'modest' as ecological and social conditions vary meaning different repercussions in different societies for different rates of growth. But clearly a per capita growth rate of 8–10 per cent a year is not modest, whereas something around 2–3 per cent might qualify.

This issue can be related to consumption, not just about whether Chinese people wish to buy ecologically preferable goods but, most importantly in this context, whether China has reached the point in its development path where economic growth begins to moderate. If this is the case then cutting carbon dioxide emissions becomes a much more practical proposition. As discussed earlier, a key implicit factor that lends hope to the notion that pollution levels and in particular changes in carbon emissions can be decoupled from economic growth is if China follows the European example of the 'saturation' of the economy with certain types of infrastructure and domestic demand for various manufactured products. This can lead, as has been the case in Europe, to a relative shift in the patterns of economic growth that are coming through services rather than more energy intensive manufacturing and construction.

Mobilising green technologies to tackle environmental problems

This involves the co-ordinated marshalling of the most effective technologies necessary to assure sustainability and the abatement of specific environmental problems. In the case of mitigating climate change this involves both supply side and demand side measures, the supply side measures involving low carbon energy sources, whilst the demand side involves measures to improve energy efficiency. Specific technological means need to be identified and deployed. In order to be effective this programme needs to be of a size appropriate for the meeting of specific environmental targets. An important conceptual distinction needs to be made between an action by the state in preferring particular technologies, or sets of technologies, and the means taken to decide policy and also to implement such a strategy. I divide this process into two streams: 'political governance' and 'economic governance'. First, the political governance stream:

Environmental governance and technological means

Although the technology-focus of EM might be parodied as involving a top-down technocratic exercise, the needs to assure political and social acceptability must be incorporated into any decision-making system. The nature of decision-making may vary from issue to issue, with some demands for environmental improvement being settled purely through decision-making by experts and some involving what Hajer calls 'reflexive mobilisation ... the mobilisation of independent opinions versus the respected power of authorities'.[39] However, the possibility that the discussion may be far-reaching and open to 'bottom-up' interventions must still remain, and moreover the environmental interest groups themselves must be able to organise and speak without having to seek the permission of government authorities to do so.

The environmental problems that need to be tackled need to be decided, and also as part of this the targets for achieving them. In addition, the technological solutions need to be evaluated in order to decide an appropriate mix of technological responses, and also appropriate means of promoting their adoption. This can only be achieved through negotiations between a wide range of relevant interest groups, including scientists, environmentalists and industrial interest groups. This occurs between informal and formal networks of interests, or policy communities, who exchange information and who collectively can make decisions with a broad basis of support. Of course, the policy outcomes will be decided by the strength of contending interest groups, with dominant industrial groups having a key if not the key influence over technology choices. However, bottom-up pressure for solutions such as renewable energy have been widely effective in several European states, shifting the industrial balance of power. There will also be an open discussion affording means of monitoring outcomes of technological solutions and means of improving outcomes if they fall short of projected outcomes. Decision makers will be accountable to the people and decisions taken in accordance and regulated in the context of a rule of law. Consumers will respond to informational, regulatory and incentivising 'smart' prompts to effectively encourage take-up of ecologically preferable technical solutions.

'Smart' market based means of promoting green technological solutions

This entails a mixture of policy instruments involving regulations, various forms of incentives (including taxes and 'feed-in' tariffs), product labelling and what are called market based instruments. These are used to promote technological solutions that have been decided as appropriate. The term 'market' here is used in the context that companies compete to provide the most efficient solutions with consumers selecting outcomes according to price and quality. A key point is that the market itself is bounded by and embedded in the various regulatory and other incentives and penalties that are being deployed to support the desired technological outcomes. State intervention exerts its influence at the macro-economic level rather than making favourites of individual companies at the micro level.

These core parts of EM are linked in various ways, but they are all under-pinned by a social consensus that sees the achievement of environmental well-being as being an essential political priority. This increasingly emerges not so much as a conflict between economic and environmental priorities in which economic priorities tend to be favoured, but rather whereby ecological and eco-nomic[40] rationalities are pursued simultaneously without one being more important than the other.

It is necessary here to make a distinction whose significance may otherwise be overlooked, between the sort of market based solution associated with EM and the 'top-down' strategy that has been dominant to date in China in the delivery of green technologies such as renewable energy. It is important to understand that whilst China's economy, since the turn of the 1980s, moved towards a more profit-oriented means of development, this does not mean that the economy is organised the same as is familiar in the case of Western capital-ism. State intervention is more widespread at the micro-level with commercial outcomes in areas such as renewable energy dependent on networks of influence rather than market competition. Such differences need to be touched on now in order to emphasise the difference between what may be understood in Europe to be associated with what Janicke calls 'decentralised' and 'smart' means of imple-menting environmental policies and the sort of practices that underpin Chinese developmental practices.

The means of implementing desired technological outcomes in China are done through using China's particular system of 'state capitalism'. The issues associated with this system will be much further discussed in Chapter 3, but in essence they include the achievement of plans set out by central government through the incentivisation (or penalisation) of local officials rather than by classic competitive market based means. Although the companies involved in achieving the government objectives will themselves have to achieve profit-ability objectives, they will be selected by state's representatives to perform par-ticular tasks and carry out volume-based deployment objectives. This is as opposed to company output and prices being decided by the company them-selves as a response to the signals they derive from the market.

Essentially the contrast between European based EM market systems for delivery of outcomes and the Chinese system is that the Western system involves the agency of the classical 'invisible hand' of the market, whereas in China outcomes are largely determined by the agency of local officials acting to carry out centrally decided policy objectives. This is the system that has been associated with the development of Chinese capitalist expansion since the 1980s, and has been summarised as entailing how 'the cadre evaluation system powerfully shaped local official behaviour by linking both the remuneration and advancement of local leaders to performance on economic as well as socio-political norms'.[41] Although increasing areas of the economy have become more market oriented, the delivery of renewable energy is still very much bound by the type of system, as described by Chen as a relationship between a controlling 'Principal' in the form of the central government and its 'agents' in the form of provincial and local government.[42] Indeed the electricity system as a whole is still dominated by state-owned-enterprises (SOEs).

Of course there are some aspects of the debate about EM that are more rel-evant to European conditions than China. For example, the debates like those in the European environmental movement between those who were 'anti-growth' or so-called 'de-industrialisers' and those who favoured an EM approach do not feature prominently in China.[43,44] There it is not usually a question of whether economic development is desirable, but how much stress should be placed on pollution control and resource conservation. However, other aspects that form a contrast are clear, even sometimes implicitly, such as the notion that the environmental movement must be an independent, autonomous, movement able to negotiate with industry and the Government without the Government or industry having an effective veto on the legitimacy of the environmental groups themselves.

Another caveat when discussing EM is a more general one. According to its critics, the problem is that EM is a process of ameliorating a condition where so-called 'advanced' industrialised countries are already over-consuming and over-polluting.[45] That is the case, certainly in the case of carbon emissions. However, the question is 'how do we go from here?' We have to answer the question of whether EM strategies can indeed take us back from this trajectory of worsening climate crisis. A key issue examined here is the extent to which China is being transformed, economically speaking, into a state whereby its development behaves more like European countries, and thus how we can deploy EM to analyse ecological progress. Looking at China, therefore, can help us examine whether EM strategies do have a possibility of ameliorating the climate change problem by promoting radical cuts in carbon emissions. We can do this by using what I describe as core essentials of EM to analyse the possibilities that China can achieve radical cuts in carbon emissions. Doing this may involve recording some salutary lessons for China. It also involves identifying avenues down which it is making progress. It involves questioning Western preconceptions about what is happening with the Chinese economy and its carbon emissions profile in particular.

Having discussed what I would see as the core essentials of EM in its 'Euro-centric' nature, I will now consider how this analysis of EM can be turned into a set of tools necessary to study the empirical subject, namely to assess the extent to which it is plausible that China can achieve radical reductions in carbon emissions sufficient to achieve the overall targets of the Paris Agreement. Of course this is much more radical than the Chinese Government's target which they have committed.

Deploying core aspects of EM

I will thus return to the core aspects of EM that I have just discussed and discuss how they can be deployed to analyse the empirical data. I need to convert the 'core' EM theory I have discussed into some tools which I can deploy to conduct the empirical investigation. I shall focus on the following things, which parallel the four key areas I have just covered.

First is the EM notion of whether an economy involves modest rates of service oriented economic growth. This will help to reconcile economic growth with environmental protection. In the case of climate change mitigation this involves achieving very radical cuts in carbon emissions, a reduction of one-half to two-thirds of 2015 Chinese levels by 2050 would be needed, as discussed in Chapter 1. Obviously such a target becomes all the more difficult if high rates of economic growth occur. However, if the Chinese economy is restructuring to a lower rate of economic growth then this strategy becomes more feasible. Hence a key aspect of this study is to examine the evidence for the emergence of such an economic restructuring.

A second focus is the degree to which technologies are being mobilised by the state to deal with the environmental challenges. In the instance of climate change low carbon energy technologies (including energy conservation methods) are the key technologies. However, the success of such a focus may be largely determined by two further lines of focus, that of environmental governance and also economic governance.

The third focus is to examine the extent to which the environmental governance system can be regarded as being analogous to those regimes normally associated with EM conditions (in Europe). This involves responsiveness to, and participation by, citizens' groups and environmental groups, the degree of effectiveness of environmental agencies in controlling pollution and the robustness of the civil legal system means of pollution abatement. The ability of environmental groups to negotiate with, and influence, industry and Government and influence outcomes is important. Of course this has to be applied to the carbon emissions reduction programme. This includes an assessment of the basis and extent to which environmental groups and movements have independent legitimacy. I will investigate how the environmental governance system impinges on this programme in China, including how it affects energy decisions and monitoring of energy outcomes.

The fourth focus is that of the economics of governance. This includes the degree to which there is a system of 'smart' instruments which are used to promote environmental objectives, in this case carbon emission reduction. Particular emphasis will be placed on the degree to which they are deployed in an environment that encourages technological improvement through competition. Both energy demand and supply will be considered. However, as has been discussed, the Chinese system of promoting carbon reductions relies heavily on what has been called a 'principal-agent'[46] system whereby the centre incentivises development through the actions of its officials which are incentivised to do so. The effectiveness of this 'top-down' system in encouraging competition (or organising an effective substitute for it) will be considered. Particular case studies will be considered, one interesting contrast being between wind power and solar power. The impact on energy demand and its conservation will also be considered.

This analysis is pursued alongside a hypothesis which says that China's progress in adopting a programme of carbon reduction can be measured according to the extent that it lives up to some 'core' aspects of 'Eurocentric'-style EM; that is, the core aspects that I have been discussing. Differences and similarities between the 'Eurocentric' core aspects of EM and Chinese practices will be examined. Of course, just because there are differences does not automatically mean that what China is doing is less effective. Indeed a key aim of the analysis will be to determine whether, and how, Chinese practices are more or less effective than what has been outlined as being 'core' elements of EM.

This does not mean of course that Eurocentric approaches, as they currently stand, are adequate to meet the challenge of climate change, or for that matter other environmental concerns. After all policies like the EU-ETS and its carbon pricing system, although ground-breaking in theory, have not been transformed into tools with major effects.[47] Renewable energy targets and energy efficiency policies may often have been pursued with greater vigour in the EU than elsewhere, but, performance has still been below what is needed to achieve the Paris targets.

If even 'Eurocentric' EM is to prove to be effective, then it has to be associated with a radical upgrade of policy initiatives to deal with climate change. 'Eurocentric' EM may still, generally speaking, the best we have (so far) got operating in large-scale practice in ameliorating the effects of developed economies. However, current concerns have shifted towards more emphasis on reducing energy costs and that may have reduced the priority of promoting energy efficiency and renewable energy, even though pursuit of such policies may reduce energy costs in the longer term. A further consideration is that green solutions may result in reductions in demand for fossil fuels, and thus fossil fuel prices may stay low, making it more difficult to reduce energy demand. This emphasises the need to increase the carbon price in order to ensure that low fossil fuel prices do not encourage increased consumption. Such measures, in addition to increased regulatory and use of incentives to implement low carbon solutions, mean that a strong version of EM needs to be deployed to achieve anything close to the targets adopted in the Paris Agreement. Langhelle has observed, 'Ecological modernization should be seen as a necessary, but not suffi-cient, condition for sustainable development'.[48] However, as discussed earlier, ecological modernisation is a moveable feast that can change and improve over time in pursuit of sustainability, which will themselves shift over time.

The EU-ETS has, since its inception in 2003, only had a modest effect to reduce carbon emissions compared to the impact of the increase in world energy prices in reducing energy demand, and renewable energy and energy efficiency have been promoted through instruments such as feed in tariffs and regulations. The carbon targets implicit in the EU-ETS have been low and given the fact that high energy prices in the decade after 2004 depressed energy consumption. It remains to be seen whether the political will exists in Europe to use the EU-ETS (as well as strengthen energy efficiency regulatory mechanisms) to compensate for more recent falls in fossil fuel prices and thus to keep energy consumption down. It also remains to be seen, given recent policy changes in countries like Poland, UK, and even Germany, whether there will be a sufficient stream of long term power purchase agreements available for renewable energy generators to help meet the Paris targets.

The limitations of the EU-ETS were one of the issues covered by Joseph Szarka as he looked at what EM strategies had achieved in Europe. He concluded that

> the capacity of technological forcing to translate ecological modernization theory into effective policy and practice has proved limited.... A key lesson is that technology-based policies need to be accompanied by economic and political strategies to counter-act the unwillingness of incumbents to cooperate. Technological acceleration does not happen simply through 'natural selection' at the level of firms and their technology choices, but requires focused and coordinated political responses to shape the business environment.[49]

An important, if not the most important, part of the argument upon which my analysis is based is that if China falls short of the core 'Eurocentric' aspects of EM, then a radical reduction of carbon emissions is certainly not going to be achieved. However, even EM in its European style needs strengthening to ensure the necessary structural technological shifts to achieve radical cuts in carbon emissions. However, as will be argued, it is plausible for China to adopt a sufficiently strong version of EM to achieve radical reductions in carbon emissions over the coming decades. That, however, may require some important changes that first catch up with European style EM and then surpass it (alongside developments to strengthen EM in the West of course).

The USA may display some, but not other aspects of European-style EM, perhaps especially in the case of carbon reduction.[50] This is illustrated by the lack of consensus on the importance of tackling climate change, with Obama's initiatives being opposed by many Republicans and states led by Republicans.[51] In the task of assessing the possibilities of China achieving radical cuts in carbon emissions it would seem helpful to do a comparison with what is happening in the case of the USA to draw up a reasonable analysis and prognosis. The EU, by contrast, has at least tried, if not always so successfully, to promote global agreement on climate change.[52] It is certainly the case that the EU has much lower per capita carbon emissions compared to the USA.[53] Of course, this may be because of structural geographical-economic reasons as much as, or as more than, government policies. However, it is opportune to study the extent to which China is more typical in terms of structural and also policy means compared to the EU (hence a reason for focus on 'Eurocentric' EM) rather than the USA.

There is another way in which the 'Eurocentric' nature of EM may be relevant to analysis of China, and that is to do with the social and physical context of European building and transport in comparison with China. As will be discussed in Chapter 4, there are some similarities between China and European urban intensities compared to the more dispersed nature of the USA, with important consequences for energy consumption. This parallel underlines the relevance of European conceptions in analysis of China.

Conclusion

I have engaged in a discussion of major contributions to EM theory with a view to establishing a means of evaluating China's progress, and potential for future progress, in curbing carbon emissions from its energy sector. I have examined approaches to EM in developing countries, and also approaches to EM in China. Some writers prefer emphasising differing aspects of EM, which in my view is in effect to argue that EM can be deployed differently in China as opposed to Europe about which the theory was initially devised. However, the approach in this chapter is to argue that there have been structural changes in European economies leading towards modest levels of economic growth and more reliance on service industries. This is associated at least with a stabilisation or decline of carbon emissions in Europe, and generally progress towards greater levels of environmental protection.

Hence my argument is that I will use what has been called a 'Eurocentric' notion of EM as a measuring stick that can help us gauge the effectiveness of China's progress towards effective carbon reduction strategies. The measures of how close Chinese economic and governance practices are to that of this

'Eurocentric' EM will be measured by how close Chinese practice tends towards the core essentials of EM that I have just discussed under the headings of: modest economic growth levels in a predominantly service-oriented economy; mobilising green technologies to tackle environmental problems; environmental governance and agreement about technological means; 'smart' market based means of promoting green technological solutions pursued in a competitive economic environment.

I can examine the extent to which China is satisfying these core criteria for EM necessary to achieve carbon reduction. If China is not satisfying some of them then there will be a discussion of the relative effectiveness of what I see as the core elements of Eurocentric EM and Chinese policy and practices.

Of course, even if 'Eurocentric' EM practices can achieve more carbon reduction than current Chinese policies this in itself, as in the case of Europe, does not assure the achievement of radical cuts in carbon emissions. As discussed, EM itself needs to be implemented in a strengthened form in the case of carbon reduction. However, if, as a result of the analysis, it is found that 'Eurocentric' EM is going to achieve more progress than current Chinese strategies then China will certainly have to change practices and policies. The EM analysis in this book can help us understand at least some of the changes that need to be made.

We can see here that EM involves both 'top-down' and 'bottom-up' aspects. A 'top-down' dimension involves setting measures that influence technological choices. A 'bottom-up' dimension consists partly of the involvement of environmental NGOs in setting environmental objectives but also of the delivery of outcomes in a market context. It is common to emphasise the top-down nature of the approach, and overlook the important 'bottom-up' nature of how EM works in practice. Indeed a much publicised public policy effort which uses a title which sounds a bit like ecological modernisation called an 'eco-modernist manifesto' seems precisely to have this problem, amongst others.[54]

In Chapter 3, as I assess the nature of the economic and political context in China. I shall discuss how different phases of economic development and state policy has affected the level and nature of economic growth. In Chapter 4, I focus on issues surrounding carbon emissions from and energy demand in China. In Chapter 5, which focuses on pollution, environmental governance forms an important part of the discussion. Then in Chapter 6, chiefly concerned with the deployment of low carbon technologies, I look at how economic governance affects technological choices and the efficiency of deployment of low carbon technology. In the concluding chapter, Chapter 7, I draw the strands together and come to a verdict on how far China has gone to meet the various criteria for EM that I have outlined in this chapter.

Notes

1 Hajer, M. (1995) *The Politics of Environmental Discourse*, Oxford: OUP, p. 26
2 Mol, A., Sonnenfield, D. and Spaargaren, G. (eds) (2009) *The Ecological Modernisation Reader*, London: Routledge
3 Janicke, M. (2009) 'On Ecological and Political Modernisation' in Mol, A., Sonnenfield,

D. and Spaargaren, G. (eds) *The Ecological Modernisation Reader*, London: Routledge, pp. 28–41, p. 35

4 Jänicke M. and Lindemann S. (2010) 'Governing environmental innovations', *Environmental Politics*, vol. 19, no. 1, 127–141

5 Ibid., p. 135

6 Janicke, M. (2008) 'Ecological modernisation: new perspectives', *Journal of Cleaner Production*, vol. 16, 557–565, p. 563

7 Ibid.

8 Spargaaren, G. (2009) 'Sustainable Consumption: A Theoretical and Environmental Policy Perspective', in Mol, A., Sonnenfield, D. and Spaargaren, G. (eds) *The Ecological Modernisation Reader*, London: Routledge, pp. 318–333

9 Herrendorf, B., Rogerson, R. and Valentinyi, A. (2013) *Growth and Structural Transformation*, NBER Working Paper No. 18996, Cambridge MA: National Bureau of Economic Research, available online at www.nber.org/papers/w18996

10 York, R. and Rosa, E. (2003) 'Key challenges to ecological modernization theory', *Organization& Environment*, vol. 16, no. 3, 273–288

11 Langhelle, O. (2009) 'Why Ecological Modernisation and Sustainable Development should not be conflated', in Mol, A., Sonnenfield, D. and Spaargaren, G. (eds) *The Ecological Modernisation Reader*, London: Routledge, pp. 391–417

12 Mol, A., Spargaaren, G. and Sonnenfeld, D. (2009) 'Ecological Modernisation: Three Decades of Policy Practice and Theoretical Reflection' in Mol, A., Sonnenfield, D. and Spaargaren, G., *The Ecological Modernisation Reader*, London: Routledge, pp. 3–16, p. 8

13 Sonnenfield, D. and Rock M. (2009) 'Ecological Modernisation in Asian and other Emerging Economies', in Sonnenfield, D. (2009) 'Contradictions of Ecological Modernisation: Pulp and Paper Manufacturing in South East Asia, in Mol, A., Sonnenfield, D. and Spaargaren, G., *The Ecological Modernisation Reader*, London: Routledge, pp. 359–371

14 Ibid., p. 360

15 Janicke, M., Monch, H., Rannenberg, T. and Simonis, U. (1989) 'Structural Change and Environmental Impact, *Environmental Monitoring and Assessment*, vol. 12 no. 2, 99–114, cited by Sonnenfield, D. (2009) 'Contradictions of Ecological Modernisation: Pulp and Paper Manufacturing in South East Asia', in Mol, A., Sonnenfield, D. and Spaargaren, G., *The Ecological Modernisation Reader*, London: Routledge, pp. 372–390, p. 373

16 Sonnenfield, D. (2009) 'Contradictions of Ecological Modernisation: Pulp and Paper Manufacturing in South East Asia, in Mol, A., Sonnenfield, D. and Spaargaren, G., *The Ecological Modernisation Reader*, London: Routledge, pp. 372–390, p. 386

17 Ibid., p. 386

18 Christoff, P. (1996) 'Ecological Modernisation, Ecological Modernities', *Environmental Politics*, vol. 5, no. 3, 476–500

19 Carter, N. (2001) *The Politics of the Environment*, Cambridge: Cambridge University Press

20 Hajer, M. (1995) op. cit.

21 Zhang, L., Mol, A. and Sonnenfeld, D. (2007) 'The interpretation of ecological modernisation in China', *Environmental Politics*, vol. 16, no. 4, 659–668, p. 665

22 Mol, A (2006) 'Environment and Modernity in transitional China: Frontiers of Ecological Modernisation' in *Development and Change*, vol. 37 no. 1, 29–56 pp. 32–33

23 Ibid., p. 36

24 Carter, N. and Mol, P. (2007) 'China and the Environment: Domestic and transnational Dynamics of a Future Hegemon', in Carter, N. and Mol, P., *Environmental Governance in China*, London: Routledge

25 Chen, C.-F. (2015) *The Politics of Renewable Energy in China: Towards a New Model of Environmental Governance?*, PhD, Bath: University of Bath, pp. 109–110, available online at http://opus.bath.ac.uk/46738/

26 Ibid.
27 Ibid., p. 175
28 Ibid., p. 95
29 Ibid., p. 100
30 Ibid., p. 284–285
31 Ibid., p. 297
32 Lai K.,*,Wong, C. and Cheng, T. (2012) 'Ecological modernisation of Chinese export manufacturing via green logistics management and its regional implications' *Technological Forecasting and Social Change*, vol. 79, 766–770
33 Zhou, Y. (2015) 'State power and environmental initiatives in China: Analyzing China's green building program through an ecological modernization Perspective', *Geoforum*, vol. 61, 1–12
34 Knutsen, H. and Ou, X. (2015) 'Ecological Modernisation and Dilemmas of Sustainable development in China', in Hansel, A. and Wethel, U. (eds) *Emerging economies and challenges to sustainability: Theories, strategies, local realities*, London: Routledge, pp. 65–78
35 Klimont, Z., Smith, S. and Cofala, J. (2013) 'The last decade of global anthropogenic sulfur dioxide: 2000–2011 emissions', *Environmental Research Letters*, vol. 8, no. 1, available online at http://iopscience.iop.org/article/10.1088/1748-9326/8/1/014003/meta
36 Blühdorn, I. (2000) 'Ecological Modernisation and Post-Ecologist Politics', in Spaargaren, G., Mol, A. and Buttel, F., *Environment and Global Modernity*, London: Sage, pp. 216–225, p. 220
37 See tables for primary energy consumption and carbon dioxide emissions in *BP Statistical Review of World Energy* (2016) available online at www.bp.com/en/global/corporate/energy-economics/statistical-review-of-world-energy.html
38 Department of Environment Food and Rural Affairs (UK) (2016) '*Official Statistics – UK's Carbon Footprint*, available online at www.gov.uk/government/statistics/uks-carbon-footprint
39 Hajer, M. (1995) *The Politics of Environmental Discourse – Ecological Modernization and the Policy Discourse*, Oxford: Oxford University Press, p. 282
40 Mol, A. (1995) *The Refinement of Production-Ecological Modernisation Theory and the Chemical Industry*, Utrecht: Van Arkel, p. 33
41 Whiting, S. (2011) *Power and Wealth in Rural China*, Cambridge: Cambridge University Press, p. 72
42 Chen, C-F. (2015) op. cit.
43 Hajer (1995) op. cit., pp. 78–103
44 Mol, A. (1995) *The Refinement of Production*, Utrecht: Van Arkel
45 York, R. and Rosa, E. (2003) 'Key Challenges to Ecological Modernization Theory – Institutional Efficacy, Case Study Evidence, Units of Analysis, and the Pace of Eco-Efficiency', Organisation and the Environment, vol. 16, no. 3, 273–288
46 Chen, C-F. (2015) op. cit.
47 Delbeke, J. and Vis, P. (2015) *EU Climate Policy Explained*, London: Routledge
48 Langhelle, O. (2000) 'Why Ecological Modernization and Sustainable Development Should Not Be Conflated', *Journal of Environmental Policy and Planning*, vol. 2, 303–322, p. 303
49 Szarka, J. (2012) 'Climate challenges, ecological modernization and technological forcing: policy lessons from a comparative US-EU analysis', *Global Environmental Politics*, vol. 12, no. 2, pp. 87–109, p. 103
50 Schlosberg, D. and Ronfret, S. (2008) 'Ecological modernisation, American style', *Environmental Politics*, vol. 17, no. 2, 254–275
51 Goldenburg, S. (2015) 'Obama's carbon reduction plan under attack from 24 states and Republicans', *Guardian*, 23 October, available online at www.theguardian.com/us-news/2015/oct/23/obama-carbon-coal-power-plant-epa-lawsuit-republicans

52 Bäckstrand, K. and Elgström, O. (2013) 'The EU's role in climate change negotiations: from leader to "leadiator"', *Journal of European Public Policy*, vol. 20, no. 10, 1369–1386

53 World Bank (2016) Carbon Emissions, available online at http://data.worldbank.org/indicator/EN.ATM.CO2E.PC

54 Asafu-Adjeye, A., *et al.* (2015) *An eco-modernist manifesto*, available online at www.ecomodernism.org/. The authors of this 'manifesto' associate 'eco-modernism' with technological emphases (such as apparent preference for nuclear power over renewable energy) that have not been generally associated with the outlooks and analysis of the academic EM literature, or indeed the priorities of most environmental NGOs from which EM takes its cue for setting environmental priorities

3 Curbing the concrete

In April 2007, an article in the official newspaper *China Daily* reported about what was seen as a particular example of excessive and unnecessary construction, the so-called 'White House' of Yingquan in Fuyang. Fuyang is regarded as a relatively poor area in the north-western province of Anhui, and the district of Yingquan needed many social improvements; better education, help for local farmers. But what they got was the demolition of a local school, the expulsion of farmers from their land with limited compensation and the erection of a massive ostentatious municipal building. This cost nearly four million dollars to build, around a third of the annual fiscal budget of the district council budget.[1] This became quite a cause celebre especially following an attempt by the local party boss to silence a whistle-blower who committed suicide following false accusations.

In many ways this was but an exaggerated example of how excessive development was occurring all over China. This was wreaking environmental havoc in the form of local pollution from the coal needed to power the construction and also ballooning quantities of carbon emissions that threatened the planet with faster climate change. But it was also wreaking economic havoc on the country.

A crazy system of politics and economics was driving China into debt caused, above all, by a senselessly excessive building boom. A lot of it resulted from corruption, not real development. The building boom, along with an excessive focus on exports was driving up debts as well as carbon emissions. Indeed, as can be seen from Figure 4.1 in Chapter 4, carbon emissions from China more than doubled in the ten years from 2002–2012. Incidentally, this period coincided with a world-wide commodities price spike, with Chinese demand forming a substantial contribution to this. As Andrews-Speed has commented, in terms of the energy impact

> Almost all past projections of energy use in China have underestimated the rate of growth and have failed to predict periods of shift to heavy industry and high energy intensity, most notoriously in the early years of the twenty-first century.[2]

At the same time, as will be discussed in Chapter 5, concern amongst Chinese people about pollution were increasing and forming into powerful demands upon the government to reduce coal burning and other causes of pollution.

At this stage it seemed that any chances for China treading a pattern of moderate increases in economic development and a focus on a much more service-based economy as have occurred in the early years of this century in Europe seemed remote. As argued in Chapter 2 this is a core condition of achieving ecological modernisation and the achievement of environmental protection alongside economic development. This chapter examines whether this implicit assumption of EM can in fact be achieved. If so carbon emissions will be stabilised or reduced.

Indeed it seemed that by 2014 things were changing in the sense that the steep upward curve in energy consumption and carbon emissions was flattening out. In 2013 the Government issued an edict saying that no new government buildings should be constructed for five years and set about discouraging excessive new building in general. There was also a clampdown on corruption – and there was a big overlap between building development and corruption, with condos often being seen as a perk for government officials when they approved development projects.

The Government put an emphasis on a need to 'rebalance' the economy towards an economy that was growing a little slower and shifting the economy towards consumption of services rather than production of goods. As in the case of the need to combat pollution, this was not (merely) the result of wisdom suddenly becoming part of the logic of the leadership of the Chinese Communist Party (CCP) but rather their acceptance of pressures from Chinese people themselves. It was also in line with what economists were saying, independent ones as well as advice from bodies like the International Monetary Fund (IMF).

Rather than rely on energy intensive activities, the future economy of China will rely much more on cleaner and much less energy intensive industries that revolve around the internet. As Mckinsey put it:

> China sorely needs a new leg of expansion because the industrial growth of recent years – driven by heavy capital expenditures in manufacturing – will be difficult to sustain. The internet, by contrast, should foster new economic activity rooted in productivity, innovation, and higher consumption…. For global companies counting on China for continued growth, the new Internet wave will change the nature of competition: it will enable the most efficient Chinese companies to grow more quickly, shine more transparency on business and consumer markets, and create conditions for a better allocation of capital.[3]

Moreover, although China is still producing goods, the hope is that it will focus much more on goods that can help reduce pollution, not increase it. In particular it is producing massive quantities of renewable energy, wind power and solar power in particular – indeed in 2014 and 2015 nearly half of all wind turbines installed in the world were installed in China.

China is at a crossroads of sustainability of both its economy, of its environment and the planet itself. The good news is that it seems to be taking the first steps towards the path of sustainability. This will not only assure a better future for the Chinese economy, but will also make an enormous and essential effort to curb emissions of greenhouse gases, especially carbon dioxide. Here sustainability, as in the idea of 'sustainable development' means the ability to carry on doing something indefinitely, without undermining the ability of future generations to carry on flourishing – both in an economic and an environmental sense. Of course, this effort could yet be derailed if the Government do not follow up its plans with action – but the reality is that if it fails then the Chinese economy, as I explain in this chapter, will collapse under a rising mountain of debt, and carbon emissions will decline as a result in any case.

In this chapter, I want to discuss the unsustainable path that China is abandoning (whether by plan or 'force majeure') as well as the direction in which it is now heading. I want to explain how the notion of economic sustainability and ecological sustainability overlap to a great degree. I will also discuss the political implications of this.

It may sound unusual to say that there is an overlap between a sustainable economy and a sustainable environment – indeed the founding bibles of modern environmentalism say they are in direct conflict with its other. Tracts like 'Limits to Growth' written in 1972 concluded that, in effect, economic growth could not continue because it was depleting resources and producing pollution at such a rate that the planet could be destroyed.[4] However, as the theory of ecological modernisation (discussed in the previous chapter) suggests, in reality there may be no such contradiction. China may have been held to represent the trend of unsustainable growth, but now, there is the possibility that it may lead the world away from calamity and towards sustainability. There are still great problems remaining, but a trend is now becoming clearer in the energy sector at least, and as I discuss further in Chapter 5, the Chinese Government is under heavy political pressure to follow this trend. In this Chapter I explain how China has no choice for economic reasons either.

Turning from production to services

For many years China's rapid economic growth has been spurred on by the fact that half of the GDP went into investment. This investment produced an excess of goods and services over and above what Chinese people could consume immediately. This excess was sent abroad as exports and also as investment in infrastructure such as roads, buildings, railway stations etc. Companies would borrow the money (from banks) that had originally come from people's savings and invest the money to produce exports and infrastructure. This used to be profitable because the Chinese companies could harness cheap resources. But this had a very high carbon price. In the first decade or so of the twenty-first century China was burning around a quarter of its carbon emissions to produce exports and around a fifth of its carbon emissions would go on construction of buildings.[5] Indeed, from 2003 to 2012, as evidenced by the big increases in energy consumption during those years, China appeared to go on a wildly energy intensive binge of construction projects. But in recent years this – what I would call 'productionist' – strategy, which involved nearly half of all China's carbon emissions, has ceased to be economically viable.

Ansar, Flyvbjerg, Budzier and Lunn are acutely critical of China's infrastructure-led economic growth model, as they comment:

> Investing in unproductive projects results initially in a boom, as long as construction is ongoing, followed by a bust, when forecasted benefits fail to materialize and projects therefore become a drag on the economy. Where investments are debt-financed, overinvesting in unproductive projects results in the build-up of debt, monetary expansion, instability in financial markets, and economic fragility, exactly as we see in China today. We conclude that poorly managed infrastructure investments are a main explanation of surfacing economic and financial problems in China. We predict that, unless China shifts to a lower level of higher-quality infrastructure investments, the country is headed for an infrastructure-led national financial and economic crisis.[6]

It used to be the case that the (buildings and export) investments that dominated the Chinese growth spurt in the early twenty-first century would prove profitable because the companies that made the investment recouped enough income to repay bank loans needed to finance them. But this is no longer the case, if it ever was. The bank loans are not being repaid. Debts are piling up. This is because the resources that used to be cheap are now much more expensive. Chinese costs have risen. Wages have risen and China needs to import more energy and other raw materials from abroad. Local government used to repay the loans they took out for construction buildings, railways, bridges etc., by taking land off the farmers for little compensation, and selling it at high prices to property developers, thus making a profit. But the money that local government used to make on selling land has fallen because property prices have fallen, so local government officials found they were not making enough money on land sales to repay the loans they had taken out to finance the building developments. In addition many investments made in export oriented goods are no longer making such a profit. The consequence has been that while official growth figures stayed high in reality this was only achieved at the expense of increasing quantities of debt.

China's former economic growth rate, running at around 10 per cent a year, has now fallen. The official figures say it has fallen to around 7 per cent per year, but even that is almost certainly a considerable exaggeration. The figures are compiled on the basis of estimates send in from the provinces. Officials are still given rewards to improve economic development, so it there is an incentive to inflate the figures. There have been admissions that the figures were inflated in the past.[7]

Apart from the ban on new government buildings being put up, a crackdown on corruption since 2012 has also been widely perceived in having an effect in cutting out unnecessary production. This has led to a sharp fall in the habit of giving expensive western goods, often watches, to government officials. Shipments of Swiss watches to China slumped 19 per cent in the first ten months of last year (2015), and are worth £700 million (about one billion dollars) less than the annual level before the crackdown.[8]

Getting Chinese people to switch to spending money rather than saving it is not as easy as just cancelling government projects. However, the economic figures do suggest that spending is at least shifting more towards services, which have much lower energy inputs compared to buildings or goods. Services as a proportion of gross domestic product have expanded from 44 per cent in 2010 to nearly 52 per cent in 2015.[9] The future lies in big increases in spending on personal welfare, development and leisure. Spending on universities has ballooned with funding from both state and private sources through fees. Student numbers have multiplied tenfold since the end of the last century. Not only that, but Chinese universities are now climbing steadily up the international league tables in larger and larger numbers.

The state capitalist economy

As I was growing up, the ideas of 'competition' and 'communism' did not really seem to gel. Well, in theory. China is run by the Chinese Communist Party, and state-owned companies are still very important in the economy, but in China state owned companies behave differently from the state owned companies that have existed in the West. From 1979 onwards, Deng Xiaopeng led the reorganisation of the Chinese economy. He crafted a system of incentives that overcame many of the lack of incentives to make profits that are inherent in the centrally planned economy. However, as we shall see, the system was rather better suited to organising great advances in production rather than protecting the environment.

Incentive structures that motivated people in state owned enterprises (SOEs) were reorganised. Managers would only advance in their careers if they achieved production and profit objectives. Similarly for employees they would advance their careers and earn bonuses if the companies made profits. Local Government was a very important part of this revolution, although its role is distinctly double-edged. Local government, especially the municipal level where many planning decisions are made, were incentivised to promote development of infrastructures and industries. The central government set targets by which local officials would be judged. In addition, local government gained money from new enterprises in various ways – from levying fees and taxes, and also by making money on selling land development rights to developers. Indeed the system of financing of local government was geared so that local government needed to derive money from developing infrastructure and local development in general, since otherwise it would not have enough funds to provide basic services. Officials from provincial, county, city and township levels of government were assessed on their success in promoting economic development. The Communist Party structure oversees many of these mechanisms.[10,11,12] It seemed straightforward for local government officials to organise large infrastructure project such as building railways, airports, roads, bridges. This, in the development phase, has assisted local economic development.

The Chinese system is very effective in marshalling resources through economies of scale and process. For example, the cars for the ten competing state-owned taxi companies in Beijing have been bulk ordered from South Korea. This will save lots of money compared to each taxi company ordering and negotiating prices to each buy a much smaller number from different car manufacturers. China is said to thrive in two forms of innovation involving first its focus on its large consumer base and second improving production processes, which achieves economies of scale.[13]

In a growing number of sectors there is more competition and China is able to utilise its massive domestic consumer base to hone its products. Examples include production and sale of mobile phones and computers as well as a range of standardised commercial and industrial equipment such as pumps. Chinese companies are also able to use its large supply chain to achieve efficiencies in processes. As I shall discuss in Chapter 6, utilising economies of scale of purchase and manufacture has served the Chinese well in the production of solar power.

However, the system, though appearing to be competitive, is in some sectors, particularly the state-owned sectors, prone to inefficiencies. For instance as I discuss in Chapter 6, in many parts of the electricity sector business contracts are achieved through networks rather than competition on price and quality.

A private sector grew, starting in the 1980s, and the state owned enterprise (SOE) sector was made much more profit-oriented. They were rationalised, especially at the end of the century, and by 2004 their numbers had fallen by around three-quarters compared to a decade earlier.[14] Private companies were also encouraged, and indeed today anybody who is unemployed is encouraged to go into business for themselves. These were periods of classic development-oriented growth organised along state capitalist lines as the economy surged ahead on the basis of increasing production for exports and the creation of infrastructure, including roads and particularly buildings.

State owned enterprises, and indeed any activity deemed important by the Chinese Government (including loans for development in Africa and other places) could rely on low interest loans backed by government guarantees. This allowed Chinese companies to make effective use of what were then under-utilised and uncoordinated Chinese resources of land, labour and capital. Companies could expand their activities rapidly without having to pay high premiums for risk capital.

Up to around 2010, this strategy still appeared to be profitable in economic terms, even though there were mounting environmental costs. The Government could boost the economy almost at will. According to Andrews-Speed, the Government retained the power to constrain or stimulate growth in the economy at short notice, and such decisions appear to outsiders to come quite suddenly. But never have the forecasters been utterly wrong-footed as they were by the surge in energy demand seen in the first few years of the twenty-first century.[15]

The Chinese strategy has helped the country make up for the many decades of under-development, made worse by the savage dislocations associated with so-called 'cultural revolution' in the 1960s. However, the system stopped producing the great benefits. Increasing debts and diminishing returns of stimulus measures have sapped the Government's ability to boost economic growth at will. In recent years there has been much talk of shifting the economy to depend much more on consumer led spending, especially on services, and less on investment led production.

An important part of increasing consumption is to reduce environmental degradation since services, which will increase in value as consumption rises, generally involves much lower levels of environmental degradation (including carbon emissions) compared to investment in industry and infrastructure. The impact on energy consumption will be further discussed in Chapter 4. As discussed in the next chapter, the growing middle classes expect that pollution will be reduced, and the Chinese leadership are under very heavy pressure to redeem pledges of environmental improvement.

The downside of Chinese state capitalism

The system of giving government guarantees as a staple diet for industrial development has proved to be unsustainable. Large debts have accumulated through state owned enterprises in the industrial sector and also to local government. Giving guarantees is fine until the point when developments become unprofitable and today's investment growth turns into long term losses. Ultimately banks and the state are laden by bad debt, and bad debts have been rising at worrying rates in recent years in China. Either the Chinese can shift their economy much more towards consumption of services or there will be mounting debts followed eventually by an economic crash.

According to Michael Pettis, who discusses how China needs to rebalance its economy, 'lagging wage growth, an undervalued currency and repressed interest rates' all shift resources from consumers to production'. He also comments: 'environmental degradation, a serious problem with China's growth model, is an important transfer of income from households to business'.[16]

As will be discussed in Chapter 5, local government's responsibility for implementing environmental regulations is often fatally compromised by its conflict of interest with promoting and receiving much of its income from precisely the developments which are responsible for the environmental degradation in the first place. Taxes and fees levied on local industry are vital sources of revenue from local government. Up until now the courts are under local authority control, which severely limits the ability of the courts to respond positively to citizens trying to protect the environment from polluting or otherwise environmentally damaging developments. As I shall discuss in Chapter 5, activists are increasingly challenging this situation, and gaining some victories. Although they are still often stymied, time and popular pressure are on their side, and the decline in the productionist model itself points in the direction of lower pollution.

The system of funding local government has long been problematic. As part of a power struggle for control of tax income the central government took away control over a large proportion of tax revenue from local and provincial government in the early 1990s. This left local government, in particular, being reliant on the centre for the funds to promote the developmental expansion that the officials were expected to generate. Because municipal authorities were not allowed to borrow money themselves they developed institutions called 'local government financing vehicles' (LGFVs) for their infrastructural investments. They raised money, at least partly, on the basis that the loans would be repaid through the proceeds from land sales conducted by the municipal authorities. However, this was, in effect, betting the house (literally in terms of buildings) on what was basically organised land speculation. Things would work out fine when land prices continued to increase, but disaster would occur if they did not, as indeed happened in 2011 when property prices crashed.[17]

Minxin Fei says 'Chinese LGFVs are known mainly for their unique ability to sink perfectly good money into bottomless holes in the ground'.[18] In 2008 (responding to the Western financial crisis), the Chinese Government effectively encouraged a step change acceleration in this process by offering large quantities of new credit facilities to help this programme, only making the impact on increasing government debt of the crash in property prices much worse. The Chinese Government is still dealing with the problem of sanitising the immense debts that resulted from the fallout. In addition to the economic debts there is the social and environmental fallout.

A phenomenon has emerged in China of the 'ghost' or 'wasted city'. In the West there are cases where the occasional new building remains unoccupied for some time or where old urban areas have decayed and become de-populated, but in China this problem is in its own dimension. A survey done in collaboration with the Chinese Academy of Sciences said:

> In 2013, around 22.4% (49 million) of the newly constructed residential buildings in urban areas remained empty…. Vacant apartments, buildings and neighborhoods come with poor or no public infrastructure, lack public services and therefore generate major economic, social, and environmental effects. The economic and social impacts include huge economic losses, property devaluation, governmental financial risks, deterioration in the investment environment, shrinking employment and labor markets, social injustice and protests, poor public health, and psychological effects.[19]

The study looked at 28 'wasted' cities and documented the wasted resources and environmental impacts associated with them:

> The vacant buildings in the 28 wasted cities consumed over 1.5 billion tons of eight construction materials (aluminum, steel, wood, cement, brick, gravel, sand, and lime). The estimated total embodied energy of the vacant buildings is as much as 7.3E9 GJ. The buildings in the wasted cities also contributes to the discharge of air pollutants such as SO_2, NOx, particulate matter ... and greenhouse gases emissions.[20]

The authors of the study recommend a series of policy changes that are needed in order to stop the problem of wasted cities growing even further. Part of this alternative strategy rests on making development a more bottom-up rather than top-down strategy, with local participation in discussion of local plans and local consent for them. Secondly there need to be a reform of the way local government is financed, and a move away from local government reliance on land sales and building developments as a major source of their income. Third, local government's activities need to become transparent and the local government needs to become more accountable for these activities. Fourth, those in the private and public sector need to take responsibility for the developments that are implemented. This connects up with my previous observation that government guarantees for loans for productionist growth are a big part of the problem of economic and environmental unsustainability that afflicts Chinese development today.

Regrettably, it seems that the wider global financial system may have become infected by this madness. This is because loans associated with the building boom were sold to Western banks in the period immediately after the 2008 banking crash on the basis that they involved a higher return than was available at the time in the West. But many of these loans have proved to be, to use the trade euphemism, 'non-performing'; that is, the loans will not be repaid. Sadly, Western bankers failed to learn the lessons of the 'sub-prime' mortgage crash and did not understand the problems of these loans they were buying from China. This leaves some Western banks with a problem.

Returning to the Chinese economy itself, there may be parallels between Japan's post-WW II state capitalist development strategy and that of China. Both systems suffered from a common malaise – overproduction. Japan's industry is all privately owned, but a coherent state bureaucracy that was pretty independent of the elected politicians coordinated an export led drive for growth that was very successful well until the 1980s. The state coordinated development – particularly through privileged access to cheap loans and a low exchange rate with industrialised economies with a large proportion of GDP channelled back into investment. Indeed there was talk of Japan challenging American commercial hegemony.

However, as the costs of Japanese production rose, its investment-led productionist strategy became less profitable. The returns on investments became smaller and debts taken out to finance investment were not paid back. Hence levels of debt in the economy increased. The increase in debts slowed the economy down. What have been called 'zombie' companies – companies kept alive by low interest rates and continual 'restructuring' of debts – crowded out growth in more profitable companies. Wages were depressed and innovative companies were left less able to compete in the markets. There was little economic growth from the early 1990s to the early 2000s in what has frequently been termed 'Japan's lost decade'. Japan's political establishment then proved to be a dead weight as it was successfully lobbied by leading 'zombie' corporations to maintain their position.[21]

Despite the Chinese Government's aim of moving towards a more services based economy, the total Chinese debts have carried on mounting.[22] Many analysts believe that China is now entering or about to enter a period of zombification leading to slower economic growth than has been the case over the previous thirty plus years.[23] The Communist Party of China's (CCP) political leadership has close links with many debt-laden state owned enterprises (SOEs) – in effect, 'zombie' companies. This situation will worsen if bank crises make the Government take on board accumulating quantities of debt.

An increasing reliance on imported oil and commodities has increased Chinese costs, and so, indirectly, may China's efforts to secure rights to oil and other commodities from other countries. Certainly China has been complimented by some (and criticised by others)[24,25] for its exercise of 'soft power' in seeking such resources – in contrast to the rather more aggressive tactics of Western countries in the past. China has lent developing countries low interest loans to build infrastructure in return for concessions on oil, minerals and food production. This is in contrast to the sad story of Western attempts to topple recalcitrant governments during the days when the Western oil companies ruled the oil world, and provides a counterpoint to the higher interest loans charged by Western banks for development purposes. On the other hand, of course, there have been accusations that the Chinese encourage poor working conditions for workers involved in projects it sponsors in developing countries.

What has been less commented upon is the degree to which this activity may in fact be a risk and a potential drain on Chinese resources. China's loans may be of a charitably low interest level – but that may be very risky for China, threatening a similar effect on its own economy as lending money to 'zombie' companies, reducing income for China compared to investing in business which produces better returns and lower default rates.

Fears about creating mass employment if (relatively) declining industries such as steel suddenly lay off workers has limited the ability of the Government to cut down on rising debt levels. Indeed, during 2015, clashes between steel workers being laid off and the authorities increased. Closing down inefficient, polluting plant seemed to be a prime aspect of policy, though this does not impress the steelworkers themselves. Debt levels continue to rise in the Chinese economy, and while many expect that the Chinese state's 'closed' system of banking can contain the fallout, it will only do so at the cost of relatively modest economic growth. Economic growth has already fallen. According to an analysis by a Swedish economist, growth in 2015 was around 3 per cent.[26] Bloomberg collected a set of figures that came to a figure slightly higher than this, but still less than the Government's claims of 7 per cent growth.[27] How long the government can maintain credibility in its own economic growth figures remains uncertain. But, more than this, the debt mountain appears to be getting worse, and economic growth could fall still further.[28]

A problem with the Chinese economy from an ecological point of view is not so much that it has state owned enterprises, but that they have tended to dominate energy intensive sectors such as steel and, as a result, will be resistant to being rationalised. In 2014 they accounted for around 22 per cent of industrial income in China.[29] Nevertheless, the industrial importance of SOEs in general in terms of contribution to the economy has been in steady decline for the last 20 years. This trend seems likely to continue, with internet companies such as Alibaba and other privately organised services oriented businesses being the biggest source of growth.

Certainly, it is likely that if unemployment increases dramatically it will be the Government and the leadership of the CCP that will be increasingly challenged, alongside other institutions like local government that could better justify themselves during the time of expansion compared to long days of stagnation. Hence the Government is likely to roll over debts and accept a long term condition of relatively low growth as a price to pay for keeping unemployment down. Low growth means that there will be a much slower growth in energy consumption. However, if the economy is to have chances of development in the future, it has to be 'rebalanced'. Two things, therefore, suggest that China's economic growth will still remain at around 3 per cent per year indefinitely. First, in the near term, the 'zombie' effect, as discussed, will keep growth rates down in the near and medium terms. Second later on, as China 'rebalances' its economy towards services growth rates will be more sustainable at a lower rate.

Rebalancing the economy

The acceptance of the need to rebalance the economy is widely expressed in Chinese Government circles. The case was explained in formal economic terms by a group of China-based economists, writing a paper for the International Monetary Fund (IMF). Indeed they begin their paper by saying 'There seems to be a growing consensus that China's growth model – heavily reliant on exports and investment – may have run its course'.[30]

They argued that increasingly in recent years much Chinese investment in infrastructure and exports is generating losses rather than long term economic development. The investment may produce notional economic growth in the short term, but generates bad debts which can only reduce growth in the longer term. The authors recommended that investment is shifted away from 'manufacturing and real estate' towards 'agriculture and services'.[31]

The allegedly high growth rates reported by the Government have not taken into account the environmental costs, both locally and globally. Moreover, even in narrow economic terms, Chinese policymakers have realised that the headline growth figures exaggerate sustainable growth. In the short term growth figures are inflated by investments backed by loans underpinned by government guarantees that later turn out to be loss making, leaving the country with increasing drains on its economy resulting from the bad debts in the longer term.

The Government is committed to rebalancing the economy through greater emphasis on consumption. It is being asked to take measures such as giving greater monetary incentives to consumers to spend rather than save. This will be helped if there is a better welfare system including pensions and health provision that reduce the need of Chinese people to save.

The building programme in China has been curbed to a certain extent, although probably even this is still bloated through attempts at promoting growth through development of infrastructure through extension of credit in 2015–2016.[32] Indeed the curbing of the programme seems to be a big factor in the slowdown in Chinese economic growth starting in 2012, and associated with that the actual fall in coal burning during 2015. Mountains of useless concrete are not being produced, at least not in such great quantities. A planet's worth of carbon emissions is no longer being generated! More on the fall in coal use will be discussed in Chapter 4. Measures such as the ban on building new government buildings for five years from 2013[33] and efforts to curb local government debts accumulated through construction projects[34] seem to have had a big effect in stemming the tide of concrete.

In fact, the Chinese leadership under Xi Jinping appears to have put a lot of effort into trying to counter corruption, although it is also said that corruption charges have been used as a selective weapon against opponents of the leadership within the CCP. Observers believe that some progress has been made in anti-corruption activities.[35] Certainly this will be a factor, perhaps a big factor, in cutting down overproduction in the Chinese economy. Jonathan Fenby comments that 'the resulting caution (of the anti-corruption campaign) … slowed down the economy given the fear of being caught out in bribery integral to the way much business is done'.[36] Ecologists, who are sometimes disdainful of economic growth in general, are likely to say, alongside others, that less economic growth is worth a step to cleaner society, especially given that the corruption is often involved in developing highly energy intensive production. The curb on new government construction projects has been a central part of the anti-corruption drive.

The Chinese Communist Party (CCP) has a strong rhetorical commitment to reorienting the economy more towards consumption and towards a more service oriented economy. Certainly, on paper, the Chinese Government's professed strategies point strongly in this direction. As described by an article published through Government run *China Daily* the Government's new Five Year Plan includes pledges to 'a major extension of health care insurance, financial reforms and liberalisation of the capital account and targets for constructing affordable housing and reducing pollution'.[37] We will have to see how much change this actually will generate over the next few years.

Certainly the Government has appeared to curb some aspects of over-production, including in the buildings sector, through restricting new debt issues and by improving management of existing debts. Economic growth since 2012 has declined to reflect this, and has cut out at least some of the investment that was generating dangerous levels of losses through a build-up of bad debts. It does seem logical that if less is taken out of consumers' pockets for investment and they thus spend more on consumption, and that the proportion of spending on services will increase. According to data produced by the Chinese Government at the end of 2015 services had increased as a proportion of GDP from around 45 per cent to 51 per cent since 2011 and consumption as opposed to invest-ment was responsible for the majority of new economic growth.[38]

Countries like Australia, who have up until now supported the energy inten-sive productionist path in China by exporting coal and metals, are expecting still to increase their trade, but to do so through services. According to a report by Bloomberg:

> Services and agriculture exports to China will grow 10 percent annually, while coal and iron ore exports stagnate, according to economists at Aus-tralia & New Zealand Banking Group Ltd.... In particular, the tourism and education sectors can expect strong growth as more Chinese citizens travel to Australia for leisure and study,

the ANZ economists said.[39]

Economic growth is highly associated with energy consumption, as has been analysed in China's case.[40] A key consequence of the shift towards a much more service-oriented economy is a reduction in rates of economic growth. Writing for the Paulson Institute Zhang Bin argues that China has recently entered an economic zone known as a 'middle income economy'. He says:

> both the general slowdown of China's economic growth and the stagnation of its industrial sector are the natural consequence of China's new status as a middle-income country. The experience of advanced economies has shown that services play a more prominent role in the economy once per capita income reaches a certain level. And since productivity growth is generally lower in service-related sectors, such an economy will inevitably slow down as these sectors become engines of growth.[41]

This conclusion is backed up by both argument and also statistical analysis of the economic transitions undertaken by already developed economies. After a certain point of economic development (which China has now passed), people's expenditure on manufactured products declines as a proportion of their total spending and their spending on services increases. At first the decline in spending on manufactured products is offset by declines in spending on agricultural products, but then services continue to increase as a proportion of GDP. This trend has been discussed by Zhang Bin who draws on analysis of economic growth statistics.[42]

According to Bin 'both the general slowdown of China's economic growth and the stagnation of its industrial sector are the natural consequences of China's new status as a middle-income country'.[43]

However, if the basis of China's high economic growth, until around 2013, has been the expansion of industrial production, and much of the continued increase in production is no longer profitable, this implies that China's main source of growth is disappearing. This may partly be replaced by a more effective service sector, but nevertheless, China may become much more like richer countries with a dominant service sector and also, lower rates of economic growth than has been the case in China's developmental phase. Certainly, lower rates of economic growth have been seen in recent years in other eastern states that have earlier followed what could be called a 'productionist' developmental path broadly similar in many respects to that followed by China. However, now that their economies have matured, including becoming much more service oriented, their per capita economic growth rates have fallen. In the cases of South Korea, Japan, Singapore and Taiwan per capita economic growth rates have all been less than 3 per cent since 2011.[44,45] Indeed, according to Robert Barro, who conducted a statistical econometric analysis of factors associated with economic growth rates in developing and emerging economies, China's economic growth rate should 'soon' decline to '3–4 per cent'.[46] Given that China's population growth is slowing, sheer population effects are likely to reduce this rate of economic growth still further.

The notion of an increasing proportion of GDP going to services as China rebalances, and the accompanying notion that there is a natural consequence of lower economic growth, has tremendous consequences for the future trajectory of energy consumption in China. Put simply this means that increases in energy consumption are likely, in the future, to slow or disappear. This is because of two inter-related factors. First, economic growth falls, which reduces the pressure for more energy consumption. Second, the fact that services become a higher proportion of the economy will mean that pressure for more energy usage will be even further reduced because services, on average, consume only a small proportion of amount of energy usage associated with manufacturing. This is even before one considers the impact of energy efficiency policies which are designed to limit energy consumption, and to which the Government is now firmly committed. In many ways these trends implicitly implement the value-preferences of green critiques of economic growth, but moves in the direction of ecological modernisation. Economic growth declines and society achieves prosperity with reduced demands on non-renewable energy resources.

The Government has taken steps to control the overspending by local and provincial governments on building developments. It has prevented local government from taking out loans to finance development unless it is done transparently and under the clear consent of the central government. However, Bin argues that the Government ls still to embrace the full set of policies that will assure a smooth transition to the more services oriented economy. Too much economic stimulus is being given to infrastructural projects (what I call here a 'productionist' path) rather than the new services economy. He argues that private, and especially, smaller, companies involved in the service sector should not be disadvantaged by having inferior access to investment capital compared to large, state owned companies.[47]

Environmentally desirable technologies need to be given advantages with the cost of incentives borne by the rest of the economy as a way of 'internalising' the 'external' environmental costs of the economy. This does not mean that environmentally desirable technologies such as green buildings or renewable energy should be cosseted from the rigours of competition, but merely that wind power developers should compete with other wind power developers etc., not with 'brown' technologies in general. Then there can be a shift from an unsustainable productionist path to an ecologically and also economically sustainable development path.

Conclusion

The main thrust of this chapter is that the over-productionist path followed hitherto by China may have served some developmental objectives, but it is unsustainable now not just in ecological terms, but also even in economic terms. China is now adopting a different economic path oriented towards consumption and low pollution and low energy intensity services. The only issue here is whether this occurs reasonably smoothly or by dint of a crisis following a banking debt crisis. The energy implications of this clearly point in one direction, that is that the hitherto seemingly unstoppable upwards curve of energy consumption is now being halted. In fact the proportion of the economy taken up by services is likely to greatly increase in the future, and as this happens so rates of economic growth will become lower. Rates of growth of energy consumption in China are likely to decline further along with the general lowering of economic growth.

Certainly there is good evidence that the tide of unnecessary construction has been greatly curbed. However, the Government still has to 'rebalance' the economy towards consumption of services, assuring high employment as well as reduction in debts. If it is the case that the Chinese Government fails to turn the ship around to a more sustainable direction, then economic collapse is likely to be the consequence, as the economy is swallowed by mounting debt problems and lack of further investment. That in itself will lead to a big drop in energy consumption. Hence, to a certain extent, it does not matter which way things go (rebalancing or collapse), carbon emissions will not rise as they have done in the past. On the other hand, whilst China may experience a much lower rate of economic growth in the next few years than since the 1980s, it may well achieve a rebalancing of the economy towards consumption of services.

The task of rebalancing will require some effective action to overcome the inbuilt bias of the current Chinese local government set-up towards development of infrastructure and manufacturing exports. The way that local government finances are currently structured means that they have an interest in supporting industry rather than environmental demands. To Western eyes there is an obvious case for democratic control of local government so that the popular demands for lowering pollution can be achieved without the local officials' associations with industry getting in the way. This issue is further discussed in Chapter 5.

There are two very important lessons here. First is that future economic growth is likely to rise at a much slower rate than has been the case over most of the last 35 years. Second is that even this extra growth is likely to be much less energy intensive than previously since it is likely to be much more oriented towards services rather than production of buildings and goods for export.

These two factors, put together, are an important part of what I have called 'Eurocentric' ecological modernisation (EM). This is implicit to developed economies that have achieved high levels of energy and materials consumption but where the increases in such consumption tend to plateau, or at least increase more slowly. The technological aspects of EM are crucial, and so are the political and economic governance aspects of EM. In the next chapter I look at how social and technological factors can, in the case of China, combine to produce a stabilisation of carbon emissions through stabilisation of energy consumption. If this occurs, this gives the possibilities for introducing low carbon energy technologies in such a manner as to steadily reduce carbon emissions. I turn to focus more on such issues in the next chapter.

Notes

1 *China Daily* (2007) 'Local Officials Need Oversight', 24 January, available online at www.chinadaily.com.cn/cndy/2007-01/24/content_790745.htm
2 Andrews-Speed, P. (2012) *The Governance of Energy in China*, London: Palgrave, p. 39
3 McKinsey Quarterly (2015) China's rising internet wave, January, available online at www.mckinsey.com/insights/high_tech_telecoms_internet/chinas_rising_internet_wave_wired_companies
4 Meadows, Donella H., *et al.* (1972) *The Limits to Growth*, New York: Universe Books
5 These calculations are based on two technical analyses: (a) A. Li, *et al.* (eds) (2014) *Proceedings of the 8th International Symposium on Heating, Ventilation and Air Conditioning*, 'Lecture Notes in Electrical Engineering 263', DOI: 10.1007/978-3-642-39578-9_52, Springer-Verlag Berlin Heidelberg, Chapter 52; Cong, X., *et al.*, Analysis on CO2 Emissions of Construction Industry in China Based on Life Cycle Assessment, pp. 499–506; (b) Minx J.C., *et al.* (2011) 'A "carbonizing dragon": China's fast growing CO2 emissions revisited'. *Environmental Science and Technology* vol. 45, no. 21, 9144–9153
6 Ansar, A., Flyvbjerg, B., Budzier A. and Lunn, D. (2016) 'Does infrastructure investment lead to economic growth or economic fragility? Evidence from China', *Oxford Review of Economic Policy*, vol. 32, no. 3, 360–390, p. 360, available online at http://oxrep.oxfordjournals.org/content/32/3/360.short

7   Chew, J. (2015) 'Chinese Officials Admit They Faked Economic Figures, Fortune, 14 December, available online at http://fortune.com/2015/12/14/china-fake-economic-data/

8   Arlidge, J. (2016) 'What's happened to the Great Malls of China?', *Sunday Times Style Magazine*, 24 January, page 22

9   Roach, S., 'China's services sector is growing, but far too few Chinese are spending,' *South China Morning Post*, November 2015, available online at www.scmp.com/comment/insight-opinion/article/1884050/chinas-services-sector-growing-far-too-few-chinese-are

10 Whiting, S. (2001) *Power and Wealth in Rural China*, Cambridge: Cambridge University Press

11 Wang, G. and Zheng, Y. (eds) (2013) *China: Development and Governance*, Singapore: World Scientific

12 Naughton, B. (2007) *The Chinese Economy*, Cambridge, Mass. MIT Press

13 Seong, J. (2015) 'What You Need to Know About China's Surprising Strengths in Innovation', *Huffington Post*, available online at www.huffingtonpost.com/jonathan-woetzel/china-strength-innovation_b_8359026.html

14 Naughton, B. (2007) *The Chinese Economy*, Cambridge, MA: MIT Press, p. 313

15 Andrews-Speed (2012) op. cit., p. 18

16 Pettis, M. (2013). *Avoiding the Fall: China's Economic Restructuring*, Washington: Carnegie Endowment for International Peace, p. 39

17 Sanderson, H., Forsyth, M. (2013) *China's Superbank*, Hoboken, New Jersey: Wiley, see section 'Manhattan in China'

18 Fei, M. (2012) Are Chinese Banks Hiding 'The Mother of All Debt Bombs'? *The Diplomat*, 10 September, available online at http://thediplomat.com/2012/09/are-chinese-banks-hiding-the-mother-of-all-debt-bombs/

19 Guizhen He. Mol, A. and Yonglong L. (in press) 'Wasted Cities in China', *Environmental Development*, p. 2

20 Ibid., p. 5

21 Johnson, C. (2001) 'Japanese Capitalism Revisited', *Japanese Policy Research Institute*, available online at www.jpri.org/publications/occasionalpapers/op22.html

22 Unsigned (2015) *Economist*, 'Deleveraging delayed, Credit growth is still outstripping economic growth', 22 October, available online at www.economist.com/news/finance-and-economics/21676837-credit-growth-still-outstripping-economic-growth-deleveraging-delayed

23 Kramer, J. (2015) 'Economic Insight: China: Zombification instead of a crash', *Commerzbank*, available online at https://research.commerzbank.com/delegate/publication?params=0%2B6I0ndQR829Lw8lNu54JbF9l3Hf2b6yTTLDsi%2BvIrG9dLM6sGJ1smz5YSY6etBo

24 Brautigam, D. (2011) *The Dragon's Gift – The real story of China in Africa*, Oxford: Oxford University Press

25 Sanderson, H. and Forsythe, M. (2013) *China's Superbank*, Singapore: John Wiley

26 Nylander, J. (2015) 'Sweden's Top Economist Puts China's GDP Growth At 3%, But Others Are Even Less Optimistic, *Forbes Magazine*, 23 September, available online at www.forbes.com/sites/jnylander/2015/09/23/swedens-top-economist-puts-chinas-gdp-growth-at-3-others-are-less-optimistic/#1a0a30c62243

27 Smith, N. (2015) 'China's economy is worse than you think', 3 November, *Bloomberg View*, available online at www.bloombergview.com/articles/2015-11-03/china-s-slump-might-be-much-worse-than-we-thought

28 Evans-Pritchard, A. (2016) 'Fitch reveals the $2 trillion black hole in China's economy that heralds a lost decade', *Daily Telegraph*, 22 September, available online at www.telegraph.co.uk/business/2016/09/22/fitch-warns-bad-debts-in-china-are-ten-times-official-claims-sta/

29 Curran, E. (2015) 'State Companies: Back on China's To-Do List', *Bloomberg*, 30

July, available online at www.bloomberg.com/news/articles/2015–07–30/china-s-state-owned-companies-may-face-reform,

30 Lee, I., M. Syed and L. Xueyan (2013) 'China's Path to Consumer-Based Growth: Reorienting Investment and Enhancing Efficiency', *IMF Working Paper 13/83*, Washington: International Monetary Fund

31 Ibid., p. 4

32 Wildau, G. and Hornby, L. (2016) 'China GDP grows 6.7 per cent in second quarter on boost from infrastructure', *Financial Times*

33 Unsigned, *Economist* (2013) 'China bans new government buildings in corruption curb', 23 July, available online at www.bbc.co.uk/news/world-asia-23422985

34 Unsigned, *Economist* (2014) 'Counting Ghosts', 4 January, available online at www.economist.com/news/china/21592628-china-opens-books-its-big-spending-local-governments-counting-ghosts

35 Pei, M. (2015) 'China's war on corruption could hasten Communist Party's decline', *Nikkei Asian Review*, 19 May, available online at http://asia.nikkei.com/Viewpoints/Perspectives/China-s-war-on-corruption-could-hasten-communist-party-s-decline?page=2

36 Fenby, J. (2014) *Will China Dominate the 21st Century?*, Cambridge: Polity

37 Moody, A. (2015) 'Dissecting China's five year plan', 23 November, *Daily Telegraph*, available online at www.telegraph.co.uk/sponsored/china-watch/politics/12006280/china-five-year-plan.html

38 Wildau, G. (2015) 'Growth data buoy China at 'pivotal moment" in economic rebalancing, *Financial Times*, 19 October, available online at www.ft.com/cms/s/2/df727b0c-763c-11e5-8564-b4bb9a521c63.html#axzz3vWZVxZY5

39 McDonald, I. (2015) 'Hang in There Australia, Your Exports to China Will Double', *Bloomberg Business*, 19 October, available online at www.bloomberg.com/news/articles/2015-10-19/hang-in-there-australia-your-exports-to-china-will-double

40 Wang S., Li, Q. and Zhou, C. (2016) 'The relationship between economic growth, energy consumption, and CO2 emissions: Empirical evidence from China', *Science of the Total Environment*, vol. 542, Part A, 15 January, 360–371

41 Bin, Z. (2016) 'Easing China's transition to a services economy', *Paulson Policy Memorandum*, London: Paulson Institute, available online at www.paulsoninstitute.org/wp-content/uploads/2016/04/PPM_Services_Zhang-Bin_English.pdf

42 Herrendorf, Berthold M., Rogerson, Richard and Valentinyi, Á, (2014) 'Growth and Structural Transformation', *Handbook of Economic Growth* 2, 855–941, as cited by Bin, Z. (2016) *Easing China's transition to a services economy*, London: Paulson Institute, available online at www.paulsoninstitute.org/wp-content/uploads/2016/04/PPM_Services_Zhang-Bin_English.pdf, p. 4

43 Ibid., p. 1

44 World Bank (2015) *Per capita economic growth data*, available online at http://data.worldbank.org/indicator/NY.GDP.PCAP.KD.ZG

45 Trading Economics (2016) *Indicators*, available online at www.tradingeconomics.com/

46 Barro, R. (2016) Economic Growth and Convergence, Applied Especially to China, *NBER Working Paper No. 21872*, Cambridge: MA, National Bureau of Economic Research, available online at www.nber.org/papers/w21872

47 Bin, Z. (2016) op. cit., pp. 7–12

4 Carbon emissions and energy consumption

In this chapter I am going to take a look at what China is doing in terms of altering patterns of energy consumption, and to look at what is happening in particular at the profile of carbon emissions that we have seen coming from China. In doing so, I will make some comparisons with the USA as well with as the EU. This will help to establish, in relative terms, the trajectory of carbon emissions from China.

Hence in this chapter I am going to look at the energy issues directly. How are China's energy and carbon emissions shaping up for the future, and what are the pressures which influence this outcome? In answering such questions, doing so I will also question the credibility of what some Western energy claims about China which creates the impression that the Chinese are the main barrier to dealing effectively with climate change. The arguments in this chapter build on the foundations in Chapter 3. The imperatives in this chapter involve a rebalanced, more services-oriented, lower growth economy and also one where the Chinese people demand low pollution technologies to be implemented with the highest priority. In this chapter I look at how such institutions and policies may emerge to influence levels of energy consumption. Regulatory responses that can be associated with Ecological modernisation (EM) include effective measures to make energy use more efficient, and energy use outcomes will be affected by the physical and social structures that underpin society such as urban density and sizes of living spaces. This chapter connects how the assertion that China is moving towards a ern style pattern of lower, more service oriented pattern of less rapid and more device oriented patterns of economic growth to less energy intensive outcomes. This trend, leading to stabilisation and reduction of carbon emissions, is an implicit part of what I have called 'Eurocentric EM.

In looking at where China's carbon emissions are going we need to look at the changing profile of the energy sources that are being utilised by China. I need also to comment on the debate about whether coal use in China is still increasing (or in fact decreasing), but mainly I will restrict this chapter's discussion to changing profiles of energy demand. My main discussion about changes in the pattern of fuels used in China will occur in Chapter 6. In this chapter I want to focus on two issues: factors affecting energy consumption and overall trends in Chinese carbon emissions.

I want to avoid the problem that is so often encountered in may discussions of energy of looking solely at energy supply, as if somehow that was fixed by projections – often influenced by the energy supply industries themselves! So this chapter looks at the changing level of carbon emissions principally from the perspective of energy demand, and then we can go on to discuss the changing nature of fuels used to supply the energy. This will be done mainly in Chapter 6 where of course I will talk about the changing balances between the various fuels, coal, oil gas, renewable energy and nuclear power.

Exploding myths about China's carbon profile

Up until 2015, it seemed an almost universal assumption that China's growing use of coal and its burning of fossil fuels in general threatened to burn the planet as carbon emissions hurtled upwards. It was claimed that if China's and India's economic growth continued the Earth's ecosystems would be overwhelmed. One report by a leading environmental group claimed that 'Earth lacks the water, energy and agricultural land to allow China and India to attain Western living standards'.[1] Another common opinion was that China's coal consumption was likely to defeat efforts to contain post-industrial global temperature rises to under 2 degrees C.[2] Sometimes the comparisons seem to be selected to favour the USA, for example one observation pointing out that in terms of power stations capacity China had moved from having less power station capacity before 2000 to double that of the USA by 2010. It was said to be heading for four times US capacity by 2040.[3] A letter in the UK's Guardian newspaper (at the time of the Paris Agreement on Climate Change in December 2015) that

> China's strategy for dealing with air pollution is a cosmetic exercise cynically timed to coincide with the Paris summit on climate change…. Despite all the fine speeches in Paris, China has 368 coal-fired power stations under construction and is planning a further 800.[4]

But are such projections alarmist? In the light of recent experience, I argue in this chapter, the answer is yes especially as building more power stations does not, in itself, create extra energy demand. By early 2016, the Chinese Government had ordered a slow down to much of the power station fleet being constructed.[5] By March 2016, coal-fired power stations were operating, on average, for less than half the time.[6]

There is an argument within the environmental movement about how far continued economic growth is compatible with ecological survival. Some would argue that it cannot be, and others (and I would agree with this strain) would argue that the important target is to reduce reliance on non-renewable resources. It is the reduction of use of materials, and protection of ecological systems that is the important bottom line, rather than data on economic growth. That having been said, of course, the source of pollution overproductionist growth that was occurring in China in the earlier years of this century was clearly at odds with sustainability, but, as argued in Chapter 3 this was unsustainable even in conventional economic terms, never mind ecological ones.

Sometimes comparisons made between the West and China and developing countries can involve implicit bias if the only metric is simply China's share of current global carbon emissions. Certainly China's contribution to global carbon emissions should not be underestimated. In 2014 China was responsible for emitting some 28 per cent of the world's carbon dioxide.[7] Some figures for 2012 are given in Figure 4.1 in comparison with the other leading emitters.

But, looked at on a historical basis, China's input is not nearly as large. China's coal and cement production has been responsible for around 8 per cent of global carbon emissions since 1750 – but then, of course, on a historical basis the West's contribution is rather larger than this. The West's investor owned oil companies alone are responsible for some 22 per cent of carbon dioxide emissions in this period, never mind counting all of the coal and natural gas and cement produced in the West over the years.[8] And counting things back to 1750 is very relevant given the fact that carbon dioxide is a very long-lasting gas in the atmosphere. China's contribution has tended to be reported purely on a current basis without reference to any historical contribution to current global warming patterns.

But perhaps even worse than this, China's contribution to carbon dioxide emissions is misleading without any reference to per capita carbon emissions. Yes, there are a lot of people in China! But is the individual Chinese person any more or less responsible for carbon emissions than the average US citizen, or any other citizen?

In fact China's emissions per person are pretty typical for an EU country – about the same as the UK, less than Germany but less than half that of the average US citizen, as can be seen in Figure 4.2. Moreover, as discussed later in this chapter, 'embedded' emissions contained in Chinese exports will reduce China's per capita emission rate compared to the EU.

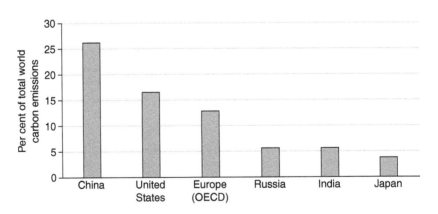

Figure 4.1 Carbon dioxide emissions by leading countries.

Source: US Energy Information Service.[9]

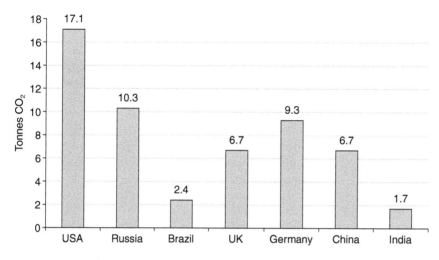

Figure 4.2 Per capita carbon emissions from leading countries.
Sources: BP[10] and World Bank.[11]

Clearly the emphasis has to be on getting the industrialised world's house in order as well as in ensuring that China's emissions decrease rather than increase. The point is that in this debate the responsibility has to be shared equally on the basis of average per capita emissions, not the largest countries picked out for blame. This is especially as on a historical basis the already industrialised world has a much heavier responsibility for past carbon emissions and thus for temperature increases so far rather than the newly industrialising nations.

This is now especially the case since China's total carbon emissions (from energy and concrete) may have stabilised or even actually fallen in the most recent period. I will discuss the mechanics of how this has happened, and what we can expect in the future, and I will suggest some results that may surprise many people, namely that Chinese carbon emissions are likely to undergo a substantial decline in the coming years.

One analysis written by Fergus Green and Nicholas Stern and published by the Grantham Institute has pointed out four key implications of what China does in the future, and my four reasons for arguing that what China does is of supreme importance in the world largely flow from them.[12] First the sheer size of China, one fifth of the world's population, means that China's impact on global outcomes is massive. Second, China is seen as a leader of poorer countries, helping to shape their development paths, often by sheer emulation, and often by the fact that China's development policies involve lending money to poorer countries for development purposes. Third, China will influence other countries on the basis that if China can reduce its emissions and grow its economy, then surely others, already much better off, can do the same. Finally, China can influence everybody because of the country's contribution to the art of marshalling resources through its wind power and solar pv deployment programmes.

What is clear, and is something that confounds earlier notions that Chinese people were less interested in environmental protection compared to Western countries, is that the Chinese seem now more concerned about climate change than much of the West. Opinion surveys conducted recently by *YouGov* indicate that Chinese people are far more concerned to counter climate change than the average person in the USA or the UK.[13] Denmark, with its wind power programme that now supplies over 42 per cent of its electricity demand, is one of the few Western countries that comes out ahead of China in terms of popular concern over global warming. Indeed, the Danish Government has given considerable advice to Chinese policymakers and regulators about how to best shift to a low carbon economy.

This does not mean that the Chinese Government is being as radical as it could afford to be on the topic of setting targets for reduction of carbon emissions. When Xi Jinping met Barack Obama in 2010 and signed an agreement declaring that China would aim to peak its carbon emissions by 2030 this looked relatively radical. Now it looks thoroughly conservative. Analysis of China's pre-Paris Agreement commitments makes them seem vague, with targets expressed in reductions in energy intensity rather than reductions in carbon emissions themselves, and an effective target of peaking of carbon emissions by 2027 if all goes well.[14]

By contrast of course the attitude of US legislators has been obstructive towards agreeing to international treaties on carbon abatement, despite some moderately hopeful efforts by Presidents Clinton and Obama. The notorious (to climate change campaigners) 'Byrd-Hagel amendment' was used as a justification for US Congressional opposition to American agreement to treaties such as the 1997 Kyoto Protocol. Kyoto set targets for emission reductions for the industrialised nation. The Byrd-Hagel amendment which was passed by a vote of 95 to 0 by the US Senate actually prevented the US from signing any climate change agreement if it did not contain commitments by developing countries such as China to 'limit or reduce greenhouse gas emissions'.

The American politicians were worried, in particular, that without such limitations on Chinese emissions they could gain a competitive economic edge over US business. One of the ironies of this position is that, as discussed in Chapter 4, the only way that China can remain competitive (and indeed survive economically) is to adopt more service oriented economic strategies that involve reductions in carbon emissions! By contrast, the USA is actually falling behind the Chinese in production of solar pv. The US response (and that of the EU), far from being competitive, is to protect its own industry.

Of course, now that China has agreed to cut emissions, does not seem to presage Congressional approval of the Paris Agreement on Climate Change which was agreed in December of 2015 by dint of it being an executive agreement rather than a Treaty. Ironically, of course, the US could (in the 1990s) have actually signed up to some emission reductions without, as it turns out, having to do anything it would not have done anyway. This is because emissions have fallen in the US since the 1990s. Not anywhere enough, of course, considering the high level of per capita emissions by the USA. This leads onto another issue which is very important to understanding how much carbon emissions will be generated by China in the future. This is the fact that future projections of energy consumption have an invariable tendency to be overestimates. Often grossly so.

Let us look at some examples I have to hand drawn from documents on my bookshelf or hard drive. In the case of the USA, the US Department of Energy projected, in 1993, that US annual energy consumption would increase from 85 quadrillion (quad) Btu in 1990 to 107 quad Btu by 2010.[15] In fact, the actual consumption in 2010 was just 98 quad Btu. If we go even farther back the projections can become even more inaccurate. In the case of the UK, in 1976 the UK Government projected that UK annual energy consumption would increase to between 500 and 550 million tonnes of coal equivalent (tce) by the year 2000.[16] In fact it has never risen above 280 million tce. Perhaps this projection seems so inaccurate because it was made before the implications of the oil price hikes of the 1970s became clear. Even more recently the EU grossly overestimated projected consumption of natural gas. In 2003, Eurogas, which represents the natural gas industry projected that EU gas demand would increase from around 400 million tonnes of oil equivalent (mtoe) to 560 mtoe by 2015.[17] In fact the figure actually declined to around 385 mtoe in 2015. Again the original projection was made before the oil price spike (which pushed up fossil fuel prices in general). Indeed, even today, many estimates of future energy consumption may not fully take into account the impact of the period of high oil prices which lasted from around 2004 to 2014.

Oil price spikes – such as occurred from 1973 to 1985, and again from 2004 to 2014 – concentrate people's minds on making improvements in energy efficiency. During the course of this new less energy intensive technologies (and products and services that have lower energy usage in general) become much more economic. Their use becomes mainstream, often universal, and such 'learning' of new techniques and adoption of the new technologies persists thereafter in the form of established routines of knowledge and practice. Hence projections of future energy consumption made before the end of an oil price spike are likely to be especially inaccurate. We can expect that, just as in the case of the oil price hike of the 1970s and 1980s, the oil price hike that occurred this century will have long-lasting depressive effect on energy consumption patterns across the world.

This trend of overestimation of future energy consumption is explainable by reference to two factors in particular. First is the fact, which governments do not like to admit, that economic growth often fails to be as high as they would like to project. A second factor is that in recent decades (and these days particularly) the new, fast expanding, technologies tend to be low energy using technologies based around information. Michael Grubb, *et al.* comment that '[t]he egregious errors in OECD forecasts tended to reflect simplistic extrapolations of past trends, with little consideration of technological changes, efficiency improvements, saturation effects, and sectoral changes in the economy'.[18]

During the nineteenth and much of the twentieth century the new technologies were often energy producing machines – steam engines, internal combustion engines and gas turbines which prompted big increases in energy consumption. Expanding industry tended to be made possible by the more efficient mobilisation of such energies and hence industrialisation was profoundly energy intensive – energy intensity being the amount of energy required to produce a given quantity of GDP.

But now it is much more the case that expansion of GDP is bound up with the deployment of information technologies which are by their very nature associated with much lower energy intensities. Of course, more traditional industries, such as construction (of which there has been a lot in China) are still energy intensive. But once countries are no longer spending so much effort in construction their energy intensities are bound to go down, and go down much further as their growth is concerned much more with the lower energy intensive growth associated with services. The energy intensity of GDP associated with services is, measured on a global basis, around 9 times less than the energy intensity of industrial production.[19] That is, services consume, for each unit of GDP, little more than 10 per cent of the energy compared to the energy consumed by a unit of GDP of manufactured product.

The relative energy efficiency of the different sectors for China can be seen in Figure 4.3 below.

A point made in Chapter 3, was that China is moving towards a more service oriented economy as it develops in the direction of already developed economies. As the proportion of GDP coming from services improves in China, so there is likely to be a dramatic decline in energy intensity of Chinese GDP and

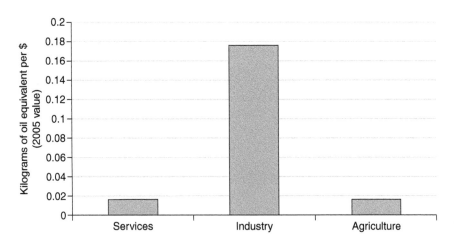

Figure 4.3 Energy intensity of different sectors of the Chinese economy.

Source: World Energy Council, www.wec-indicators.enerdata.eu/.

thus, as also economic growth declines, a stabilisation, or even, with effective energy efficiency policies, a fall, in energy consumption overall. The high proportion of services as opposed to manufacturing and agriculture in developed countries can be seen in Figure 4.4 below.

A further factor is simply that in the future energy intensity even of traditional types of production tends to decline. Moreover, newly industrialising countries tend to industrialise using much lower amounts of energy consumption than was used by earlier industrialisers. This concept has been called 'dematerialisation'.[20] These factors which are reducing energy intensity are, as discussed earlier, given a major boost as a result of oil price spikes. The impact on energy projections for China will be considerable, as for the rest of the World, and may not have been fully factored in through projections that have been made for government. On top of this, as discussed in Chapter 3, as economies develop their proportion of services in GDP increases, and as this happens, economic growth tends to decline, thus putting further downward pressure on the amount of energy the economy consumes.

This discussion is part of an introduction to considering projections of future energy consumption in China. We need to do this in order to make some intelligent guesses on what levels of carbon emissions China is likely to produce in the future. You may ask whether my guesses are useful or plausible. I would argue that they are likely to be a lot more plausible than official projections which make the mistake of over-estimation of energy consumption that are likely to occur. Generally speaking, also (and with much relevance to China), projections based on past behaviour are likely to be very wide of the mark.

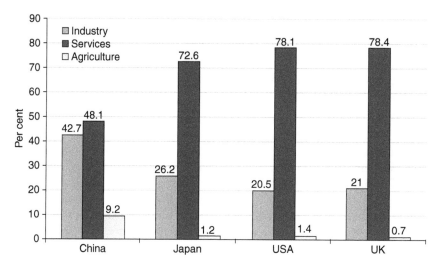

Figure 4.4 Percentage shares of different sectors of GDP in selected countries in 2014.

Source: World Bank, http://data.worldbank.org/.

In analyses and projections of future carbon emissions, there is all too often far too little attention paid to energy consumption. Even when energy consumption is modelled, Grubb, *et al.* report that the tendency has been to assume that China's industrial structure will remain much the same, thus inflating expectations of energy demand.[21] Instead, emphasis and analysis may be placed on the technologies used to supply the energy. I mentioned near the start of this chapter the 'counterintuitive' notion that the fact that China was building a lot of new coal-fired power stations is likely to reduce, not increase, carbon emissions. The point is that the power stations can only ever generate the amount of electricity that is consumed. So if more power plants are built than are needed in terms of having generation able to supply all of the electricity demanded, then the result is likely to be that either the new plant will not be used or old plant will be closed down. In fact, the latter will be the case because the operating costs of the new plant will be rather lower, and their energy efficiency will be rather higher than that of the old plant. Older, less efficient, power stations are being closed down in large numbers.[22] Hence the average energy efficiency of the coal power plant fleet will increase, meaning that the amount of coal needed to generate the electricity demand will fall. There seems little likelihood that the system will allow electricity prices to fall significantly to encourage demand, since they are controlled by the Government and the producers would not sanction a fall in prices.

Of course, the Chinese Government does not, initially, expect the outcome of sluggish growth in electricity demand. It is trying to say that growth will maintain at around 7 per cent per annum in order to satisfy its own public relations, steel industry workers and so on. But as argued in the last chapter, this is unlikely to happen. In an effective at least partial recognition of this fact, in March 2016, the Government stopped a range of provinces from building power stations and opening new coal mines. Many existing coal mines are being shut down.[23]

China's energy consumption and carbon emissions – slowdown or decline?

As is well known, China's energy consumption is dominated by coal. In 2013, 66 per cent of the country's primary energy consumption came from coal. 18.4 per cent came from petroleum, 9.8 per cent from natural gas and non-fossil fuels (renewable energy and nuclear power) accounted for 9.8 per cent of consumption.[24] Primary energy consumption is a measure of the total initial input into energy production. This figure is rather larger than final energy consumed of course, the difference between the two figures being very large in the case of electricity consumption because of the large amounts of energy wasted during production of electricity when fossil fuels are used.

Coal consumption is falling as a proportion of national energy consumption, whilst the other categories are increasing. Around half of coal consumption is used in power stations, most of the rest by industry. I will discuss the other fuels used in electricity generation and the changing proportional share of their use to generate electricity in Chapter 6.

Purely in conventional energy security terms, China has faced increasing strains on its energy economy. If you go back to 1998, China had relatively little need to import energy. True, its coal production managed to mostly keep up with its ever-increasing appetite, especially in the decade from 2003, although even here net imports increased to around 6 per cent of total consumption. But its oil deficit had grown to massive proportions by 2014. Whereas in 1998 it had been able to produce over 80 per cent of the volume of oil consumption from Chinese sources, by 2014 this dropped to around half of this, that is, 40 per cent. There was also a natural gas supply gap building up as well. In 1998, China's level of natural gas production was around 90 per cent of its consumption, but by 2014, despite a big increase in domestic Chinese gas production, it was producing only 71 per cent of the level of Chinese consumption.[25] In the period 1990 to 2005, for example, 'China's per capita-emission rate grew at an annual rate of 7.25 per cent'.[26] Indeed, as can be seen in Figure 4.5 below, China's output of carbon emissions was increasing at a particularly rapid rate in the period 2002 to 2013.

There are, of course, great pressures on China to reduce its coal consumption in order to reduce air pollution, as can be been seen in Chapter 6. The Government is organising the closure of coal mines as well as reducing reliance on coal imports. However, there is also concern about the increased need to import oil to fuel its expanding use of motor vehicles and also there is concern about the increase in imports of natural gas which are needed to substitute for coal. Natural gas, of course, is seen as a much cleaner alternative for heating purposes in particular. All of this adds to the pressure to use its fossil fuels more efficiently. The needs to reduce emissions and defend China's energy security are perceived to overlap to a degree that is much more virtuous than in many other countries. Indeed, compared with the USA, China has the reduction of energy consumption much more on its energy security agenda compared to the USA, since it faces much greater relative reliance on energy imports compared to the USA.

There seems to be clear evidence that China's carbon dioxide emissions have at least levelled off, and perhaps even fallen in 2015. However, there is still some disagreement about the figures and their interpretation. Greenpeace has said that that not just coal consumption but also carbon emissions actually fell in 2014–2015.[27] Others, however, including the US Government's Energy Information Agency (EIA) are more cautious and argue that carbon emissions may have levelled off, but maybe not fallen. EIA seem to accept that coal consumption has fallen – the implication being that the EIA assumes that the energy content of coal that is consumed has increased in 2014 compared to previous years.[28] This approach is generally supported by a team from the Norwegian based Cicero centre who specialise on climate change issues. They argue that whilst coal consumption has clearly fallen since 2013, an increase in use of other fossil fuels as well as an increase in the energy content in the coal actually

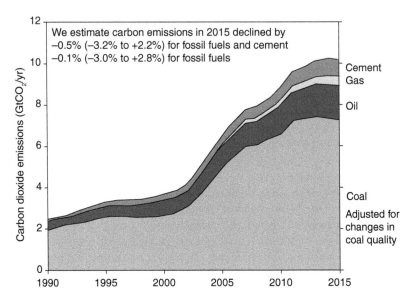

Figure 4.5 Carbon dioxide emissions in China to 2015. Figure prepared and supplied by Jan Ivar Korsbakken and Glen Peters on 22 March, 2016 to accompany publication of paper published in Nature Climate Change.[29,30]

burned means that in 2015 carbon dioxide emissions may have only fallen marginally and in 2014 not at all; Figure 4.5 above, expresses the changing picture in recent years according to their analysis.

Indeed, a continued decline in coal consumption would seem to tally with other data, including the sluggish nature of production of electricity, which according the figures available from the Chinese Government's National Energy Administration only increased by 0.5 per cent in 2015.[31] That implies a decrease in coal use since there has been (a) a substantial expansion in generation of electricity by renewable and nuclear sources, these displacing coal consumption and (b) much less coal will be used to produce a given amount of electricity because new more efficient coal-fired power stations are taking the place of older, smaller and less efficient coal power plant.

Of course, as the authors of the Nature and Climate paper quoted earlier insist,[32] there are considerable uncertainties about the figures which may not be fully resolved until revised estimates have been finalised by the Chinese statisticians, which takes years. However, the energy statistics may have a greater degree of robustness compared to some economic statistics. As mentioned in Chapter 3, there is an incentive in China to manipulate the economic growth data artificially in an upwards direction, since local officials gain career advancement through being perceived as contributing to economic growth. But there is no clear motivation in presenting artificially low figures for energy production. Indeed, in the run-up to the Paris Climate Change Agreement (concluded in

December 2015), if anything, the Chinese Government would have had an incentive to keep the energy consumption figures up, because it resisted accepting a target of capping carbon dioxide emissions before 2030. The Chinese Government has a big incentive to show reductions in air pollution, but as discussed in the last chapter, air pollution is (now well) measured directly, and the Chinese public will be influenced by these direct indicators of air pollution and not by data on carbon dioxide emissions, which does not actually produce the local smogs. In any case, Chinese energy data comes from a variety of sources and so is difficult to 'fix'.

At the end of the day if, as many economists believe, Chinese economic growth has fallen steeply from around 10 per cent in the decade up to 2013 to maybe as low as around 3 per cent in 2014 and 2015, then one would expect growth in Chinese energy consumption to have sharply declined. Indeed the decline in coal consumption and perhaps (in 2015) slight decline in total carbon emissions may be associated with an economic growth of 3–4 per cent per annum.

How China could slow and even stabilise its energy consumption

Much of the reason why energy growth in China has been curbed has been covered in Chapter 3; it has been concerned with rebalancing the economy away from what has become an unprofitable 'productionist' economy and towards more spending on less energy intensive services. Indeed much of the decline in energy growth can be attributed to the decline in China's building construction programme, an activity which has taken up around a fifth of China's total energy consumption. However, there is a lot more to things than this, and there are a lot of reasons why we may look forward to a continuing lack of energy growth. If there is little or no energy growth, then measures to shift fuel use from coal to less carbon intensive fuels will generate large cuts in carbon emissions – as well, of course, in reductions in local pollution.

Of course, many people might find this notion of China actually reducing its emissions now and in the near future to be a strange one. After all, is not China still a country with a relatively low per capita GDP compared to 'developed' nations? However, when this is examined carefully the notion becomes much less strange. Perhaps we should turn the issue around, and ponder, why should Chinese emissions rise any more rather than fall?

For one thing, China's population growth is lower than for the average country, at just 0.5 per cent per year, and even this is falling.[33,34] Second, academics have argued that China seems to be heading for quite radical reductions in energy intensity, perhaps more radical than has occurred in the cases of other formerly state capitalist states such as Korea and Japan.[35] In short, China's apparent energy profligacy has been associated with some very inefficient practices which are being discarded.

The causes of this likely tendency towards much lower energy intensity can be divided into two factors. One is the physical structure of the human infrastructure in China, in particular its pattern of buildings and settlements. We can use a comparison with the USA to illustrate this. The USA's infamously high per capita energy usage is associated with its urban structure. It has a low urban energy density, something which leads to much higher rates of car travel than, for example, European cities. Partly because of the low urban density in the USA, there are political pressures to restrain taxation of gasoline used for motor vehicle transport. This, in turn, makes car travel even less energy efficient since there are fewer price incentives to buy energy efficient vehicles compared to European conditions where motor vehicle fuel taxes are generally high by comparison. But Chinese conditions of urban structure are much more analogous to that of Europe rather than the USA. Chinese cities such as Shanghai, Shenzhen and Beijing have urban densities that are 2–4 times the urban densities of US cities such as New York and Los Angeles.[36]

Another key factor which pushes up per capita energy consumption in the USA higher than most countries, is the sheer size of US buildings, especially residences, compared to other countries, including Europe and of course China. Large buildings mean large energy consumption figures, and so uses such as air conditioning consume vast energy resources. In the winter, which is cold in many parts of the USA, energy consumption will be very high. However, again, China is much more analogous to European conditions than that of the USA. Indeed, house sizes in China are currently much smaller even than European ones, which are in turn rather smaller than house sizes in countries such as Australia and the USA[37] (both of which countries having per capita carbon emissions which are among the highest in the world). However, there is still upwards pressure on electricity consumption coming from air conditioning. It is estimated that by 2025, use of air conditioners will constitute around 10–12 per cent of 2015 levels of electricity consumption. Strengthened energy efficiency standards for energy using equipment are essential for keeping this increase down.[38]

I have used a general comparison with Europe here, but the point I go on to make is that China's urban infrastructure is, in its density, much closer to European patterns than that of the USA. In other words, structurally, Chinese energy consumption is naturally going to be like European ones, and unlike that of the USA. Whatever the criticisms may be of Chinese planning or urban centres, it is still very dense in many senses. Indeed, recent policy discussions indicate that there is now a trend towards emphasising increasing urban energy density to reduce strain on the environment and also new demands for road building.[39] Moreover, the living spaces are much, much smaller than American ones, and still very small even by European standards. Hence there is a physical structural pressure for Chinese energy consumption to be like European levels. The Chinese Government is pressing for 'gated communities' to lose their enclosed status in order to make ways for easier transportation and more concentrated amenities for local residents, although this meeting resistance from rich condo residents.[40]

A further fact, of course, is the proportion of services as a contribution to the Chinese economy, as has been mentioned previously. At the moment the

Chinese economy involves about half the GDP coming from services compared to approaching 80 per cent in countries such as the USA and the UK. Yet this proportion of services in the Chinese economy is rapidly increasing, meaning that we can expect great downwards pressure on Chinese energy consumption compared to already developed countries in the next few years.

Then there are the policy influences in China which need to be taken into account in any discussion of factors that will put downward pressure on energy consumption in China. There are great pressures to reduce air pollution in China. The responses to such heightened Chinese concerns about local air pollution coincidentally involve measures that will reduce energy consumption and carbon emissions as a result.

Indeed, all other things being equal, one might assume an even greater rate of carbon reduction in China compared to that of the EU given the combination of political pressures to reduce the use of coal and also the fact that the Chinese economy is still very inefficient compared to that of the EU. China's energy economy is approximately half as energy efficient as the average EU country; that is, it uses twice as much energy to produce a unit of GDP compared to that of the EU.[41] Even before we take account of China's considerable programme to shift energy supply away from coal and particularly towards renewable energy sources, this may suggest that China's carbon emissions may decline. Of course if China's economic growth rate is a lot more than that of the EU, such effects may be neutralised. As argued in Chapter 3, in reality China's economic growth rate now seems to be modest by past standards.

There is a danger that continued attempts by the Chinese Government to prop-up declining energy intensive state owned enterprises (SOEs) may derail the carbon reduction strategies. Certainly there are strong pressures to keep up employment in carbon intensive industries like steel and keep producing volumes that are excess to the needs of the global market. However, as discussed in Chapter 3, such a strategy has declining effectiveness, and if this carries on indefinitely then debts will accumulate still farther which will make economic problems worse in the long run.

Certainly China's record is as a net carbon exporter; that is, of products in which a lot of carbon emissions are 'embedded'. This means that China tends to export a lot of products using more carbon than the carbon burned to manufacture the products that it imports. Grubb, *et al.* comment that 'both single country studies for China and global studies show a significant proportion of China's CO2 emissions are associated with its exports.... Thus China's per capita 'consumption footprint' remains substantially lower than that of the EU'.[42] It is likely to be the case that this situation (that is amount of embedded carbon in products imported from China) will be eased as China reduces the focus on manufacturing. Hence, in sum, the trend is likely to be that the reduction in China's carbon exports will further add to reduce its own domestic carbon emissions.

Policies

China is implementing a range of policies that will reinforce downward pressure on energy usage and carbon emissions. Let us just run through a few of these – and we can note how they compare with the policies being pursued in the USA. For a start, China is rolling out a 'carbon market' plan that has already been piloted in some selected cities. The idea behind a carbon market is that the Government can set a cap on carbon emissions. Companies may be given emission allowances based on a proportion of their past emissions, and they can buy or sell their emissions according to whether they find it relatively cheaper or more expensive to reduce their emissions. In the USA, Democratic Presidents Clinton and Obama have favoured introducing carbon markets, but Congressional opposition has always been too great. China's carbon market was being introduced in 2016. However, we should not throw our hats in the air too quickly over such developments. As one analysis of the introduction of 'pilot' schemes to deal with air and water pollution in China puts it:

> Constrained by policy design, policy conflicts, and excessive state intervention, the market has not played an effective and 'decisive' role, resulting in low market thickness for participants and transactions, market congestion on prices, and inadequate market safety for genuine emissions trading. Better emissions trading for conventional pollutants and CO_2 requires better market-oriented rules, improved policy coordination, and stronger implementation while minimizing state intervention.[43]

The Chinese Government has also increased taxes on petroleum products in 2015, although this still only parallels rates of fuel tax in the USA which are well below the rates levied in Europe. In fact, China's efforts to improve its car fuel economy have so far been relatively ineffective.

A contrast in policies between China and the USA can be seen in the case of trying to phase out inefficient tungsten light bulbs. In China, like the EU, tungsten lightbulbs are being effectively banned. But in the USA there was such an outcry from defenders of alleged 'free choice' (free choice to waste money and pollute the world?) that the most that the US Environmental Protection Agency was allowed to do was to ensure that old style tungsten lightbulbs were required to be a bit more energy efficient.

Energy use in Chinese homes is still relatively small. This is associated with large amounts of fuel poverty, with Chinese people not being able to enjoy warm homes. However, this issue seems likely to be resolved with more energy efficient homes rather than increases in energy consumption. Building efficiency standards have been upgraded in China and superior 'green building' standards have been established by the Chinese Government with the idea of expanding the proportion of new buildings which achieve the highest levels of energy efficiency. The state-directed approach seems to be veering towards the command-and-control adopted by (it seems with increasing impact) Singapore rather than the 'market' approach adopted in the USA whereby green building is merely encouraged. Interestingly, key ideas that form the basis of China's green building standards have been influenced by the US Government's own 'Leadership in Energy and Environmental Design' (LEED) standards, the difference being that in China the Government is putting much more effort into promoting its adoption compared to the USA.[44]

The USA started off ahead, but in the next future years China seems likely to draw ahead of efforts began in the USA. A housing official from the Chinese Ministry of Housing and Urban–Rural Development commented: 'Now green buildings account for 20 per cent of the property market. The target for five years is 50 per cent. But I think that after 2020 green buildings will become a basic requirement for every construction project'.[45] The Government is providing low interest loans for such purposes (a policy which goes beyond that of most Western governments). The Government is also increasing the requirements on energy efficiency for appliances, including motor vehicles, and especially heavy goods vehicles. Much attention has been on the increase in use of electric cars, a topic that will be discussed in Chapter 6. These will make a difference in time, but earlier progress in constraining emissions from the rapidly increasing motor vehicle fleet is likely to come from more energy efficient vehicles.

China's energy efficiency in building programmes initiatives needs to become much more oriented towards 'bottom-up' initiatives involving participation of people involved rather than top-down ones. Research suggests that such participatory strategies optimise outcomes when buildings are retrofitted for conservation purposes.[46] Indeed some of the 'top-down' strategies, in particular associated with 'eco-cities', seem to be at best to be mixed blessings, if not part of the problem which needs to be stopped. The 'eco-city' development in Tianjin, for example, has been criticised for being such a top-down affair whereby central planners tried to design a city without really knowing how people were actually going to live there – with the consequence that many of the buildings are still not occupied.[47] Of course, part of the alternative to this sort of development is precisely to plan buildings to respond to local demands, plans and market possibilities rather than Beijing or even some provincial government envisioning new cities and expecting millions of people to suddenly move to them. Indeed, this type of development forms part of China's accumulating debt problem.

A key problem is that local authorities have too little incentive to check whether the buildings meet prescribed energy efficiency standards, and hence there may well be large gaps between the standards and performance. The central government in Beijing checks the paperwork produced by local authorities on building standards, but the task of checking compliance for individual buildings is left to the local officials. With shortages of staff, and concerns about corruption, there must be doubts about how well the building standards are enforced in practice.[48] Price, *et al.* report that enforcement of building standards has improved greatly, but they have called for a major improvement in the capacity to monitor energy performance in buildings.[49]

One technology with a big energy saving which is being imported from Denmark is district heating systems to provide affordable heating to people. This sort of system is particularly viable in the densely organised cities that make up much of China. There is immense potential in simply using heat generated for industrial production that would otherwise be wasted. Indeed it has been calculated that such heating can provide 'can meet almost 70% of the heat demand of North China's mandated heating regions'.[50] One example of this technology being implemented can be seen in the north-eastern city of Anshan. In this project otherwise waste heat from the third largest (AngGang) steelworks in China will provide heating for around half the city's 3.5 million inhabitants.[51] In future, the district heating could be supplied through heat pumps powered by non-fossil energy sources. Heat pumps can convert electricity in heating, and may be especially useful in feeding into heat stores (hot water tanks) when there is more renewable energy being generated at a particular time than is needed to meet demand.

In general, China is moving towards adopting a range of regulatory and tax and incentive policies designed to promote reduction of energy consumption, and, as we shall see in Chapter 6, towards switching to fuels than involve lower production of pollution. This is a much more interventionist strategy than is happening to the US, and as strong or even, in some respects, stronger compared to what is happening in Europe.

The optimum strategy is neither to leave energy to the present structure of the 'market', which does not take into account environmental costs ('externalities') and nor is it for some central authority to decide which individual projects should or should not happen. Rather the best strategy is to set regulations, taxes and incentives, and offer 'soft' loans that ensure that it is in the financial interest of companies and local authorities to move towards preferred technological outcomes in whatever projects or end-uses companies are planning. That is part of a 'smart' policy instruments strategy associated with ecological modernisation.

Of course, as I have discussed, there is much greater pressure from the Chinese public to reduce air pollution compared to that of the USA. Admittedly this may to a great extent be put down to the fact that air pollution is usually a lot worse in China compared to the USA, but such Chinese pressure on the government has a collateral effect of generating pressure to reduce carbon dioxide emissions, since local and global air pollution abatement respond to many of the same techniques. However, on top of this is the pressure in China to reduce its import dependency, especially in the areas of oil and natural gas. Once again we can see that the Chinese thus have greater pressures on them to reduce energy consumption, and thus put in place more effective policies to do this, compared to the USA. Many in the USA complain about excessive influence from environmentalists, but, when comparisons are made with China, it is evident that the pressures from US environmentalists are not nearly enough to make up what is needed to bring the USA onto a more sustainable course.

The policies in China are themselves in a process of transition from one where developmentalist, and productionist led growth is superseded by sustainability objectives, which, as discussed in Chapter 3 include both producing a sustainable economy and a sustainable environment. So there are still many deficiencies in the energy related policies in China, not to mention the 'top-down' basis upon which the economy is run, of which energy management forms a part. However, they appear to moving ahead of the USA in a number of respects, which does not reflect well on the USA. It is curious to think back to the environmental debates of the 1960s and 1970s where the stereotype was of Northern environmentalists arguing with Southern based developmentalists about whether environment or development should take priority. At least that is the stereotype around which the first major environmentalist conference in Stockholm in 1972 was formed. Things have changed radically since those days, and now it seems that we are moving towards a position where China at least, may plausibly, in some respects at least be in position to challenge countries like the USA that they are not putting sufficient weight on climate change objectives and outcomes compared to that being put on them by China.

Of course, the EU has been seen as being ahead of the USA when it comes to lobbying at the climate change 'Conferences of the Parties' (COP). It has been more fastidious in implementing policies such as carbon emissions trading, banning tungsten lightbulbs, and in mandating relatively ambitious targets for renewable energy deployment by 2020. Yet there are signs that China may overtake the EU in such carbon reduction policies. There is an increasing concern to keep energy costs down, and a report produced by the European Environment argued that 'while projections show further decreases in EU GHG emissions beyond 2020 (EU) Member States project that the pace of these reductions will slow down'.[52]

China's Carbon emissions – what about the future?

As discussed earlier, emissions of carbon dioxide resulting from economic activity in China seem, on the basis of a median estimate, to have at least levelled off. But the future trend is likely, on the basis of the arguments deployed in this book, to be one of significant declines in carbon emissions, lower than what seems to have been the case in the 2014–2015 period. This is for two reasons: first, as argued in Chapter 3, the transition of China to a middle income economy with a higher proportion of GDP coming from services means that economic growth rates are likely to fall as the proportion of services of GDP increases. Second, China is putting into place policies to reduce energy consumption. Energy consumption as a whole increased by just 1.5 per cent in 2015,[53] with fuel switching to lower carbon fuels leading to a probable marginal overall decline in carbon emissions, as discussed earlier. Electricity consumption increased only slowly during the year.[54] There is every reason to believe, based on the foregoing arguments about a shift to a lower growth service economy and the increasing effects of policies making more efficient use of energy, that within a few short years' time energy consumption will not increase at all. Given that, in addition, the Chinese energy economy is shifting towards use of more lower carbon fuels, this implies that there will be a substantial year-on-year reduction in carbon emissions over the coming decades. Either the slowdown in growth and shift to more services happens through intentional restructuring by Government policy, or it will be a consequence of economic crisis caused by continued accumulation of bad debts that accrue because of the failure to restructure the economy.

One widely cited study published by the Grantham Institute in the summer of 2015 suggested that carbon emissions would be slightly lower by 2020 compared to 2014.[55] The Grantham Institute's study based their analysis on the assumption of a rapid decline in energy intensity of GDP of around 4 per cent per year, which would reduce carbon emissions by the same amount.[56] They also assume a considerable switching of fuel away from coal, including a big build-up of renewable energy (which also reduces carbon emissions), slightly faster than the Chinese Government projects, by 2020. They assume that carbon reduction trends will intensify in the 2020s and 2030s.

Their assessments are based on an economic growth rate of around 6 per cent[57] in the next few years, a rate that thereafter declines as 'rebalancing' takes effect. Of course, in Chapter 3 I suggested that economic growth could have been no more than around 3–4 per cent per annum in 2014–2015 and that this may continue in the future. If the figures used by the Grantham Institute were recalculated using this lower figure for economic growth, and other assumptions remained the same, then we would in fact be seeing substantial annual declines in carbon emissions over the next few years – and also thereafter, when, in any case, the growth rates may gradually decline. Of course we do not know what is happening in the future, but I would argue that, as energy growth rates generally decline, and as deployment of non-fossil fuels increase it is now plausible to foresee a scenario involving declines in consistent declines in carbon emissions from China starting in the next few years.

This analysis conflicts with the Chinese Government's current pledges to cap its carbon emissions by 2030, in the sense that the Chinese Government may be far too conservative. Of course, the Chinese Government is wishing that economic growth is rather higher than 3–4 per cent, and indeed its own (arguably optimistic figures) figures suggest that it is. Certainly the official economic growth figure for 2015 of close to 7 per cent seems at odds with overall energy growth of only around 1.5 per cent.[58] This gap may or may not close in another year, but it does seem that the Government is being very conservative in its commitments on carbon reduction. If it wants to achieve its own economic and environmental targets to achieve sustainable types of development and also dramatically reduce its pollution levels then China's carbon emission levels will peak at levels roughly as they were in 2015–2016, and they will decline from this level.

I would say that the Chinese Government's projections are based on pressures from their industries and about what it hopes will happen as far as economic growth is concerned, rather than what is or what is likely to happen. Perhaps also, politically, the Government is worried that it may set targets that they struggle to achieve later, and face criticism as a result. Yet in this it is simply being much too conservative. Indeed if the Government wants to wage an effective battle against local air pollution, then carbon emissions will simply have to come down in the coming years, rather than increase before a peak in around 2030 as it projects.

The most recent analysis (available, that is at the time of writing this chapter) from the Grantham Institute in fact recognised that '[i]t is just possible that emissions will fall modestly from now on, implying that 2014 was the peak'. They imply that the only main circumstances that will stop this happening is 'if oil and gas demands grow faster than expected, or if companies and local governments make unauthorised expansions in new coal-based industries'.[59] Of course, if it is the case that China's economic growth will be much reduced by a debt crisis in the medium terms, then energy consumption is likely to be even more restrained.

A stabilisation in energy usage would actually translate into a substantial annual carbon reduction, maybe 2 per cent per annum. I will discuss the size of, plausibility of, and pressures behind this trend towards fuel switching to lower carbon fuels in Chapter 6.

One has to remember, of course, that the work on projections done so far is based on, to an extent at least, assessments of what has happened in the past, and the technologies that underpin those assessments. But, as has been demonstrated earlier, past projections of future energy consumption in particular have often proved to be hopelessly exaggerated. We do appear to be moving into an era which is dominated by low energy technologies. As such we may find that even the projections which show declines in Chinese carbon emissions may prove to be underestimates because of overestimates of future energy consumption.

But the bottom line is that we may be able to expect annual average reduction in carbon emissions from China's economy of around 2 per cent for the next few years, with the prospect of increasing this percentage reduction in the 2020s not least because, as will be discussed in the next chapter, the impacts of fuel switching accelerates. If an annual 2–3 per cent decline in carbon emissions was replicated for the whole of the world on average from now on, then some good initial progress might be made towards the Paris target of keeping the global temperature rise below 2 degrees above pre-industrial levels. I say 'initial' progress, because the trend of carbon emission reduction will need to speed up, especially in the 2020s and 2030s, beyond an annual 2 per cent reduction to meet this objective. However, the build-up of renewable energy, which is already making significant inroads into coal use, will continue and increase as costs fall. The growth of fuel switching away from coal, especially the growth in non-fossil fuels is, of course, the central topic of the next chapter.

Conclusion

A discussion of China's contribution towards reducing energy consumption and reducing carbon emissions suggests that China is not the worst obstacle in the world in the task of reducing carbon emissions from energy sources. Indeed in per capita terms the present position, and likely future profile, seems to one of keeping and reducing its emissions well below that of, for example, the USA.

There appears to be a turnaround that China appears to be instrumental in engineering an actual fall in global carbon emissions, at least in the year 2015. China's own emissions may be stabilising and long before the Chinese Government predicted.

The key background to this turnaround compared to the narrative of rapidly increasing carbon emissions that threaten to burn the planet can be explained by the economic pressures and economic rebalancing discussed in Chapter 3 and, as discussed in Chapter 5, the mounting pressure from Chinese people for pollution to be reduced as a top political priority. Many of the means of achieving this through changed governance regulations are through 'top-down' methods. However, this top-down method is limited and given the economic pressures for development local authorities are not currently an effective instrument to ensure that policies for energy conservation are properly adopted. The key lesson is that popular political will for more sustainable energy practices should allow the objectives to be achieved through greater local consent rather than through the 'top-down' rule that prevails at the moment. However, regardless of this, the direction of policy towards a lower energy economy seems clear.

In terms of the developmental path that now seems to be adopted China is much more likely to be seen in the future as an energy leader, although that in itself depends on more decentralisation. Such leadership includes a range of policies and initiatives to support this. This can be contrasted with the lacklustre efforts of the USA, and also it may overtake the EU whose efforts may be seen as becoming more complacent as of late. It is certainly the case that the prospects for substantial reductions in Chinese carbon emissions owe much to a reduced economic growth rate compared to the past, as well as policies designed to reduce energy and encourage fuel switching to lower carbon energy sources.

The economic growth rates likely to be achieved are certainly below what the Chinese Government projects, but in fact are in line with the implications of its declared strategy of rebalancing the economy to a more sustainable one in all senses (as discussed in Chapter 3). If we factor in expected reductions in energy intensity to economic growth rates of between 3 and 4 per cent over the next few years, and then also factor in increases in non-fossil generation (discussed later in this book) then we can expect reductions in annual carbon emissions from China. Of course, Government efforts to boost energy intensive industries by offering more credit may keep emissions up to an extent, but as discussed this is a literally bankrupt strategy that will unwind before too long.

Hence we can reflect on some of the implicit processes of ecological modernisation that, in European countries, have led to relative stabilisation of energy consumption. This includes lower economic growth rates and also a shift to service industries which are less energy intensive than manufacturing and infrastructure. This more European-style path is being adopted by China. In addition, China's patterns of urban density mark a closer parallel in energy terms to Europe rather than the USA. China is adopting some energy efficiency techniques that parallel what has happened in the West, and to that extent it can be said to be moving towards EM style means of ecological management. However, it is still a top-down system that is still at odds with what I have described as core features of Eurocentric EM and which will hold back reduction of energy use. EM involves bottom-up as well as top-down economic and political governance. The topic of governance is discussed in the next chapter.

Nevertheless the idea that the USA – or other nations – can afford to deflect taking action to reduce carbon emissions because China will benefit may be dangerously out of sync with what is emerging as a new reality. This reality is that China's energy path is becoming much more sustainable, and nations who cannot keep up with that are not only letting the world down, but are likely to lose out in competition with China in trade.

Of course, this path includes not only the reductions in energy usage that I have talked about in this chapter, but also fuel switching to lower carbon fuels. It is to this topic of fuel switching that I turn to in the next chapter.

Notes

1 Unsigned (2006) 'Booming nations "threaten Earth"', *BBC News*, 12 January, available online at http://news.bbc.co.uk/1/hi/sci/tech/4604556.stm
2 Larson, E. (2014) 'China's Growing Coal Use Is World's Growing Problem', 27 January, available online at www.climatecentral.org/blogs/chinas-growing-coal-use-is-worlds-growing-problem-16999
3 Ibid.
4 Russell Jones, R. (2015) 'To destroy human civilisation we just need to continue with business as usual', *Guardian*, letter, 10 December
5 Ng, E. (2016) 'China Shenhua delays coal power plant construction on orders from Beijing', *South China Morning Post*, 29 March, available online at www.scmp.com/business/companies/article/1931597/china-shenhua-delays-coal-power-plant-construction-orders-beijing
6 Davies Boren, Z. (2016) 'Global coal bubble: Power plants in the pipeline to cost $1 trillion', *Greenpeace Energy Desk*, 30 March, available online at http://energydesk.greenpeace.org/2016/03/30/global-coal-boom-bust/
7 US Environmental Protection Agency (2015) *Global Greenhouse Gas Emissions Data*, www3.epa.gov/climatechange/ghgemissions/global.html
8 Clark, D. and Kiln (2013) 'Which fossil fuel companies are most responsible for climate change?' *Guardian*, 20 November, available online at www.theguardian.com/environment/interactive/2013/nov/20/which-fossil-fuel-companies-responsible-climate-change-interactive?CMP=twt_gu
9 US Energy Information Service (2016) *International Energy Outlook 2016*, Table 9.2, p. 143, available online at www.eia.gov/forecasts/ieo/pdf/emissions.pdf
10 BP (2016) *BP Statistical Review of World Energy*, available online at www.bp.com/en/global/corporate/energy-economics/statistical-review-of-world-energy.html
11 World Bank (2015) *Population Totals*, available online at http://data.worldbank.org/indicator/SP.POP.TOTL

12 Green, F. and Stern, N. (2015) 'China's 'new normal': structural change, better growth and peak emissions', *Grantham Institute on Climate Change and the Environment/ Centre for Climate Change and Economics Policy*, pp. 43–44, available online at www.lse.ac.uk/GranthamInstitute/wp-content/uploads/2015/06/China_new_normal_web1.pdf

13 Jordan, W. (2015) 'Global survey: Chinese most in favour of action on climate change', *YouGov*, 10 June, available online at https://yougov.co.uk/news/2015/06/07/Global-survey-Chinese-most-favour-action-climate-c/

14 Evans, S. (2015) 'Climate pledge puts China on course to peak emissions as early as 2027', *Carbon Brief*, 1 July, available online at www.carbonbrief.org/climate-pledge-puts-china-on-course-to-peak-emissions-as-early-as-2027

15 Department of Energy/Energy Information Administration (1993) *Annual Energy Outlook 1993*, Washington DC: Energy Information Service, pp. 173 and 191 (note: a mean has been taken between the small difference between the low and high estimates)

16 Elliott, D. (1978) *The Politics of Nuclear Power*, London: Pluto Press, p. 86

17 E3G (2015) *Europe's Declining Gas Demand*, 15 June, available online at www.e3g.org/news/media-room/europes-declining-gas-demand

18 Grubb, M., Sha, F., Spencer, T., Hughes, N., Zhang Z. and Agnolucci P. (2015) 'A review of Chinese CO2 emission projections to 2030: the role of economic structure and policy', *Climate Policy*, vol. = 15, sup1, s7–s39, p. s11

19 World Energy Council (2015) 'Energy Efficiency Indicators', available online at www.wec-indicators.enerdata.eu/

20 Bernardini, O. and Galli, R. (1993) 'Dematerialization: long term trends in the intensity of use of materials and energy', *Futures*, 25, 431–448

21 Grubb (2015) op. cit., p. s28

22 Chen, K. and Chen, A. (2016) 'China faces massive closures of small thermal power plants', *Bloomberg Business News*, 29 August, available online at www.reuters.com/article/us-china-power-idUSKCN114103

23 Davies Boren, Z. (2016) 'China stops building new coal-fired power plants', *Greenpeace Energydesk*, 24 March, available online at http://energydesk.greenpeace.org/2016/03/24/china-crackdown-new-coal-power-plants/

24 National Bureau of Statistics of China (2014) 'Total Consumption of Energy and its Composition', available online at www.stats.gov.cn/tjsj/ndsj/2014/indexeh.htm

25 BP (2015) *Statistical Review of World Energy*, available online at www.bp.com/en/global/corporate/energy-economics/statistical-review-of-world-energy.html

26 Koehn, P. (2016) *China Confronts Climate Change*, London: Routledge, p. 29

27 Myllyvyrta, L. (2015) 'China coal use falls: CO2 reduction this year could equal UK total emissions over same period', *Greenpeace Energy Desk*, 14 May, available online at http://energydesk.greenpeace.org/2015/05/14/china-coal-consumption-drops-further-carbon-emissions-set-to-fall-by-equivalent-of-uk-total-in-one-year/

28 Energy Information Administration (2015) 'Coal Use in China is Slowing', 17 September, available online at www.eia.gov/todayinenergy/detail.cfm?id=22972

29 Korsbakken, J. and Peters, G. (2016) 'China CO$_2$ emissions growth slowed in 2014 and 2015'. 'Maybe down in 2015, but too close to call' supplemental to Korsbakken, *et al.* (2016) available online at https://twitter.com/jikorsbakken

30 Korsbakken, J., Peters, G. and Andrew, R. (2016) 'Uncertainties around reductions in China's coal use and CO2 emissions', *Nature Climate Change*, published online 28 March, available online at www.nature.com/nclimate/journal/vaop/ncurrent/full/nclimate2963.html

31 National Energy Administration (2016) 国家能源局发布2015年全社会用电量, 15 January, available online at www.nea.gov.cn/2016–01/15/c_135013789.htm

32 Op. cit., Korsbakken, *et al.* (2016)

33 World Bank (2015) *Population Growth*', available online at http://data.worldbank.org/indicator/SP.POP.GROW

34 Fong, M. (2016) *One Child*, New York: Houghton Mifflin Harcourt, pp. 208–210
35 Wu, Y. (2012) 'Energy intensity and its determinants in China's regional economies', *Energy Policy*, 41, 703–711, p. 704
36 Cox, W. (2012) 'World Urban Areas Population Density – a 2012 update', *New Geography*, 3 May, available online at www.newgeography.com/content/002808-world-urban-areas-population-and-density-a-2012-update
37 Wilson, L. (2014) 'How big is a house', *Shrink That Footprint*, available online at http://shrinkthatfootprint.com/how-big-is-a-house
38 Yu, H., Tang, B., Yuan., X., Wang, S. and Wei, M. (2015) 'How do the appliance energy standards work in China? Evidence from room air conditioners', *Energy in Buildings*, vol. 86, 833–840
39 The World Bank/Development Centre for Research of the State Council of the People's Republic of China (2014) *Urban China*, Washington DC: World Bank Group, available online at www.worldbank.org/content/dam/Worldbank/document/EAP/China/WEB-Urban-China.pdf
40 Bloomberg News (2016) 'China plans to tear down walls of gated condos and let public in', *Bloomberg*, 11 April, available online at www.bloomberg.com/news/articles/2016-04-11/china-plans-to-tear-down-walls-of-gated-condos-and-let-public-in
41 US Environmental Protection Agency (2015) op. cit.
42 Grubb, *et al.* (2015) op. cit., p. s15
43 Zhang, B., Fei, H., He, P., Xu, Y., Zhanfeng, D. and Young, O. (2016) 'The indecisive role of the market in China's SO_2 and COD emissions trading', *Environmental Politics*, vol. 25, no. 5, 875–898
44 Zhou, Y. (2015) 'State power and environmental initiatives in China: Analyzing China's green building program through an ecological modernization Perspective', *Geoforum*, vol. 61, 1–12
45 Yunfei, Ge. (2015) 'China will increase green buildings to 50% by 2020', *CCTV*, 10 December, available online at http://english.cntv.cn/2015/12/10/VIDE1449722762008895.shtml
46 Liu, W., Zhang, J., Bluemling, B., Mol, A. and Wan, C. (2015) 'Public participation in energy saving retrofitting of residential buildings in China', *Applied Energy*, vol. 147, 287–296
47 Kaiman, J. (2014) 'China's eco-cities: empty of hospitals, shopping centres and people', *Guardian*, 14 April, available online at www.theguardian.com/cities/2014/apr/14/china-tianjin-eco-city-empty-hospitals-people
48 Liu, C. (2011) 'China Tackles Energy-Wasting Buildings', *Scientific American*, 27 July, available online at www.scientificAmerican.com/article/china-tackles-energy-wasting-bulidings/
49 Price, L., Levine, M., Zhou, N., Fridley, D., Aden, N., Lu, H., McNeil, M., Zheng, N., Qin, Y. and Yowargana, P. (2011) 'Assessment of China's energy-saving and emission-reduction accomplishments and opportunities during the 11th Five Year Plan', *Energy Policy*, vol. 39, 2165–2178, p. 2165
50 Zhang, L., Gudmundsson, O., Thorsen,J., Lia, H. and Svendse, S. (2014) 'Optimization of China´s centralized domestic hot water system by applying Danish elements', *The 6th International Conference on Applied Energy* – ICAE2014, *Energy Procedia 61*, pp. 2833–2840, p. 2835, available online at www.sciencedirect.com/science/article/pii/S1876610214033463
51 State of Green (2015) District Heating in the Chinese City Anshan, *Danfoss*, available online at https://stateofgreen.com/en/profiles/danfoss/solutions/district-heating-in-the-chinese-city-anshan
52 European Environment Agency (2015) 'Trends and projections in Europe 2015 Tracking progress towards Europe's climate and energy targets', Copenhagen: *European Environment Agency*, file:///C:/Users/Toke/Downloads/Trends%20and%20projections%20in%20Europe%202015.pdf.pdf

53 BP (2016) *Statistical Review of World Energy*, June 2016, available online at www.
bp.com/content/dam/bp/pdf/energy-economics/statistical-review-2016/bp-statistical-
review-of-world-energy-2016-full-report.pdf
54 Unsigned (2016) 'China's electricity mix: changing so fast that CO_2 emissions may
have peaked', *Energy Post*, 1 March, available online at www.energypost.eu/chinas-
electricity-mix-changing-fast-co2-emissions-may-peaked/
55 Green, F. and Stern, N., 'China's 'new normal': structural change, better growth and
peak emissions' *Grantham Institute on Climate Change and the Environment/ Centre for
Climate Change and Economics Policy*, pp. 52–53, London: Grantham Institute, available online at www.lse.ac.uk/GranthamInstitute/wp-content/uploads/2015/06/China_
new_normal_web1.pdf
56 Ibid.
57 Ibid.
58 BP (2016) op. cit.
59 Grantham Research Institute (2016) 'China's 2030 peak-emissions target likely to be
met within the next 10 years', 7 March, available online at www.lse.ac.uk/
GranthamInstitute/news/chinese-emissions-may-already-have-peaked/

5 Pollution

From protest to good governance?

Introduction

Jonathan Watts, author of the book *When a Billion Chinese Jump*, published in 2010, reports being told a joke about the city Tianjin.

> An enemy bomber is on a mission to blow up Tianjin. He flies across the Bohai Sea, but, when he reaches the city, he turns the plane around and returns without dropping a bomb. 'What are you doing?' asks his commander on the radio. The pilot replies, 'We don't need to waste our explosives. It looks like someone has already destroyed it.'[1]

In August 2015, the city was rocked by a terrible explosive accident killing over a 100 people and releasing toxic chemicals at a chemical complex at that city. There was no joking. However, in today's China, such events are not greeted by fatalistic humour that may have dominated earlier responses. The battle against pollution and accidents caused by industry has risen to the top of the agenda in China today.

This chapter sets the scene to enable us to understand how, and the extent to which, it is that China is now beginning to make great efforts to curb the problem that threatens the world – that of climate change induced by human made greenhouse gas emissions (mainly through energy production and consumption). The strength that helps this project move forward is derived from a need felt by the Chinese Government, Chinese NGOs and generally the Chinese people to take action to improve their environmental quality of life in a number of ways.

Pollution is the scourge of industrialisation, and China is in the thick of this scourge. In this chapter there is an outline of some of the pollution problems in the context of looking at the pressure for action to combat pollution. Some key controversies will be discussed, and there will be a discussion of the groups and forces that are seeking to tackle environmental pollution in China and also the challenges and opportunities that face this struggle. As part of this I will consider the extent to which environmental governance institutions are capable of coping with the task of reducing pollution, and particularly with reducing carbon emissions. This will help us understand the extent to which China matches up with core elements of what I have described as a notion of ecological modernisation derived from European origins.

First there is a discussion of the general pressure on the Chinese Government to take action on pollution, and the extent to which it needs to do this to preserve its own legitimacy. I shall look at some key indicators of pollution – I focus on air pollution since this is a topic of central debate – and place it in context, both in comparison with other places and also with the past. I focus in particular on controversies about air pollution and Beijing – this is because it is a topic that has generated much controversy, and also for practical reasons because there is so much data on this.

I then spend a major part of this chapter looking at, first, the campaigns and the campaigners that make up the pressure both on, and with, the Government to tackle the pollution problem. This includes people that are regarded as helpful by the Government, those that are regarded as less helpful, and governmental dilemmas in relying on societal forces to tackle pollution. Second, I look at key governance structures themselves to see how effectively they are dealing with these pressures. I end by examining some themes about how the battle on pollution is going, including what has been a conventional notion that pollution inevitably goes hand in hand with industrialisation.

Pressure for pollution control

The Chinese Government is tackling pollution, perhaps above all, because it has risen up the political agenda, and measures of whether the Government is delivering the goods that people want will now be based partly on how it is seen to be taking all reasonable steps to tackle pollution. It may be that the economy is still the number one concern of Chinese citizens, but barring major breakdowns in China's economic fortunes, pollution issues now seriously rival economic concerns. Indeed, according to a *YouGov* opinion poll, Chinese are actually more worried about pollution than they are about economic instability.[2] As discussed in Chapter 4, opinion poll evidence suggests also that Chinese have become more concerned about climate change than opinion in many Western states.[3] This implies that the public has accepted the key lynchpin of ecological modernisation, namely that economic development has to be accompanied by environmental improvement, including pollution reduction. It may have been that as late as 2003 that the majority of the Chinese people saw rapid economic growth as practically the be-all and end-all of policy. But if recent opinion polls and also recent upsurge in concern about pollution (discussed later) is anything to go by, things have changed.[4] People crave a solution to the pollution problem, especially to the sun-blocking smog that envelopes China's cities. The following commentaries may serve as a context:

Wade Shepherd, who has written about China's 'ghost cities', said in April 2015:

The question facing the Communist Party is how it can balance public opinion, governmental fissures, industrial profit motives, and the stability of the domestic economy. An unrequited commitment to improving air quality at this point could backfire and make the Party look inept and weak – exactly how an authoritarian regime cannot afford to look, if it easy to retain the legitimacy to continue ruling. 'If things get worse and our Government still does nothing, I'm not sure what will happen,' a woman from Jiangsu province told me. 'It's not like anything else. It's survival.'[5]

Such statements might have seemed odd at the beginning of this century, when development and making money were the only seemingly important objectives. Raising living standards is still of paramount importance, but so, now, is reducing pollution. As a writer in *Fortune* magazine put it: 'Some China watchers are describing pollution – along with corruption – as one of the most significant threats to the legitimacy and continued rule of the Communist party'.[6]

Pollution problems

There are some terrible statistics. In 2013 a study reported that 'in Guangzhou – the capital of Guangdong province in southern China 44 percent of rice samples were found to contain poisonous levels of cadmium. That rice was being served to unsuspecting diners in restaurants around Guangzhou.'[7] This is one of many stories of metal poisoning that affect large proportions of the countryside. Many Chinese people do not trust food production after various scandals, one of the worst being a poisoned milk scandal in 2008 – something which accounts for the popularity of imported milk formula on the shelves of Chinese supermarkets. As will be discussed later in this chapter, fear of poisoning from the production of chemical factories has been a particular cause of mass protests.

Water pollution is particularly acute, especially in the south of the country. For example the Hai River, with serves Beijing and Tianjin has 70 per cent of its flows in the 1966–2005 period compared with the period between 1951 and 1966.[8] Also, 'The World Bank estimates the cost of water scarcity and air pollution at around 2.3 per cent of GDP'.[9] Moreover, 'One-fifth of farmland is too polluted to grow crops, nearly 60% of groundwater is unfit for human use and air pollution is 20 times the recommended safe levels.'[10] In April 2016, there were press reports that '[m]ore than 80% of China's underground water drawn from relatively shallow wells used by farms, factories and mostly rural households is unsafe for drinking because of pollution, a Government report says', and the report goes on to say that the problem is 'largely due to fertiliser run-off and the dumping of untreated factory waste'. Water shortages loomed in the north of the country as water table levels fell.[11]

The case of heavy metals

A prime example of the unsustainable nature of productionism is the environmentally disastrous exploitation of resources in Inner Mongolia to produce rare earth metals. These include cerium, Neodymium, yttrium and dysprosium. These types of metals are used widely as essential ingredients in making magnets and many electronic products, including wind turbines, it is sad to say. However, the problem, as this story implies, is not so much with wind turbines as the lack of pollution control in China and the implicit collaboration of the World Trade organization (WTO) in not helping the problem.

The area around Baotao, at the centre of the industry, has been described as a 'hell on earth'.[12] Carcinogenic heavy metals such as cadmium seep into the surrounding environment, toxic fluoride and other gases are emitted in large quantities. Large quantities of strong acids used to leach out the metals are discarded. A large toxic lake sits near the industrial complex near Baotao. In general, there is a 'dystopian' landscape around the area.

China supplies most of the production of rare earth metals. It is not that China has a monopoly of the elements themselves – the bulk of the resources are in fact outside China – it is just that China has specialised in developing the extractive and processing industry necessary for the production of the metals.

The point about this industry in this context is that, first, this is a leading example of how China has used its lax attitude towards environmental degradation to subsidise its industrial costs of producing rare earth metals. Second, the industry is an example of a highly energy intensive (as well as very locally polluting) industry that is owned by the state and which thus has cheap loan facilities from the Government underpinned by Government guarantees. The industry involves such state owned giants as Baotou Steel, a leading example of the sort of energy intensive, polluting industry that the state supports directly. Indeed Baotou has been listed as an important case of state actor which has built up debts.[13] In 2014–2015 Baotou Steel was the fourth largest steel producer in the world, and the second largest in China, just behind Herbei Steel in term of tonnage produced.[14]

Other countries find that the costs of extracting and processing the rare earth metals are rather higher because the environmental costs of reducing the pollution that goes along with the industry are incorporated into the price of the production that is sold. In economics this is known as internalising external (i.e. the environmental) costs. If China's environmental standards are higher than the industrial costs will rise and the international prices of rare earth commodities will rise. This will allow other countries to compete with China, and, of course, the pollution associated with rare earth metal production in China will decline.

Environmental laws passed in 2014 should mean a clampdown on the pollution levels around Baotao. However, such regulation still has to be effected. Unfortunately the actions of the World Trade Organisation (WTO) appear not to be helping in that they supported complaints that China was reserving production of rare earth metals for its own consumption. Indeed other countries appear to be most interested in keeping prices of rare earth metals low rather than curbing pollution in China. This is because actions by China to restrict exports were actually attacked by the WTO because they increased world prices of rare earth metals.[15] Of course it is far better for China to impose greater environmental controls to ensure that its production of rare earth metals is less environmentally damaging (which does not contravene WTO rules), but what also needs to happen is for production in other parts of the world to take place using cleaner methods. The WTO certainly has not helped this process. Free trade regulations may often help ensure more effective use of resources and thus reduce pollution, but they can also act as a 'double-edged sword'.

A particularly high profile case of pollution in China is the thick smog which engulfs China's major cities. In this case at least, as will be discussed later, there is increasing transparency – though for the moment in the measurement of pollution rather than the atmosphere itself! It is also of central relevance to this book since its causes are very often energy related, especially from coal burning and use of motor vehicles.

We need to look at this problem in particular also since it occupies an especially high profile level of public controversy. We also need to compare this with elsewhere, to achieve perspective, and in doing so take a historical perspective to see how China's perceived and actual pollution crisis compares with the reduction of pollution in developed nations.

Air pollution in China – a comparison with the West

The air pollution levels in Chinese cities are far higher – four of five times as high – compared to cities such as London or New York. A study by Berkeley University estimated that air pollution kills 1.6 million Chinese people every year.[16]

Certainly Western countries have had their own severe air pollution problems in the past – the smogs in Los Angeles and the 'pea soupers' in London are well-known cases. In fact, the smoke levels during the infamous London smog of 1952 were astounding high, even by contemporary Beijing standards. During the days of 6 to 8 December, 1952 the smoke levels in London (which I assume to be analogous to PM10 as smoke tends to be called today) were recorded as being around 1,600 micrograms (ug/m^3) per cubic metre of air, and at least 4,000 people were estimated to have died around this period as a result of the smog.[17] No measurement is available for the smaller particles. However, it may safely be assumed that they were extremely high as well in the case of the London pea souper since the WHO data indicates that smaller particulate concentrations are proportionate to the concentrations of the larger particles. It should be remembered that London, and other Western cities suffered from this type of pollution for many decades, in London case, arguably, for centuries.

This compares to the annual mean measurement of PM10 of Beijing in 2013 of 108 micrograms per cubic metre,[18] although, for example, in one smoggy January day measurements in central Beijing were recorded of between 300 and 560 micrograms per cubic metre.[19]

Of course, the problems in Western cities were abated after Government took a number of measures, although there are still occasional 'blackspots' and even the usual much lower concentrations in Western cities are still associated with many excess deaths. In 2015 and 2016 concern increased about the emissions from diesel cars which were said to be covered up by car manufacturers.

However, in the case of China today the pollution crisis occurs at a time when reducing carbon emissions is a vital global priority, so this in itself changes the character of what sort of response will be favoured by the public as a means of reducing the pollution. Measures which simultaneously reduce both local and global pollution will be preferred. Hence it is the coincidence of the local and global air pollution priorities that puts an emphasis on implementation of technologies that can achieve both objectives; that is, the reduction of both local and global pollution. This means that the tremendous pressure on the Chinese Government to abate local air pollution can lead to China taking action to make a huge difference to the problem the world faces in the shape of climate change. For example, merely shifting to 'cleaner' coal will be seen as a less valuable response compared to reducing the need for energy consumption or shifting to using non-fossil fuels.

China's cities rank as some of the more polluted cities in the world according to data available from the World Health Organisation.[20] In order to compare pollution levels I utilise one simple measure that is PM2.5 – I agree that there are various other measures of air pollution, but PM2.5 is widely regarded as important since these particulates are regarded as being especially harmful. This means small particulates of dust or prices of matter less than 2.5 microns in size. Here I just want to draw a general comparison of scale with other parts of the world rather than do a detailed analysis.

Mean annual levels of PM2.5 (ug/m^3) are measured at being invariably below 20 in Western Europe and the USA. This compares with 85 in Beijing, and even higher, at 128, in Xingtai in Hebei province (not far from Beijing). Xingtai boasts a complex of mining operations that prepare coal for power stations.[21] Baoding, also in Hebei Province has an average annual PM2.5 reading almost as high, at 126. According to a newspaper report 'much of Baoding's pollution comes from coal-fired steam boiler systems used in more than 100 provincial villages close to the city. These boilers are extremely polluting'.[22] On the other hand, there are several cities in India, which have much higher readings than in China. According to the WHO data PM2.5 mean annual levels in Allahabad in Pakistan registers at 170, Delhi at 122 and Gwalior a (literally) eye watering 176.

But it should be remembered that in order to reach the high standards in most places in the West there have been changes that took many years. Indeed, when one looks at the place where the industrial revolution started – the United Kingdom – it took centuries before the pollution problems of the industrial revolution were conquered. Indeed talk of the London 'pea soupers' was part of the London scene described by the writer Dickens, yet this scourge was dealt with only a century later. Of course, Chinese citizens expect progress to be a lot quicker than that in China today!

Blue skies and red alerts in Beijing

There has been increasing concern in the Chinese Government about what could be called the 'flagship' nature of the pollution crisis in the capital Beijing. As China has emerged as a country which wishes to present itself as a major power in many economic, military cultural and sporting areas, it has become sensitive to the damage that the Beijing smog does to its international reputations. This has led to efforts to create 'blue skies' for important events likely to attract widespread attention in the global media.

A well-known 'blue sky' effort to cleanse the skies of Beijing took place at the time of the Beijing Olympics in 2008. During the two months of the 2008 Olympics there were restrictions on automobile use and also closure or restrictions on factory production to produce the required 'blue skies'. Since then there have been further blue sky events. These have become a key feature of the battle over pollution in China whereby the authorities have tried to put forward a facade of clean air – 'blue skies' – at key events.

Embarrassingly for the national Government (since it is based in Beijing), pollution is especially concentrated in the Hebei Province. This province includes Beijing where the key events occur, and producing 'blue skies' means closing down much or all of the heavy industry such as steel production facilities that generate the pollution, mainly from coal burning. This was much reported at the Asia-Pacific Economic Cooperation summit which occurred in November 2014. It was reported in *The Diplomat* that

> Factory owners, aware of the upcoming APEC Summit and pre-empting the shutdowns, shifted production elsewhere. Steel production in Hebei fell 2.9 percent in the first nine months of 2014, although this has been offset by a 9.3 percent increase in Jiangsu province near Shanghai. The planned closures ahead of APEC have not so much solved the problem as merely pushed it southwards. On November 6, Beijing's AQI was a blissful 25; meanwhile Shanghai languished at 217, the iconic vista of the Bund hazy, as if hastily sketched in charcoal.[23]

Besides this there was a holiday order for six days, which had the effect of considerably reducing vehicle traffic and the associated pollution.

The following year, in September 2015, there was a military parade which coincided with a Government orchestrated 'blue sky' effort. Once again industry was restricted and cars were restricted on which days they could be on the roads according to their number plates.

However, such 'blue sky' periods have served as an indicator that the Government has taken the issue of air pollution seriously. However, as ever, this sort of staged pollution slowdown – for a day or a short period of days – may be necessary for the Government in an effort to persuade the public that it is serious about tackling the question, but it is a double-edged sword. This is because its very recognition of the importance of the issue makes it legitimate for people to debate the issue and criticise the Government's actions, or inactions. Failure to achieve targets for reducing pollution will threaten the legitimacy of the Government. As discussed earlier, the Government is 'riding a tiger' which it cannot get off. In short, the 'blue sky measures' may have saved foreign visitors from being dismayed and polluted themselves, but they have shown Chinese citizens what things could be like and they have stoked the hunger of Chinese citizens for serious action to tackle the problem.

Some progress has been made. In 2014 and 2015 coal consumption began to fall and also the Government had established a system, with the help of experts like Ma Jun, to more effectively monitor pollution levels in a transparent manner. A system of alerts was developed, and in December 2015 this generated the first 'red alert' which triggered emergency measures of restricting which vehicles could be used and closing schools and factories. Once again, it seems likely that public relations rather than consistent policy was the key motivator since these restrictions happened to coincide with the negotiations, which were taking place in Paris, leading up to the Climate Change Agreement. Nevertheless, there are concentrated efforts by municipal authorities to cut down on pollution in Beijing. Climate Action reports that 'Beijing is aiming to eliminate the use of coal in six districts over two years and help 600,000 households shift from coal to clean energy by 2020'.[24]

In Beijing itself there were signs that ordinary citizens were dissatisfied with the 'red alert' policy of the Government to tackle severe pollution episodes. One concerned mother (who was buying bottled 'clean air' sent from the Canadian Rocky Mountains to give her small child) told the BBC that:

> We don't like the (red alert) policy. We don't want students to be home. If we close down more factories and coal mining companies it will really solve the problem. However, it will affect the economy of the whole society. We are waiting for the wise people to give us a better solution.[25]

The mother's mention of buying clean air from China underlines that the key interest is in tackling local air pollution, given that bottled air from Canada could be quite energy intensive! But in the case of the key strategic policies aimed at tackling air pollution, reducing coal use through energy efficiency and shifts to lower carbon fuels, policies aimed to tackle local pollution will reduce carbon emissions.

Campaigns against pollution have formed an important spur to changes in both Government policy and mobilisation of public opinion. It is now time to look at such campaigns and the campaigners that have been active.

The anti-pollution campaigners

Nowadays, there is more monitoring of pollution levels of various sorts around China. Indeed, leading Chinese environmentalists such as Ma Jun have paved the ways towards establishing systems where you can check up instantly on your smartphone or watch the levels of air pollutants such as PM2.5, nitrogen oxides or whatever. However, it was not always this way. What have been some key actions that have produced changes? Let us focus on the case of smog in Beijing.

Since 2008, the US Embassy in Beijing had taken to tweeting information about air pollution in the city according to its own measurements. However, at the beginning of 2012 controversy erupted when it appeared there was a big disparity between official measurements of air pollution and that coming from the US Embassy.[26] The Chinese Government attacked the US Embassy for its data releases, but Chinese citizens appeared much more angry with their own Government about the disparity.

The evidence of pollution was/is all too apparent to ordinary people – they can see the sun blotted out and fear the effects on their health. Campaigns on the subject spread quickly on the internet. It actually does not require a tremendous degree of IT geekery to access Western messages that are otherwise disallowed by the Government, and if a story is important enough it will be replicated soon enough on the 'internal' web through WeChat and Weibo. There was a lot of anger at the inadequacies of Government data on pollution and, of course, the underlying pollution crisis. So it was not possible to block out the news from the US Embassy. Rather, the authorities were forced to improve and make more relevant their reporting of pollution data. This is now so much the case that pollution data is now more available for China than many other parts of the world.

But what is this anti-pollution movement in China? Perhaps we can usefully talk of a movement in three parts: 'elite', non-governmental and dissenting. These three categories merge into each other, but nevertheless using these three categories may help us have an overall picture of what is happening.

The elite campaigners

In 2015, the most high profile anti-pollution campaigner was probably Chai Jing, a former investigative reporter and news presenter for China Central TV. Fired up by her new born daughter's need to have an operation to remove a growth, and blaming this on pollution, she made a film called 'Under the Dome' which exposed the pollution problems and the complacent attitudes towards the problem. The film emphasises the deadly effect of PM2.5. This is especially damaging to the lungs and circulatory system.

The film was a runaway sensation when it was posted on the internet and was downloaded millions of times. In fact the film was very careful to avoid challenging the legitimacy of the Government, or calling for democracy or such things. It was focussed clearly on the 'technical' aspects of the environmental problem. This is the narrow, but distinct path that elite anti-pollution campaigners can tread.

They can even win the support of the Government, as did Chai Jing, insofar that, of course, the Government would like the problem to be tackled.

But within a few days the Government became worried that the film was, albeit indirectly, promoting unlicensed dissent, demonstrations and direct criticism from the public. The film was taken down from the Chinese intranet and state bodies feared retributions would be made if they promoted the film. Even so, by the time it had been taken down, it had been downloaded two hundred million times.[27] However, you can see it on *YouTube*, with an English translation.[28] But this episode highlighted a dilemma for the Government. They could try and be on the side of the environmentalists, but if they do so they risk stoking expectations that they are unable or unwilling to fulfil. As one Government sponsored report which came out shortly after the release of 'Under the Dome' put it: 'There is a huge gap between how fast the environment is being improved and the how fast the public is demanding it to be improved, and environmental problems could easily become a tipping point that leads to social risks'.[29]

Another elite campaigner is Ma Jun, who, as mentioned earlier has been leading efforts to make air pollution data available to the general public. He is well known for his campaigning on water pollution issues, including his book, published in China in 1999, entitled 'China's Water Pollution Crisis'.[30] He, like Chai Jing, started as a journalist and wrote widely about water issues, which he summarised in what is his most famous book. He wrote about water shortages as the Yellow River dries out, floods from the Yangtze, and the water pollution in south China. He documents the causes of all of this, the developing industrialism in China which pays little regard to finite water supplies and cares little about dumping its toxic chemicals in lakes and rivers. Yet Ma Jun's approach is cautious with regard to the authorities.

He seeks to cooperate with, and to encourage, the Government in the right direction, rather than confront it. You will not find a specific direct attack on a specific Government agency or official in his book on the water problem. Even in the case of the controversy surrounding the 'Three Gorges Dam' hydro project, which resulted in many people being displaced, his criticism is carefully couched. He points to severe environmental problems with the project, yet comments 'The Three Gorges Dam project needs to be approached carefully'.[31]

Yet Ma Jun appears to have been very influential in educating people about the water problem and in giving people the knowledge which they can use to campaign for improvements. He has been especially effective on the air pollution issue. He played a pivotal role in 2012, in making the Chinese authorities release data on PM2.5 air pollution. Indeed he coordinated the establishment of an instantaneously and easily accessible database on air pollution levels of various sorts in China, wherever you happen to be. When I spoke to an adviser to the Government in Beijing, who arrived by bicycle, he showed me the setting on his watch which showed the current level of pollution. It would be better for cycling! As in many places, however, he was also worried about his bicycle being stolen!

Ma certainly has a big international profile, although he rarely gives interviews. He is Director of the Institute for Public and Environmental Affairs. However, he stresses that since his most famous book on water problems was published in 1995, many aspects of the pollution problem have got no better.

The Institute for Public and Environmental Affairs (IPE) coordinates a 'green choice alliance' of environmental NGOs, including Friends of Nature (equivalent to Friends of the Earth in the US and UK), aiming to monitor and influence corporate behaviour to improve environmental performance.[32] The IPE focuses, in particular, on influencing multinational corporations since then their consumers can be asked to pressurise the companies to behave better. The IPE publishes the environmental supervision monitoring records of companies (reports published by the Governmental environmental inspectors). This is an aid to local campaigners to pressure the companies to improve their practices. Anybody can read, online, about reports of illegal discharges and fines imposed by the authorities. Indeed, as Munro[33] puts it, summarising some research by Zhang:[34] 'polluting enterprises were even more nervous about the effects of hostile media reports than about EPB [governmental Environmental Protection Bureaux] fines'.

Despite the cynicism about the alleged double face of Chinese Government actions on pollution (publicly strong on action, but privately struggling with dominant industrial interests), independent evidence does indicate that there has been some improvement in local air pollution. As will be discussed in the rest of the book, there is increasing hope that China may be treading on the first steps of a path where the world may be successful in constraining carbon dioxide emissions which affect the world through climate change.

Whereas by the summer of 2015 it seems that list in some cities (including Shanghai) air pollution had actually gotten worse, overall there seemed to be some reduction in the country taken as a whole. There were records of a 16 per cent reduction in levels of PM2.5 in Beijing air in the year up to the summer of 2015. This progress was put down to the economic decline in heavy industry to some extent, but also positive measures including the closure of inefficient coal burning power stations, their replacement by natural gas power plant, restrictions on motor vehicles and closure or moving of heavy industry in the area surrounding Beijing.[35]

Elite campaigners such as Ma Jun have (so far) done well in the art of providing nourishment to the cause of environmental protection without making the Government feel that they are a significant threat to its stability. That way is the path to stay out of jail! Rather, they inform people, apply commercial pressure to companies, without questioning the legitimacy of the Government or directly encouraging protests. However, when public opinion is aroused they provide the expertise to enable concern to be effective and to enable the Government to implement reform. Or at least that is the hope.

The 'official' campaigners

There is room for groups, which are given state permission, to conduct public campaigns for pollution reduction. There are over 700 officially recognised NGOs that, in theory at least, are encouraged by the state to pursue polluters through legal action. Indeed, at the beginning of 2015, the Supreme People's

Court said that such groups would receive privileges and reduced court costs to take action against companies that breach pollution laws. The Government points to instances where companies are forced to pay millions of dollars in fines after social groups took them to court for flouting pollution regulations.[36]

Certainly the environmental NGOs, by being subject to Government registration and limits on the extent to which they can criticize the agencies of the Government (and most notably they cannot challenge the leading role of the Communist Party), have limits on how they can challenge the Government. Indeed, the phenomenon of 'Government organised non-Government organisations' (GONGOS) is widespread. They have advantages for the Government in terms of implementing changes they favour although as Martens puts it: 'Some observers regard the presence of GONGOs as an intermediate step towards a more mature civil society, while others consider them to be illegitimate frauds undermining the development of true social forces'.[37]

It may be argued that a key aspect of ecological modernization is that Government has to negotiate with established policy networks of NGOs about environmental objectives. The Government, by accepting such a large and well organized set of NGO networks into their governance arrangements, becomes limited itself in its ability to ignore the influence of environmental NGOs in its day to day work and its policy making activities. This may be true to some extent, but then the Government knows that the environmental NGOs are subject to the consent of the Government for their operations, and so this may limit the bargaining power of the NGOs. Nevertheless, if the Government is not going to suffer defections and shifts towards more outright opposition from the NGOs it seeks to control and which it has taken on as a process of shoring up its own legitimacy, then it needs to offer the prospect of serious involvement in policy decisions.

The Government certainly does lay claim to stepping up efforts to control pollution. According to reports compiled by a Greenpeace media team, in 2015 the Chinese Government shut down some 9,300 factories after negative environmental monitoring reports. A further 15,000 firms were shut down. A total of 630,000 companies were inspected and large fines imposed on many companies.[38] As yet, however, many feel that the jury is out on what effect this will have. In cases such as that of the polluted Lake Tai for which Wu Luhong has campaigned so much (which is discussed later) Government authorities point to closures of factories that were responsible for pollution. Yet pollution levels did not subside, and some felt that the Government was merely closing loss-making companies that may have closed anyway.

In many ways the 'official' environmental groups are also limited in what they can do. They most certainly cannot challenge the legitimacy of the Government or criticise the role of the Communist Party. They can call for changes in Government policies provided they do not attack particular members of the Government. The environmental groups that are able to campaign are allowed so long as they are seen as helping state agencies whose work it is to uphold Government policy. Hence a clear demarcation line will be drawn between such 'helpful' activities and those which threaten in any way to undermine the legitimacy of the authorities or who are seen to be encouraging civil unrest.

The Government needs such groups to help them ameliorate environmental problems which it very much needs to tackle. However, the problem faced by the Government is that such activities may also empower those who are opposed to the Government as well as helping reforms. Hence the Government often shows ambivalence by, for example, the termination of official promotion of 'Under the Dome', and, as we shall see, cases such as Wu Lihong who campaigned over Lake Tai being lionised as an environmental hero but later being thrown into jail as a subversive.

But clearly the initiatives organised by the 'official' groups, though they may be carefully monitored by the authorities, are still useful to them – and also useful of course to the general cause of environmental improvement. Campaigns such as the 'Climate Youth Movement' for example, which operates across campuses which seek practical progress in gaining energy can be given as examples of activity that begun several years ago.[39]

Other campaigns may conflict with the interests of local industry, but use tactics which do not lead to civil unrest. Campaigns on the internet and social media can fall into this category. A typical one may involve a local conservation group campaigning against a factory's use of local water resources or a use by a factory of local land which impacts on local farmers.

In one instance that is given coverage on the website of The Center for Legal Assistance to pollution victims (CLAPV), success was realised through the usage of micro-blogging and the combined strength of numerous environmental protection personages and NGOs. Through mutual forwarding and initiatives, the case received much attention and a large range of responses, which ultimately included a public response from the State Forestry Administration's official Weibo account. In it, the SFA stated that Xiaopo Lake Wetland's ecosystem is very fragile and should be protected.

One case representing this approach concerns the opposition to the development of the wetlands around Lake Xiaopo in Qinghai Province. Local farmers and conservationists mounted a campaign against proposals for a dock and throughways to complement planned tourist developments, which included the construction of a hotel. Particular attention was paid to the threat to the rare black-necked crane and other endangered animals. In addition and damage to the wetland would setback the fight against desertification that is a major problem in the region.

The case arose when local people and environmentalists saw that companies seeking to implement the plans began tearing down fences erected by local farmers. The farmers used surrounding land to provide pasture for their animals. Lawyers and environmental NGOs mounted a campaign through Weibo and WeChat to mobilise opposition to the development. Documents were obtained from state environmental agencies with whom the applications for development were lodged and the lawyers were able to pinpoint several violations of the law in respect to environmental impact statement that were necessary, but not properly done. It was claimed that local farmers were duped into signing documents permitting the development. However, after the controversy blew up on the internet the State Forestry Commission sent a Weibo statement saying that 'Xiaopo Lake Wetland's ecosystem is very fragile and should be protected'.[40] Soon after that the developers abandoned the proposals.

The Center for Legal Assistance to pollution victims (CLAPV) is a law firm, which is a key member of the 'Green Choice Alliance' coordinated by Ma Jun's IPE. The CLAPV have helped many groups to obtain justice for environmental crimes. It is led by the award winning lawyer Wang Canfa, who justifies being placed in the category of an elite campaigner himself.

Of course they (the CLAPV) reckon that their activities are educating the courts and industry to be more aware of environmental laws. A lot of the legal work is done on a 'pro bono' basis. Environmental lawyer Liu Jinmei is most proud of one particular case she took up while working for the Center: 'I helped nearly 400 villagers from Minhou county in Fujian province win compensation totalling 6 million yuan (HK$7.6 million) after an incineration company illegally discharged waste gases containing carcinogenic dioxins'.[41] What is clear from Liu's statements is that they are able to do their work (without falling foul of the Government) by stressing how the law can work for people. They clearly work within, rather than against, the system. However, their impact may be, at the moment, fairly limited.

In a review of the politics of climate change in China Miranda Schreurs argues that:

> [e]nvironmental NGOs are increasingly accepted by the state and may even become necessary for the government to achieve its internal goals and portray a degree of pluralism internationally. The existence of an NGO community bolsters China's leadership's efforts to portray itself as having a benevolent form of environmental authoritarianism.... The ability of the NGOs to influence Government policy, however, remains limited.[42]

Beyond the GONGOs, however, lie other layers of NGOs. According to Koehn there are also 'PONGOs (emerging Party-organised NGOs), about 8,000 registered NGOs ... and perhaps 100,000 grass roots environmental NGOs that receive no Government funding and act outside the official NGO-registration process'.[43]

The 'over-enthusiastic' campaigners

The unregistered grass roots campaigners tend to live in a tolerated grey area observing a set of poorly defined rules and understandings with Government. Yet many other campaigners who do not follow these rules, or who are simply not in a position to follow them, have not been so fortunate. This includes the longstanding anti-water pollution campaigner Wu Lihong. His campaign focus has been a decades' long attempt to stem the scourge of industrial pollution in

Lake Tai (Taihu), one of China's biggest lakes south-west of Shanghai. He used to swim in the lake as a youngster, but thereafter noticed how it was becoming polluted. His story has been extensively reported.[44,45]

He went around collecting evidence of pollution and dangerous discharges from local factories and linking this to the pollution levels in the lake. He campaigned for the companies to stop doing this. His campaigning attracted widespread local support. Indeed he attracted the general support of the wider Communist leadership and was awarded the title of 'environmental warrior' at the 2005 National People's Congress.

However, local factory owners and their workers grew angry with this as factories were threatened with shutdowns because of their pollution discharges. On the other hand, local people who were affected by the pollution were enraged, and direct action followed – for example, peasants blocking a road in protest against the way pollution damaged their farms. This is when Wu began to find himself in increasing trouble with the authorities. He supported demonstrations by local people that involved blocking a road. He wanted to cooperate with the officials, but they rejected his applications to be a registered environmental NGO. Nevertheless his efforts received widespread support, both in the local media and nationally where he was even given and award by the central Government for being one of the nation's top local environmental campaigners. Wu organised petitions, lobbied various levels of Government.

However, local officials allied to local industry closed in on him and arrested him, charging him with what are seen as trumped up charges of extortion, and sent him to jail. He had accepted a contract to help clean up the pollution from local Government, ignoring advice from friends that this was a trap set for him.[46,47]

The authorities claimed that the pollution was being curbed, but then pollution seemed to become worse with a terrible toxic algae bloom in 2007. This poisoned the water making it unfit to drink. Fish died, destroying fishermen's livelihoods. Wu was arrested. He ended up being sent to jail for three years. After he was released he continued to campaign against the pollution which is still much in evidence, but is subject to constant monitoring and restriction by the local police.

Wu Lihong is an example of what happens when an initially 'constitutional' protestor runs into a brick wall, and is perceived as a threat to the local industrial establishment. But there are thousands of protests each year which are certainly not wanted by the Government.

Mass demonstrations and violent protests

Then there are the so-called 'mass events' that start out as being against the wishes of the Government. All in all, environmental protests have become the biggest source of local protests in China. Total 'mass incidents' (meaning protest demonstrations) were estimated by a former high ranking Communist Party official and were said to be running at between 30,000 and 50,000 a year.[48] According to a study conducted in 2014 by the Chinese Academy of Sciences' Institute of Law, 'environmental protests in China have been growing by 29% a year since 1996'.[49] According to a leading Chinese think-tank, 'Over the past 20 years mass incidents have increased 10 times, of which the mass incidents caused by interest conflicts including land requisition, housing demolition, environmental pollution account for more than 80 per cent'.[50]

According to an article in *Forbes* magazine about the demonstrations against chemical plants and other environmental threats

> These waves of protest are unique in that they are uniting China's working and middle classes under a common grievance. Party leaders fret about political stability and potential challenges to the regime; pollution is one of their greatest concerns. But the Chinese Government is failing to address the underlying cause of this discontent – an entrenched public distrust of officialdom – and, in the long term, is risking the possible 'joining up' of environmental protests into a widespread movement.[51]

Protests at chemical plants that are feared to be producing carcinogenic substances produce some of the most high profile, and violent, responses bringing out tens of thousands of demonstrators. Protests against building of facilities to produce para xylene (PX) have been especially confrontational resulting in demonstrations that turned violent.

The *Forbes* report also said:

> The last eight years have seen large-scale and violent anti-PX protests in the southern provinces of Guangdong and Yunnan, the eastern provinces of Zhejiang and Fujian, the northern province of Liaoning and the western province of Sichuan. The recent accident in Fujian, where the anti-PX movement began in 2007, has brought the problem full circle, and reveals the paucity of options in the Government's playbook.[52]

The 'recent accident in Fujian' resulted in around 30,000 people being evacuated and six people dying in the immediate aftermath.[53] To add to the chagrin of many locals there had been big demonstrations, in 2007, before the plant was built. The original project was planned for Xiamen. The protests only succeeded in having the plant relocated to Zhangzhou, not far away. But since then the plant has had two major accidents, including the most recent event.[54]

Many environmental protests go unreported, or censorship takes place to remove reportage. Some, however, are reported in visual terms. One example of this is a report, complete with a photograph (sent via Weibo) showing toxic-looking orange smoke pouring from a chemical factory in Neijiang in Sichuan Province in May 2015.[55] According to the report, 'The local police department said it had detained seven people who had spread rumours, damaged public property and used violence to hinder law enforcement'.[56] The same report also mentioned plans for an incinerator in Luodong being abandoned after violent

protests and also how there was a demonstration in the same province, Guangdong, against plans to build a new coal-fired power stations.

Protests can sometimes lead to the cancellations of projects – some nuclear
power projects have been halted this way.[57] In August 2016, a scheme to build a
nuclear reprocessing plant in the Eastern city of Llanyungang was halted after
several days of protests, some of which had violent incidents. According to a
report in the Wall Street Journal, a 'local resident' commented: 'I love this city
and I don't care how great the GDP is. I just want a quiet and healthy neighbor-
hood without risks.'[58]

Governance and pollution

As already argued in Chapter 2, whilst the Government under Xi Yinping has
taken a more hard-line authoritarian turn and repressed its opponents more
severely in recent times, it has limited its own options. It options are limited
through the expansion of the area in which civil society groups have compet-
ence in what the Government says are 'technical', 'non-political' concerns, that
of achieving environmental targets and combating pollution.

However, such a narrative is constrained by criticisms of how environmental
governance systems work in practice. The Government has, since the 1980s, set
up an array of regulations to control environmental performance and institutions to regulate them. These include the State Environmental Protection
Agency (SEPA) and a large network of Environmental Protection Bureaus
(EPBs). However, these have long been criticised for their links with local
private interests who provide them with financial resources.[59] Koehn reports (on
the basis of a number of cited publications) that

> [i]n most places, EPB's are weakened by insufficient funding, staffing, skills,
> fining authority networks and technical capacity. Equally authoritative or
> even more powerful units at the same administrative level within a local
> Government cannot easily be restrained by the EPB.[60]

Altogether, then, China's system of relations between Government and civil
society has been characterised by Jessica Teets, in a quote reproduced by Judith
Shapiro,[61] as

> 'consultative authoritarianism' whereby the Government and civil society
> learn from each other and groups tacitly agree to provide some public goods
> that the Government cannot. However, such groups struggle to define their
> political space, as freedoms are constantly shifting. They contract during
> major Party congresses, for example, and during anniversaries of civil
> unrest. Often the demarcation line is not visible until it has been crossed.[62]

Some analysts contend that in some places and times at least, citizens' participation in policy evaluation goes beyond mere consultation. In a study of participative

governance in one of the wealthy cities on the East coast, Hangzhou, Duckett and Wang say that

> [t]he local Government has created a range of platforms using traditional and new media that enable citizens to voice their opinions on local issues…. These mechanisms help citizens shape policy agendas, inform and influence decision-making, and provide policy feedback to modify existing policies, and so involve citizens through different stages of the policy process. They are more than simply a deliberative or consultative mechanism because they not only involve consulting citizens on particular policies or budgets but also enable them to evaluate government performance, sit in on government meetings that discuss a wide range of policies and influence policy agendas.[63]

I want to focus some attention on estimations of outcomes of the environmental governance system itself, since this is the process through which the official NGO environmental campaigners work. This is of particular importance to a study involving ecological modernization, since European style EM needs to involve effective environmental governance.

Research on what influences Chinese companies does not support the notion that environmental regulation is particularly important in promoting carbon reduction and resource conservation in general. One study of such outcomes as delivered by Chinese companies involved in exporting manufactured products found that only 'customer pressure' was significantly associated with improved environmental performance, with regulatory policies not being important.[64]

Lawyers actively work to defend environmental rights, and provided they do not challenge the legitimacy of the Government, they can be successful. However, the court system is itself run by local Government which has interests in protecting local industry. There are proposals to move control of the courts out of the control of municipal authorities. The Government is proposing to transfer responsibility for courts to the provincial level and away from the county level. This might make the courts more likely to clamp down on pollution since they will no longer be influenced by local Government officials who have an interest in supporting polluting local industry who may be targets of the law cases.[65] However, until this is implemented and followed through there are only limited possibilities of gaining success for environmental causes through court action alone. Although the number of environmental law cases is increasing, the numbers are not startlingly high for such a large country as China, considering the size of environmental problems. In 2016, some 48 cases were brought, although this in itself is an increase given that from 2007 to 2014 only 65 cases were brought to the courts. Indeed the law has only recently been changed to allow environmental NGOs to take cases which allow allegedly negligent EPBs to be forced to enforce environmental regulations. However, as yet the use of this facility is limited.[66] Moreover local environmental inspectors can face hostility, even attacks, from local industrial interests, with one case being reported in *China Daily*.[67]

Although the task of reducing pollutants from coal-fired power stations is at the top of the political agenda, there is a lack of confidence in the ability to even measure pollution from the power plant. One report commented that

> 'There is no guarantee of avoiding under-reporting (of emissions) at local plants located far away from supervisory bodies. Coal data is very fuzzy,' said a manager with a state-owned power company, who did not want to be named because he is not authorised to speak to the media. The manager said firms could easily exaggerate coal efficiency by manipulating their numbers. For example, power companies that also provided heating for local communities could overstate the amount of coal used for heat generation, which is not subject to direct monitoring, and understate the amount used for power.[68]

In 2014, a new Environmental Protection Act was promulgated in China which claimed to do much to advance environmental protection, including giving local government new responsibilities to ensure environmental protection. However, this legislation has been criticised as being heavily flawed. Zhang and Cao argue that there are four basic limitations with the new Environmental Protection Law (EPL). First, 'The EPL can be trumped by other legislation such as the specific agriculture, forestry, grassland and water laws'. Second, 'enforcement of the EPL will be hampered by the fragmented and overlapping structure of environmental governance in China'. Third, 'the new EPL fails to acknowledge citizens' basic right to an environment fit for life' and fourth 'enforcement and implementation of the law may be foiled by a lack of capacity and by conflicts of interest'.[69]

It is suspected that, in practice, there is considerable corruption amongst bodies responsible for environmental monitoring and the system of monitoring is itself very patchy in many circumstances. Various mechanisms are cited as being used to under-report polluting emissions. This is despite China passing tough new laws to punish polluters[70] Ma Jun, feels that it may take until at least 2030 to make Beijing air clean.[71]

Certainly there is a big problem with enforcing environmental laws. According to Ma Jun

> It's the local environmental officials that are in charge of enforcement, but they are subordinate to local Government. Their heads are appointed by local Government. Those who want to stick to the laws could be replaced. This is the very harsh reality. It won't be easy to change that.[72]

As discussed in Chapter 3, local Government has been a key agent, perhaps the key agent, in Chinese economic development. The local Government authorities have various incentives impelling them to promote local economic development. They have environmental responsibilities, but the incentive to execute them is in conflict with what may be seen by local officials as more pressing and often more tangible drivers for economic development. As discussed in Chapter 3, there are great pressures to increase developments which usually involve more building. However, the task of ensuring that the buildings meets energy efficiency standards are burdensome and tasks for which the local authorities may not have sufficient resources.

Indeed, despite the system being generally regarded as a 'top-down' one, in practice officials enjoy considerable autonomy in how to promote economic development, doing so in a market environment which implicitly decides, for example, how much energy is consumed. Although energy conservation targets are set, in practice they are ineffective. The authoritarian system may encourage production but not conservation.[73] Hence there is a conflict between the interests of local officials whose careers and financial interests are intrinsically bound up with the performance of local industry and enforcing environmental regulations and judgments which may reduce that performance in terms of financial returns. Under the Government's latest (thirteenth) Five Year Plan, officials will now be audited for their environmental performance upon leaving office. However, we shall have to wait and see how much difference this makes in practice, and how much weight this has in comparison with the overweening drive by local officials for cooperation with industry to increase development.

This top-down approach to environmental protection has been reinforced in recent years, under the leadership of Xi Jinping, to try to overcome the social and environmental problems caused by economic decentralization. According to Chen, Noesselt and Witt:

> The Chinese Communist Party did not seek to set its policy in accordance to the global environmental governance paradigm – sustainable development – to delegate the policy decision-making power to the lower level of government and to cultivate dialogue in the civil society. On the contrary, they have sought to implement the opposite institutional reconfigurations of 'New Urbanization': 'defragmented instruments' that use cohesive political control mechanisms to re-centralize policy incentives and enforcement implementations with the aim of reduce negative consequences of rapid modernization.[74]

Jonathan Fenby, who outlines some of the seamier sides of Chinese political economy, comments that the security apparatus has been strengthened under the leadership of Xi Jinping, but he also remarks that 'China is in many ways a far freer place for its citizens. Material progress and modernity have brought considerable individual liberation'.[75]

Ma Jun's views echo research quoted earlier which concludes that consumer pressure is much more effective than the regulatory system when it comes to reducing pollution in China. He comments: 'We can't go to courts in China, so we have to find alternate ways, like working with brands to try and create a level playing field by identifying the most obvious polluters.'[76] According to the news-paper report in which this quote is carried, 'He has already had success in getting multinationals like Apple, Hewlett-Packard, H&M and Gap to root out the worst polluters from their supply chain in China'.[77]

Moreover, what the environmental cases reveal is that the present planning system seems to be implicitly tilted towards developers rather than environ-mental interests of a wide range of types. The most glaring problems are the lack of public consultation before proposals for development are made. This is com-pounded by the lack of a defined political process where planning consent is considered and where the interest groups involved can lobby in favour of their attitudes and proposals.

As Andrews-Speed comments

> [T]he law in China is notorious for failing to secure property rights. Rights are poorly defined in law and Government agencies at all levels of govern-ment exercise their 'right' to transfer rights with little due process.... Despite the considerable progress that has been made to modernize and improve China's legal system, a fundamental contradiction remains between the (Communist) Party's stated policy to promote the rule of law and its efforts to retain the monopoly of power.[78]

If developers can merely submit proposals to the relevant state agencies without public consultation then it is not surprising that confrontation can occur when local citizens suddenly see the bulldozers in action – without any prior notion that developments are taking place. One can almost hear people saying 'if it happened in our town there would be riots'. In fact, in China, there frequently are!

Some environmental analysts have commented that 'authoritarian' govern-ance may be inevitable. Mark Beeson commented, in 2010, in discussing China's approach to environmental problems, that 'one possible consequence of environmental degradation is the development or consolidation of authoritarian rule as political elites come to privilege regime maintenance and internal stability over political liberalisation'.[79] He dismisses the possibility of 'an envir-onmentally conscious, politically-savvy, effective civil society that can trans-form environmental practices'.[80] His argument assumes that the force majeure of environmental decay will compel the authorities along a road of repression to suppress the consequences of economic development, economic development being demanded by the populace as the priority. Admittedly, China did have in place a 'one child' policy, but this has now ended, and informed opinion on the subject says that China's population will not increase as a result.[81]

However, the sort of logic expressed by Mark Beeson is different from what I argue in this book. Clearly China's policy implementation style is a 'top-down' one. But they are still following popular demands for an improved environment and, to that extent, general objectives of improving energy efficiency and imple-menting ambitious targets for deploying renewable energy (such as wind power and solar power) are consensus objectives. So, if writers are implying that somehow the Chinese Government is forcing environmental improvements on an unwilling populace, then I think they are wrong. Indeed, the contrary appears to be the case, judging by the evidence discussed here. Not only this but, as argued here, the top-down strategy simply will not be as effective as a more decentralised strategy where local government officials are accountable to local people. This is as opposed to being accountable to the central Government and its pressures on local officials to promote economic development.

There are popular demands for more action from local Government to meet environmental targets, not opposition to such things. There is pressure for more accountability on achieving environmental goals. Gilley[82] has criticised 'authoritarian environmentalism' in China for being unable to transform policies into effective outcomes. He argues that

> where state actors are fragmented, the aims of 'ecoelites' can easily be undermined at the implementation stage. Moreover, the exclusion of social actors and representatives creates a malign lock-in effect in which low social concern makes authoritarian approaches both more necessary and more difficult.[83]

His assumption, perhaps reasonable a few years ago, was that there was insufficient concern by ordinary citizens about issues such as climate change to ensure pressure from below to achieve outcomes that radically reduced pollution. However, the evidence is, as discussed earlier, that this is changing and that Chinese citizens are as concerned as ones in Europe about this issue, and perhaps more concerned to take measures to counter it since the measures complement the fight against local pollution. Hence we can argue plausibly now that not only is authoritarian environmentalism not working in China, but also that making local Government more accountable to ordinary citizens would lead to substantially greater effective pressure for sustainable energy strategies being implemented.

The survival of the Government depends on what are probably best seen as pragmatic rather than ideological or cultural dispositions by Chinese people towards different types of rule. Ben Chu criticises notions that Chinese people are, for cultural reasons, less well disposed towards democracy than the West. He points to the attitudes of the very large Chinese diaspora who fit in well with democracy abroad, and also the case of Taiwan, which appears now to be a relatively stable democracy.[84]

Nevertheless, Daniel Bell, a political scientist from Tsinghua University in Beijing, talks about how the Chinese Government is maintained through a 'political meritocracy'. However, he says that

> [i]n traditional China people judged the performance of the state not just in terms of its economic performance, but also how well it does at dealing with crises, and the same is true today … a prolonged economic crisis that undermines faith in the Government's economic performance combined with

perceptions of a heavy-handed or incompetent response to a social crisis or natural disaster may be the tipping point.[85]

The Chinese Communist Party (CCP) is very large – at 85 million out of the around 1.35 billion total Chinese population. This means that around one on 12 people are members. It seems unlikely that the Government could fall because of solely outside pressures although, as in the case of the Soviet Union, communist rule could end through a lack of internal will to continue. China is not Russia of course – in the case of Russia, communism lost power in the context of a massive loss of revenue from oil and gas as prices declined in the late 1980s.

However, to maintain an unquestioned grip on power the CCP must, as Daniel Bell observes, avoid a situation where there is long-term economic decline. The economy may still be more important than environmental issues, although the Government is now expected to achieve economic development and environmental protection simultaneously. The Government faces severe challenges in meeting all of these expectations.

New trends in tackling pollution

The received wisdom about developing countries and their efforts in dealing with pollution have been characterised by something called the 'environmental Kuznets curve'. The theory behind this is that as a country develops and economic output increases, so do pollution levels (such as sulphur or particulate emissions). However, eventually, pollution output peaks. Then pollution begins to decline – hence typically a sort of upturned U graph is used to represent the relationship between economic development and pollution. However, by the start of the twentieth century it was becoming apparent that this curve was becoming a lot shorter and flatter – in other words it was taking a lot shorter time for pollution levels to peak.[86] Indeed 'developing countries are addressing environmental issues, sometimes adopting developed country standards with a short time lag and sometimes performing better than some wealthy countries'.[87]

The standard stereotype for China has for a long time been that it will carry on churning out increasing levels of carbon dioxide (if not a lot of other types of pollution) as its economic growth continues. But this stereotype, as we discuss later, is seriously flawed. There are good reasons in theory why this should be the case. Technology has moved on a lot since the days of industrialisation in the West. The shape of economic growth itself is changing. Moreover, an increasingly affluent middle class in China knows from seeing the regulation in the West that clean air is very possible and achievable. In the context of studying opposition to a waste incineration plant in Guangzhou Province, Thomas Johnson observes that '[m]iddle class environmental mobilization in urban China – which takes place in a context of regulatory uncertainty – highlights growing contestation over what regulation comprises, who should regulate, and what should be regulated'.[88] The Chinese middle class is expanding at a very rapid pace. In 2013, McKinsey calculated that the percentage of urban Chinese consumers earning between $9,000 and $34,000 a year had increased from 4 per cent in 2000 to 68 per cent in 2012.[89] In October 2015, it was reported that, according to a report by a Swiss bank, 'China's middle class has overtaken the United States to become the largest in the world'.[90]

Rising affluence has been associated with the rise of environmental concerns among citizens in the West since the 1950s. As Philip Shabecoff has commented on the rise of environmentalism in the USA, 'our very affluence prompted many Americans to see environmental degradation as an obstacle to their search for a higher standard of living.'[91] It is therefore hardly surprising that as China's living standards rise, as it moves towards a consumer economy rather than one oriented towards industrial investments, and as services become much more prominent, that environmental standards loom larger, and in the mode of ecological modernization, become fused with economic priorities.. The new technologies that are now available make it even more plausible than in the past to achieve much greater environmental standards.

Climate change can be placed effectively centre-stage in policy by bundling it together with tackling local and immediate air pollution problems. Koehn describes this as a process of 'sub-national framing'. Combating climate change becomes a 'co-benefit' of this strategy.[92] The Government is struggling to keep up with these expectations, but it knows it must succeed, for the political consequences of failure will be severe.

Conclusion

The argument in this chapter has been that the fight against pollution is seen as an increasingly high priority in China, by the Chinese people themselves. It is such a high priority that the Chinese Government is impelled to be seen to take strong action in order to justify and preserve its legitimacy. I have discussed the evidence for this in this chapter, and it includes discussion of the various strands of the pollution abatement movement: leading intellectuals who have achieved a massive popular response; the strength of people and groups on the social media campaigning on environmental issues; the growth of environmental NGOs which the Government has subsumed into its policymaking apparatus; the growth of campaigners seeking to push the courts into making judgments favourable to anti-pollution campaigners rather than productionist-oriented local officials and commercial interests; the growth of active campaigns, demonstrations and other forms of direct action taken to support campaigns against environmental improvements, and also the evidence of opinion polling which itself suggests that the Chinese people are keener on taking action to counter climate change than many people in the West.

The old political stereotype (which I have taught as an energy and environmental academic for decades) that the 'North' favours environmental protection while the 'South' favours economic development, is breaking down. The

Chinese people are concerned to combat pollution in all its forms. Indeed, the fact that local pollution is worse in China than the West inclines them to, in effect, favour action to counter climate change even more strongly than many Western populations. Why? One very good reason is simply that the measures required to make a fundamental reduction in local pollution are usually very similar to those that are required to combat climate change: improvements in energy efficiency; shifting to low carbon fuels, especially renewable energy; and in general shifting to economic activities – particularly service industries – that involve production of much lower pollution levels than traditional heavy industry.

However, on the other hand, the modes of environmental governance that are now dominant in China are slow to respond to these changes. Improvements occur so long as the centre responds to what it sees are pressures from citizens to improve environmental conditions. It happens that, in the case of energy, the drive to reduce carbon emissions overlaps with other state priorities of improving energy security. However, the system is held back by its authoritarian nature and the lack of a fully functioning rule of law. So long as environmental NGOs are dependent on state approval to take part in discussions about environmental or climate policy then there will always be suspicions that debate is being sanitised for the convenience of Government.

At a local level there is a basic contradiction between officials that are incentivised for their ability to pursue economic development and the need to protect the environment.

The Communist Party can incorporate environmental audits on these officials. However, this requires the exercise of local knowledge, and environmental NGOs are themselves limited in what they can say and do by the fact that they cannot challenge the legitimacy of the local governments themselves. The obvious solution is to have local officials elected and thus be accountable directly to the local population. At present there are only elections to the most local parishes, which in practice have few powers or responsibilities. But if officials are elected then they are likely to be put under greater pressure to achieve environmental objectives and improve supervision of the performance of regulations governing energy use. However, inception of elections at the local level seems politically unlikely at the time of writing.

In terms of ecological modernisation (EM), the drive to achieve EM's central goal of combining business development with ecological protection is intermittent so long as it remains the case that polluting industries have a political advantage over environmental NGOs. The basic necessity (for EM) of having autonomous environmental NGOs able to negotiate with, and exert pressure on, industry in Government does not seem to be the case in China. Environmental NGOs have increased, and are increasing, their influence, but the core impulses involved in EM style environmental governance are yet to be satisfied.

In Chapter 4, I established how, first, the Chinese economy is (one way or another) rebalancing to involve much lower levels of carbon emissions as overproduction (for example of buildings) is reduced. In this chapter I have discussed how political priorities are swinging to put more and more emphasis on combating pollution. We can see from the reports about air pollution in the worst affected cities that such pollution is associated with centres of burning and mining and processing of coal. Curbing pollution from fossil fuels is the key to attaining the objective of reducing air pollution, so reducing consumption of fossil fuels and switching to cleaner fuels are natural results of a shift towards a sustainable economy in both economic and environmental senses. We turn to look at how such fuel switching is occurring and how it might develop.

Notes

1 Watts, J. (2010) *When a Billion Chinese Jump*, London: Faber and Faber, p. 277
2 Dahlgreen, W. (2016) 'Global survey: Britain among least concerned in the world about climate change', *YouGov*, 29 January, available online at https://yougov.co.uk/news/2016/01/29/global-issues/
3 Jordan, W. (2015) 'Global survey: Chinese most in favour of action on climate change', 10 June, available online at https://yougov.co.uk/news/2015/06/07/Global-survey-Chinese-most-favour-action-climate-c/
4 Schneider, F. (2013) 'The Crisis of China's Environmental Pollution: What does it Take to Clean Up the PRC?' *Politics East Asia*, available online at www.politicseast asia.com/studying/chinas-environmental-pollution/
5 Shepherd, W. (2015) 'After "Under the Dome": Can China solve its air pollution crisis?', *City Metrics*, 25 March, available online at www.citymetric.com/horizons/after-under-dome-can-china-solve-its-air-pollution-crisis-877
6 Ghemawat, P. (2013) 'Why China's middle class will solve its air pollution problems', *Fortune*, 7 November, available online at http://fortune.com/2013/11/07/why-chinas-middle-class-will-solve-its-air-pollution-problems/
7 Guildford, G. (2013) 'Half of the Rice in Guangzhou Is Polluted', *The Atlantic*, 21 May, available online at www.theatlantic.com/china/archive/2013/05/half-of-the-rice-in-guangzhou-is-polluted/276098/
8 Guoqing, W., Nadin, R. and Opitz-Stapleton, S. (2016) 'A balancing act: China's water resources and climate change', p. 104, in Nadin, R., Opitz-Stapleton, S. and Yinlong, X., *Climate Risk and Resilience in China*, London: Routledge, pp. 96–128
9 Ibid., p. 105
10 Levitt, T. (2015) 'Ma Jun: China has reached its environmental tipping point', *Guardian*, 19 May, available online at www.theguardian.com/sustainable-business/2015/may/19/ma-jun-china-has-reached-its-environmental-tipping-point?utm_medium=twitter&utm_source=dlvr.it
11 Associated Press (2016) 'Four-fifths of China's water from wells 'unsafe because of pollution', *Guardian*, 12 April, available online at www.theguardian.com/environment/2016/apr/12/four-fifths-of-chinas-water-from-wells-unsafe-because-of-pollution
12 Maughan, T. (2015) 'The dystopian lake filled by the world's tech lust', BBC, 2 April, available online at www.bbc.com/future/story/20150402-the-worst-place-on-earth
13 Wall Street Journal Staff (2013) 'Loans to Steel traders Pose Risk', *Wall Street Journal*, 4 February, available online at http://blogs.wsj.com/deals/2013/02/04/loans-to-steel-traders-in-china-pose-risk/
14 World Steel Association (2016) *Top Steel Producing Companies*, available online at www.worldsteel.org/statistics/top-producers.html
15 Stringer, D. (2014) 'China's rare earth toxic time bomb to spur mining boom', *Bloomberg Business*, 4 July, available online at www.bloomberg.com/news/articles/2014-06-03/china-s-rare-earth-toxic-time-bomb-to-spur-12-billion-of-mines

16 Unsigned (2015) 'Study: China's Air Pollution Kills 1.6 Million a Year', *China Digital Times*, available online at https://chinadigitaltimes.net/2015/08/study-chinas-air-pollution-kills-1-6-million-a-year/

17 Watkins, E. (1954) 'Air pollution aspects of the London fog of December 1952', *Quarterly Journal of the Royal Meteorological Society*, vol. 80, no. 344, 267–271 (see abstract p. 267). It should be noted that these levels were recorded as being in milligrams as opposed to the microgram used more commonly today – a microgram is 1000 times smaller than a milligram

18 World Health Organisation (2016) 'Ambient (outdoor) air pollution in cities database (2016) *World Health Organisation*, available online at www.who.int/phe/health_topics/outdoorair/databases/cities/en/, see 'urban outdoor air pollution database, by country and city'

19 Jingrong, L. (2012) 'Beijing releases PM10 density figures', *China.org.cn*, 12 January, available online at www.china.org.cn/environment/2012-01/12/content_24390197.htm

20 See World Health Organisation (2016) 'Ambient (outdoor) air pollution in cities database (2016) available online at www.who.int/phe/health_topics/outdoorair/databases/cities/en/, see 'urban outdoor air pollution database, by country and city'

21 Ma, W. (2014) 'Meet the Biggest Polluter in China's Most Polluted City', *Wall Street Journal*, 16 September, available online at www.wsj.com/articles/economics-versus-pollution-in-chinas-dirtiest-city-1410901992

22 Duggan J. (2015) 'Welcome to Baoding, China's most polluted city', *Guardian*, 22 May, available online at www.theguardian.com/cities/2015/may/22/baoding-china-most-polluted-city-air-pollution-beijing-hebei

23 Shoemaker, B. (2014) China Pollution – Blue Skies over Beijing', *The Diplomat*, 10 November, available online at http://thediplomat.com/2014/11/china-pollution-blue-skies-over-beijing/

24 Unsigned (2016) 'Beijing will close 2,500 polluting firms in 2016', *Climate Action*, 11 January, available online at www.climateactionprogramme.org/news/beijing_will_close_2500_polluting_firms_in_2016

25 Anonymous reporting (2015) 'China smog: Beijing residents buy fresh air from Canada', *BBC online*, 21 December, available online at www.bbc.co.uk/news/world-asia-35155357

26 Unsigned (2012) 'Dirty Air & Succession Jitters in Beijing', *China Digital Times*, 12 August, available online at http://chinadigitaltimes.net/2012/06/dirty-air-and-succession-jitters-cloud-beijings-judgment/

27 Ibid.

28 Unsigned (2015) *Under the Dome*, available online at www.youtube.com/watch?v=T6X2uwlQGQM

29 Stanway, S. (2015) 'China risks social conflict if war on pollution lags – govt researchers', *Reuters*, 10 April, available online at www.reuters.com/article/china-environment-idUSL4N0X733P20150410

30 Ma, J. (2004 – English edition) *China's Water Crisis*, Norwalk CT: EastBridge

31 Ibid., p. 60

32 IPE (2015) available online at www.ipe.org.cn/index.aspx

33 Munro, N. (2014) 'Profiling the Victims: public awareness of pollution-related harm in China', *Journal of Contemporary China*, vol. 23, no. 86, 314–329, p. 320

34 Zhang, H. (2011) 'Green bounty hunters: engaging Chinese citizens in local environmental enforcement', *China Environment Series* 11, 137–153, cited by Munro (2014) op. cit.

35 Larson, C., 'China gets a little more fresh air', *Bloomberg Business Week*, 16 August, available online at www.bloomberg.com/news/articles/2015-08-06/pollution-china-gets-a-little-more-fresh-air

36 Agence-France Presse (2015) 'China encourages environmental groups to sue polluters',

Guardian, 7 January, available online at www.theguardian.com/environment/2015/jan/07/china-encourages-environmental-groups-to-sue-polluters

37 Martens, S. (2007) 'Public Participation with Chinese Characteristics: Citizen Consumers in China's Environmental Management', p. 66, in Carter, N. and Mol, P., 'China and the Environment: Domestic and transnational Dynamics of a Future Hegemon', in Carter, N. and Mol, P., *Environmental Governance in China*, London: Routledge, pp. 63–82

38 Kahya, D. (2015) *Greenpeace Energy Desk Dispatch*, 6 August, 2015, available online at http://energydesk.greenpeace.org/2015/08/06/daily-dispatch-china-media-monitoring-uk-oil-nuclear-world-wind/

39 Unsigned (2010) 'Budding Greens', 15 June, *The Economist* available online at www.economist.com/node/16592268

40 Xiaopo Lake Wetland Tourism Development Damage Case available online at www.clapv.org/english_lvshi/ZhiChiAnJian_content.asp?id=70&title=Support%20cases&titlecontent=PD_zhichianjian

41 Center for Legal Assistance to Pollution Victims (2015) 'Chinese environmental lawyer takes on the powerful to give voice to vulnerable pollution victims', 22 March, available online at www.clapv.org/english_lvshi/meitibaodao_content.asp?id=59&title=Media&titlecontent=meitibaodao_list&lei1=107

42 Schreurs, M. (2013) 'Climate Change in an Authoritarian State: The Ambivalent Case of China', p. 459, in Dryzel, J., Norgaard, R. and Schlosberg D., *The Oxford Handbook of Climate Change and Society*, Oxford: Oxford University Press, pp. 449–463

43 Koehn, P. (2015) *China Confronts Climate Change*, London: Routledge, p. 96

44 Guorui, L., Hanfu, H. (2012) 'Long struggle for a cleaner Lake Tai', *China Dialogue*, 14 February, available online at www.chinadialogue.net/article/4767-Long-struggle-for-a-cleaner-Lake-Tai-; and Hager, M. (2014) China's Wu Hong continues to speak out on pollution in Lake Tai, available online at www.planetexperts.com/chinas-wu-lihong-continues-speak-pollution-lake-tai/

45 Unsigned (2008) 'A lot to be angry about', *Economist*, 1 May, available online at www.economist.com/node/11293734

46 Guorui, L. and Hanfu, H. (2012) 'Long struggle for a cleaner Lake Tai', *China Dialogue*, 14 February, available online at www.chinadialogue.net/article/4767-Long-struggle-for-a-cleaner-Lake-Tai-; and Hager, M. (2014) China's Wu Hong continues to speak out on pollution in Lake Tai, available online at www.planetexperts.com/chinas-wu-lihong-continues-speak-pollution-lake-tai/

47 Unsigned (2008) 'A lot to be angry about', *Economist*, 1 May, available online at www.economist.com/node/11293734

48 Geal, S. and Hilton, I. (2014) 'China's Environmental Governance Challenge', p. 130 in *Governing for Sustainability*, Worldwatch Institute, Washington: Island Press, pp. 129–137

49 Qin, L. (2014) 'China's pollution protests could be slowed by stronger rule of law,' *China Dialogue*, 12 November, available online at www.chinadialogue.net/article/show/single/en/7483-China-s-pollution-protests-could-be-slowed-by-stronger-rule-of-law

50 Fulin, C. (ed.) (2014) 'Decisive Role of the Market – China Reform Research Report', *China Institute for Reform and Development*, Haikou, Hainan: China Intercontinental Press, p. 8

51 Hoffamn, S, Sullivan, J. (2015) 'Environmental Protests Expose Weakness In China's Leadership', *Forbes*, 22 June, available online at www.forbes.com/sites/forbesasia/2015/06/22/environmental-protests-expose-weakness-in-chinas-leadership/

52 Ibid.

53 Jingxi, X. (2015) 'Blast in Fujian plant blamed on poor equipment', *China Daily*, 22 April, available online at www.chinadaily.com.cn/china/2015-04/22/content_20508516.htm

54 Kyo, L. (2015) 'A contentious chemical plant in China has exploded for the second time in two years', *Quartz*, 7 April, available online at http://qz.com/377929/a-contentious-chemical-plant-in-china-has-exploded-for-the-second-time-in-two-years/

55 Chun, Z. (2015) 'Residents of SW China City protest against foul air', *China Dialogue*, 15 April, available online at www.chinadialogue.net/blog/7844-Residents-of-SW-China-city-protest-against-foul-air/en

56 Ibid.

57 Hornby, L. and Lin, L. (2016) 'China Protest Against Nuclear Waste Plan', *Financial Times*, 7 August, available online at www.ft.com/content/dacb775a-5c7f-11e6-bb77-a121aa8abd95

58 Spegele, B. (2016) 'China Looks to Placate Nuclear-Project Protesters', *Wall Street Journal*, available online at www.wsj.com/articles/china-cracks-down-on-nuclear-project-protests-1470734568

59 Shi, H. and Zhang, L. (2007) 'China's Environmental Governance of Rapid Industrialisation', pp. 132–133 in Carter, N. and Mol, P., 'China and the Environment: Domestic and transnational Dynamics of a Future Hegemon', in Carter, N. and Mol, P., *Environmental Governance in China*, London: Routledge, pp. 123–144

60 Koehn, P. (2015) *China Confronts Climate Change*, London: Routledge, p. 103

61 Teets, J. (2014) *Civil Society under Authoritarianism: The China Model*, Cambridge: Cambridge University Press, cited by Shapiro, J. (2016) *China's Environmental Challenges*, Cambridge: Polity Press, p. 97

62 Shapiro, J. (2016) *China's Environmental Challenges*, Cambridge: Polity Press, p. 97

63 Duckett, J. and Wang, H. (2013) 'Extending political participation in China: new opportunities for citizens in the policy process', *Journal of Asian Public Policy*, vol. 6, no. 3, 263–276

64 Lai, k.-H,*, Wong, C. and Cheng, T. (2012) 'Ecological modernisation of Chinese export manufacturing via green logistics management and its regional implications', *Technological Forecasting & Social Change*, vol. 79, 766–770

65 Johnson, A. (2016) China Grants Courts Greater Autonomy on Limited Matters, *New York Times*, 2 January, available online at www.nytimes.com/2016/01/03/world/asia/china-grants-courts-greater-autonomy-on-limited-matters.html?_r=0

66 Yin, C. (2016) 'Failing eco-protection bureaus in the firing line', *China Daily*, 17 February, available online at http://europe.chinadaily.com.cn/china/2016-02/17/content_23515142.htm

67 Ibid

68 Stanway, D. and Chen, K. (2016) 'False Emissions Reporting Undermines China's Pollution Fight', *Reuters*, 16 January, available online at http://uk.reuters.com/article/us-china-power-emissions-idUKKCN0UV0XS

69 Zhang, B. and Cao., C. (2015) 'Policy: Four gaps in China's new environmental law', *Nature*, 517, 433–434, available online at www.nature.com/news/policy-four-gaps-in-china-s-new-environmental-law-1.16736

70 Stanway, D. and Chen. K. (2016) 'False emissions reporting undermines China's pollution fight', *Reuters*, 17 January, available online at http://uk.reuters.com/article/us-china-power-emissions-idUKKCN0UV0XS

71 Larson, C. (2012) 'China's Ma Jun on the fight to clean up Beijing's dirty air', *Yale Environment 360*, available online at http://e360.yale.edu/feature/chinas_ma_jun_on_the_fight_to_clean_up_beijings_dirty_air/2515/

72 Levitt, T. (2015) 'Ma Jun: China has reached its environmental tipping point', *Guardian*, 19 May, available online at www.theguardian.com/sustainable-business/2015/may/19/ma-jun-china-has-reached-its-environmental-tipping-point

73 Lo, K. (2015) 'How authoritarian is the environmental governance of China?', *Environment Science & Policy*, vol. 54, 152–159

74 Chen, C., Noesselt, N. and Witt, L., 'Environmentalism without Democracy? Green

Urbanization in China', Paper to 2016 Political Studies Association (UK), Brighton, 21–23 March, pp. 22–23, available online at www.psa.ac.uk/sites/default/files/conference/papers/2016/Conference%20Paper_PSA2016_3.pdf

75 Fenby, J. (2014) *Will China Dominate the 21st Century?*, Cambridge: Polity Press
76 Levitt, T. (2015) op. cit.
77 Ibid.
78 Andrews-Speed, P. (2012) *The Governance of Energy in China*, Houndmills, Basingstoke: Palgrave, p.134
79 Beeson, M. (2010) 'The coming of environmental authoritarianism', *Environmental Politics*, vol. 19, no. 2, 276–294, p. 276
80 Ibid., p. 277
81 Fong, M. (2016) *One Child*, New York: Houghton Mifflin Harcourt, pp. 208–210
82 Gilley, B. (2012) 'Authoritarian environmentalism and China's response to climate change', *Environmental Politics*, vol. 21, no. 2, 287–307
83 Ibid., p. 300
84 Chu, B. (2013) *Chinese Whispers*, London: Phoenix, pp. 76–104
85 Bell, D. (2015) *Political Meritocracy and the Limits of Democracy*, New Jersey: Princeton
86 Stern, D. (2004) 'The Rise and Fall of the Environmental Kuznets Curve', *World Development*, vol. 32, no. 8, 1419–1439
87 Ibid., p. 1419
88 Johnson, T. (2016) 'Regulatory dynamism of environmental mobilization in urban China', *Regulation & Governance*, vol. 10, 14–28, p. 24
89 Barton, D., Chen, Y. and Chun, A. (2013) 'Mapping China's middle class' *McKinsey Quarterly*, June, available online at www.mckinsey.com/insights/consumer_and_retail/mapping_chinas_middle_class
90 Agency Reporter (2015) 'China's middle class overtakes US as largest in world', *The Telegraph*, 14 October, available online at www.telegraph.co.uk/finance/china-business/11929794/Chinas-middle-class-overtakes-US-as-largest-in-the-world.html
91 Shabecoff, P. (2000) *Earth Rising – American Environmentalism in the 21st century*, Washington DC: Island Press, p. 5
92 Koehn, P. (2015) op. cit., pp. 118–139

6 Fuel switching to cut carbon

We have seen how Chinese energy consumption may have stabilised, and that carbon emissions may be declining. The translation of stability in energy consumption into declining emissions is brought about by fuel switching to lower carbon fuels. I will look at the details of how this, and how much of this, can be achieved. I will use the evidence in this chapter to assess how far China fits in with core notions of what I call 'Eurocentric' ecological modernisation. I shall discuss the extent to which Chinese strategies for fuel switching match up to the (EM) criteria I have identified, and using this discussion examine the effectiveness of Chinese strategies and practice. Key aspects which apply to this chapter are the extent to which green energy supply technologies, or at least low carbon technologies, can be installed in the right numbers. However, another key issue is whether, and to what extent, the economic governance arrangements are appropriate to overcome the hurdles that face a successful transition to a low carbon economy. To what extent does the electricity and especially renewable energy arrangements reflect the need for EM style 'smart' economic instruments? Does this sector suffer from a more general malaise of political economy in China whereby local government selects company winners rather than selection being through the market?

In the world, as a whole, investment in renewable energy is outstripping that of investment in fossil fuels.[1] On top of that, China has opened up a very large lead in absolute numbers installing renewable energy and other clean energy investments. As the European environmental consultancy E3G declared: 'China has caught up to and overtaken the EU across a range of low carbon economic sectors, including clean energy investment, R&D spending, power transmission grids and production and sales of electric vehicles.'[2] Indeed, data published by Bloomberg indicates that total investment in renewable energy in China in 2015 was easily more than the combined total investment in renewable energy made by both the USA and the EU.[3]

In 2015, China installed 15 GW of solar pv, or around 35 per cent of the world's total. In the case of wind power, 33 GW or nearly half of the world's wind power capacity installed in 2015 was deployed in China. Both figures, of course, substantially exceed China's proportion of the world population (about 20 per cent). This expansion is typical of the productionism that was discussed in Chapter 2, with the sharp difference that this productionism was promoting an ecologically sustainable product as opposed to the often polluting products that were being manufactured or constructed in the form of excessive building.

This activity helps to instil credibility in the pledge made to the Paris Agreement where China said that by 2030, 20 per cent of its energy would come from non-fossil energy sources. This was agreed as part of its thirteenth Five Year Plan (announced in April 2016).[4]

Note that this says 'energy', not 'electricity' because to reach that goal from electricity alone then 50 per cent of electricity would need to be generated from non-fossil energy sources. In fact, contrary to what is often said about hopeful targets being inserted into five year plans which are seen as being unachievable, to me, this target looks to be an underestimate of what could, or even will be, achieved. The Chinese Government has, as was discussed in Chapter 4, over-estimated the likely level of energy consumption in the future, so in fact so long as current levels of development of non-fossil electricity projects continue then the likely out-turn is that the Chinese Government's own target of 20 per cent of energy from non-fossil sources by 2030 may turn out to be an underestimate. As E3G commented: 'Many believe that the Chinese government will over-achieve its 2030 targets, just as it is going to over-achieve its 2020 target'.[5]

Some would regard the provision of energy security to China as at least as important as the lowering of carbon emissions. Mathews and Tan comment that 'We argue that the key to success in the renewable transition is not so much as sources of lower carbon emissions (decarbonisation) but as sources of energy security – what might be called "energy security through manufacturing"'.[6] Indeed, the manufacturing gains of such a strategy will be great, amounting, on one estimate to 3.4 per cent of Chinese GDP by 2050, larger than the economic contribution of steel or agriculture.[7]

The technological focus on developing renewable energy certainly falls in with a general ecological modernisation thrust. Of course, the top-down nature of the development of the industry differs, in historical terms, from what happened in Europe where much of the political pressure for support for renewable energy, and even some of the early technical development, came from the grass roots – 'bottom-up'. However, this deviation from European practice is, in itself, not restrictive of the development of renewable energy. Indeed the degree of bottom-up as opposed to top-down organisation of the renewable energy programme itself varies across Europe.[8] It does reflect a tendency for developing countries to be able to benefit from technologies developed in the West. Perhaps an issue now is how far China can contribute to technical innovation. As is implied in this chapter, perhaps this is stronger in the solar pv sector so far rather than wind power, despite the rapid deployment of wind power in China.

Fuel switching to non-fossil energy sources

In this chapter, then, I want to study the fuel switching that is taking place and also might take place to reduce carbon emissions in China. This means I will be looking mostly at non-fossil fuels, particularly renewable energy. I argue that the biggest growth, in the long term, is likely to be in wind power and solar power so I will look at these. There are possibilities for the expansion of biomass sources, and no doubt there are substantial possibilities for carbon reduction here. However, there are also controversies with some applications of biomass fuel on account of whether the wood feedstock is used sustainably through replanting of trees, and also whether particulates are sufficiently controlled when the wood is burned. In view of this I assume that the large bulk of non-hydro renewable will come from wind power and solar power, so I will focus on these fuels as providing the main bulk of 'new' types of renewable energy in the future. Then there is 'old' renewable energy in the form of the conventional hydro power sector, which I will also discuss. The Chinese Government has set a lot of store in its nuclear owner construction programme, so I will look at this as well. The non-fossil technologies overwhelmingly generate electricity, so I will also comment on the use of technologies that can plausibly convert this energy into heat and motive power. These include heat pumps and electric cars, the latter which I will discuss at some length. Such techniques have the crucial advantage, especially in a Chinese context, of reducing local pollution compared to the burning of coal and petroleum-based products that would otherwise be used.

Given that non-fossil sources will substitute for the inefficient process of coal burning to generate electricity the impact of such substitution in reducing carbon emissions is greater than would appear from the energy actually supplied. One MWh of wind or solar power will substitute for more than 2 MWh of energy content of coal since coal-fired power stations are no more than about 40 per cent efficient. So each one per cent addition of say, wind power, substituted for coal in the electricity mix will reduce the carbon output by over 2 per cent.

Electric cars powered by renewable energy will also cut carbon emissions very robustly compared to motor vehicles powered by petroleum fuels. This is because the overwhelming proportion of electrical energy used in cars is converted into motive force compared to around only about a quarter of the energy in the petroleum used in vehicles powered by internal combustion engines. Hence fuel switching from fossil fuels to renewable energy achieves gains through being more energy efficient as well as being low carbon compared to fossil fuels. Their contribution to carbon reduction will be proportionately much larger than the renewable energy production output figures themselves.

Then, of course, there is the possibility of substituting natural gas for coal which will certainly reduce local pollution, and also carbon emissions. There are possibilities for substitution of coal use by natural gas in sectors such as providing heating services for industrial, commercial and residential uses. Indeed cities like Beijing are expanding their district heating network to be supplied by natural gas. As already mentioned in Chapter 4, natural gas use has expanded substantially in recent years. This expansion is likely to continue, but only up to a point. China is likely to be much more amenable, costs being equal, to substituting renewable energy for coal rather than using natural gas. That is because extra supplies of natural gas will have to be imported. In fact even if natural gas is cheaper than renewable energy, China may, and often will, have a preference for renewable energy which does not further undermine the country's energy security. Besides which, building Liquefied Natural Gas (LNG) handling facilities to import natural gas from the USA or agreeing terms for lengthy pipelines needed to receive supplies from Russia, may not after all be that cheap.

Indeed, on balance, therefore, natural gas consumption is likely to increase substantially, but not nearly as much as renewable energy. China is reliant on increasing proportions of natural gas from foreign sources and so would prefer, where possible, to utilise home grown sources to protect energy security. Coal is now to be avoided because of the need to cut down on localised air pollution (never mind to achieve climate change targets), and so there is quite a favourable synergy of policy pressures favouring building up renewable energy. That is even before the advantages of renewable energy in reducing carbon emissions are taken into account.

Using electricity as a heat source by using techniques such as heat pumps may be seen as being desirable in an effort to reduce local air pollution. I introduce here the notion of heat pumps as a technology that may be regarded as a quasi-renewable energy technology. This is because it utilises energy from rivers, or the ground or air to act as a sort of reverse refrigerator to generate heat. The heat produced will be 2–4 times the amount of electricity input. Heat pumps can be used either in individual buildings, or, perhaps more cost effectively, to supply district heating systems. Indeed, by storing hot water in big tanks, this is a way of storing the converted heat output of electricity generated by quantities of renewable energy that are surplus to current grid requirements.

At the moment, using heat pumps will not beat natural gas in reducing carbon emissions because three quarters of the fuel used to create the electricity is coal. In the medium term, building up renewable energy in the electricity supply system will start to reduce carbon emissions using heat pumps even in comparison with natural gas.

It is important to distinguish between 'energy' and 'electricity' in stating proportions of various fuels. This is a frequent source of confusion. In the year 2014, 25.6 per cent of China's electricity came from non-fossil sources,[9] this being most of the non-fossil contribution to the energy economy as a whole, meaning that around 10 per cent of energy in the whole economy came from non-fossil sources. Most of this came from renewable energy sources. So this means that in order for China to play a full role in achieving the global Paris target of keeping post-industrial temperature rises below 2 degrees, this proportion will have to be at least doubled by 2030. This means that, by 2030, around 50 per cent of Chinese electricity will have to be sourced from renewable energy.

The target is definitely plausible given the current rate of increase in non-fossil sources, most of which is coming from renewable and some from nuclear power. The non-fossil share increased by 3.4 per cent over in 2014 and above the 22.2 per cent contribution the previous year.[10] If this percentage growth rate was continued at this velocity then the bulk of Chinese electricity would come

from non-fossil sources in 2030. Out of the 25.6 per cent of electricity generated by non-fossil sources in 2014, hydropower was easily the largest source,
contributing 19 per cent of the 5,550 TWh of total Chinese electricity generation.[11 12 13] The second largest non-fossil source is now wind power, which has
edged nuclear power into third place. Solar pv is in fourth place, but, alongside wind power, is expanding rapidly. From 2014 to 2015 nuclear power's
share of electricity production increased from 2.3 to 2.9 per cent and non-
hydro renewable (mostly wind power and solar pv) increased from 3.9 per cent
to 4.7 per cent. Altogether, there was 135 TWh more non-fossil generation in
2015 compared to 2014.[14] China's electricity supply is massive compared to
other countries, although with a fifth of the world's population this should not
be a surprise.

In fact, China is not short of non-fossil energy potential. The Government's
last Five Year Plan (2010–2015) aimed at increasing non-fossil energy supplies
to 11.4 per cent of total primary energy, and. as energy growth slows, so it is
easier to achieve percentage increases in non-fossil generation. Currently the
Government is planning massive investments in non-fossil energy resources,
and as time goes on and decisions become based more on price-oriented market
based judgements, nuclear power and hydroelectricity are likely to be disadvantaged. Their costs, especially that of nuclear power, have tended to increase as
demands for environmental improvements and, in nuclear power's case,
demands for safety improvements have proliferated. Some arguments for this
will be developed later in this chapter.

Meanwhile, the costs of wind power and that of solar power have declined.
This has been the pattern in Western countries where investment in wind and
solar has easily outpaced investment in nuclear and hydro. Certainly, investment in wind and solar is far outstripping investment in nuclear power and
hydro in the rest of the world (where more market forces tend to predominate),[15] and as China adopts a lot of the market and environmental pathologies
of Western economies, the trend may be in the direction of increasing the
emphasis on new renewable as opposed to hydro and nuclear power in China.
But for the moment China is surging ahead with deployment of large hydro and
nuclear power schemes as well as renewable energy.

I compare the installation of non-fossil fuels in the USA, EU and China in
two tables below, Tables 6.1 and 6.2. I include a comparison of per capita installation for renewable energy, although this is pointless for nuclear and hydroelectricity as the USA and EU installed hardly any hydro or nuclear power.

As can be seen, there is an approximate similarity between solar and wind
installation on a per capita (per million people) basis for the three 'empires'
(EU, USA and China). However, in the case of hydro and nuclear power China
is doing a lot whilst the EU and the USA are doing very little. Overall, then,
China is installing a lot more non-fossil energy sources compared to the USA
and the EU. Note that in comparing the actual energy production from a GWe
of electrical capacity, on a very broad rule of thumb (I stress the word 'very')
you should multiply installed nuclear capacity three times to equal wind in

Table 6.1 Wind and solar installed in 2015 in the EU, USA and China

	GW wind power	MW wind power million people	GW solar power	MW solar pv per million people
USA	8.3	26	7	21.9
EU	12.8	25.2	8	15.7
China	32.5	24.1	19	14.0

Source: European Wind Energy Association, www.ewea.org/statistics/european/; American Wind Energy Association, www.awea.org/MediaCenter/pressrelease.aspx?ItemNumber=8393; PV Tech, www.pv-tech.org/news/global-solar-installations-hit-59gw-in-2015-gtm; Institute for Energy Economics and Financial Analysis, http://ieefa.org/tongue-river-arch-coal-northern-plains-resource-council/; Renewable Energy World, www.renewableenergyworld.com/articles/2016/02/china-added-30–5-gw-of-installed-wind-power-capacity-in-2015.html; Cleantechnicahttp://cleantechnica.com/2016/02/18/solarpower-europe-uk-installed-3–5-gw-solar-pv-2015-installations-set-remain-high-2016/

Table 6.2 Nuclear and hydro power installed in 2015 in the EU, USA and China

	GW Nuclear power	GW Hydro-electricity
USA	0.0	0.4
EU	0.0	0.3
China	7.6	18.2

Source: International Hydro Association, www.hydropower.org/sites/default/files/publications-docs/2016%20Key%20Trends%20in%20Hydropower.pdf, www.hydropower.org/country-profiles/canada, World Nuclear Association www.world-nuclear.org/

terms of production and six times to equal solar, and you can multiply hydro by twice to equal wind and three times to equal solar.

In March 2016, Leonardo De Caprio said

> As we all know, the United States and China are the two biggest contributors (to carbon emissions), and I think that China has made radical movements forward as far as alternative energy and ways to be sustainable.... I really think that China can be the hero of the environmental movement, they can be the hero of the climate change movement.[16]

China is certainly the (apparent) hero of non-fossil energy sources in general, although that having been said many environmentalists don't regard nuclear and/or hydro as being especially heroic. Certainly China beats the USA and the EU in absolute numbers of renewable energy being deployed. But then China is a much poorer country than either the USA or the EU. Indeed, China's proportion of wind and solar power as a proportion of electricity generation is still much smaller than several European countries such as Germany, Denmark, Spain, Portugal, UK, France and also the USA. In as much as China can be said to be affording to spend more recently (e.g. 2014 and 2015) on renewable energy than Western states, then, relatively it does deserve a medal. But then, perhaps, in the future with costs coming down, renewable energy is the cheapest option anyway. So countries that deploy renewable energy in the future may just be 'smart' rather than 'heroic'.

But, even here, a nuanced assessment would question the degree to which the tremendous Chinese spurt in non-fossil energy represents purely a desire to reduce fossil fuel dependence. I say this because the proportionate increase in non-fossil fuels only appears to be so great in 2015 because the increase in electricity consumption has been relatively modest in that year (under 1 per cent in fact). This is as opposed to the period from 2002 to 2013 when electricity consumption increased by around 10 per cent a year.[17] Could it be that the Chinese Government's massive expansion of renewable energy (and nuclear power for that matter) is predicated on the assumption of continued increases in fossil fuel consumption, at least until 2020 or so? This would account for the over-expansion of capacity of coal-fired power plant which has resulted, combined with sluggish growth in electricity demand since 2014, in coal-fired power plant being used for a relatively low percentage of the time. So is the apparently rapid Chinese growth in renewable energy just an accident?

In one sense, it does not matter if the expansion of renewable energy is an accident, so long as carbon emissions are substantially reduced. The 'proof of the pudding' will be seen if, as expected, growth in electricity demand is now much lower than in the decade until 2013, yet the Chinese Government keeps up or expands installation of renewable energy compared to levels in 2014 and 2015. The extent of the green commitments will then be seen, and we shall see the extent to which the Chinese Government can override the wishes of the lobby of the owners and developers of coal-fired power stations.

Increasing renewable energy

The USA's population is little more than a quarter the size of that of China. We can see here that the Chinese have recently done more than the USA in increasing their proportion of renewable energy. In 2014 in the USA total non-fossil electricity consumption increased by barely 1 per cent,[18] less than a third of the proportional increase in Chinese non-fossil electricity consumption.

In May 2015, China's National Renewable Energy Centre issued a report concluding that '[t]he study shows that it is both technically and economically feasible for renewable energy to satisfy over 60 percent of China's primary energy consumption and 85 percent of electricity consumption by 2050'.[19] If, as we argue in Chapter 4, that energy growth declines so that energy growth is stabilised or reduced below current levels, then this fuel switching would mean reductions of at least two-thirds of current levels of carbon emissions by the year 2050. The 60 per cent of energy coming from renewable would be enhanced, in terms of carbon production, by production from nuclear power, by fuel switching away from coal to natural gas and also some reduction in energy consumption.

Of course, China started off well behind Europe and the USA in its build-up of new renewable energies, but it is certainly now making up for lost time. Of course, the pace needs to quicken faster still, and also energy saving needs to quicken as well, if anywhere near the Paris targets for carbon abatement are to be achieved. Nevertheless, China now leads in terms of installed capacity in both wind power and solar pv, with the USA and Germany being in second place, respectively for the two fuels. However, there are some striking differences in the degree to which the Chinese solar pv and Chinese wind power has achieved sales in markets outside China.

I want now to focus on some commercial and policy-oriented details of the low carbon sources that are rapidly expanding at the moment – namely wind power, solar power, hydro power and nuclear power. We will look at wind power first.

Wind power

Wind power in China got off to a late start compared to the West. In the late 1970s, as China struggled to throw off the legacy of the disasters of Mao's rule, the often anti-nuclear activists in places like Denmark and then the west coast of the USA became interested in modernising wind power. Nevertheless, by the 1990s, a fledgling Chinese wind turbine industry has begun, nurtured at the start (and to a certain extent still nurtured) by Danish expertise in the new wind power industry. In more recent years the Chinese wind turbine industry has surpassed the production capabilities of Western countries. In 2015, Goldwind, a Chinese state-owned enterprise became the largest wind generator manufacturer in the world, ahead of Vestas of Denmark and General Electric (GE) of the USA. However, whilst these two other companies were genuinely multinational in their sales, Goldwind's sales were almost exclusively restricted to the Chinese market.[20] A report in March 2016, which said that the Danish wind manufacturer Vestas had edged Goldwind to regain its place as the leading world wind generator manufacturer in terms of capacity sold, said that:

> Six Chinese turbine OEMs (original equipment manufacturers) in the top 15 global ranking averaged 30% year-over-year growth…. A dearth of Chinese turbine OEM activity outside of China, however, kept western turbine OEMs from losing ground globally to Chinese turbine OEMs despite China's record year.[21]

The Chinese expansion of wind power was predicated on the developmental system of centrally preferred industrial expansion that has been described earlier in this book. Central, provincial and local government officials have been induced through the system of career advancement to meeting targets to go for volume of capacity. Hence quantity of capacity seems to have taken preference over quality of production.

An important feature of the system of deploying wind power is that the domestic wind industry interests are protected from foreign competition, a key part of the developmental approach. Chen says that '[w]hile learning the technology and related policies from abroad during the process of modernisation, the policy elites have deliberately developed institutional configurations to protect domestic industry, crowding out attempts at foreign competition in the domestic market'.[22]

The lack of focus on quality of wind turbine performance, not to mention the virtual monopoly of domestic wind turbine manufacturers on the Chinese market, is associated with the integrated, one might say in Chinese industrial family terms, incestuous, relationship between wind turbine manufacturers and wind farm developers. The lack of competition in wind power in China (and its consequences) is discussed at length by Gosens and Lu. They say that the 'formal connections between wind farm developers and turbine manufacturers … may help reduce investment costs for wind farm developers…. However, this trend also reduces competition, as a connection with a turbine manufacturer will also make it the preferred turbine supplier'.[23] Gosens and Lu also discuss the lack of independent evaluation and monitoring of wind turbine performance, a key factor which militates against selling exports since potential customers will have little knowledge about performance. Arguments about the provenance of intellectual properties compound the difficulties in selling turbines abroad. This is opposed to turbines from Western countries which go through standardised testing procedures associated with governmental regulation. Of course, if manufacturers do not have to worry about being challenged over intellectual property rights in a 'captive' (Chinese) home market, then there is less incentive for them to be especially careful.

This reliance on informal networks echoes analysis by Andrews-Speed about how the Chinese system of commerce in general relies on networks or groups of alliance ('guanxi') rather than commercial agreements being reached on the basis of more transparent basis of legal rights.[24] There must be questions about the market efficiency of such practices, or at least in the absence of other competitive pressures such as the need to compete on an open, international, market with other producers (such as is apparent in the case of solar pv exports for China).

Chinese wind turbines are said to suffer from a lack of quality control and local content requirements, which require many parts to be manufactured locally to where the project is installed; this is also said to lead to inefficiencies and lack of quality. In addition, contracts may often be given to developers on the basis of personal relationships rather than which bids are most competitive. These are some of the conclusions of Chen who comments that

> the lower quality of domestically manufactured wind turbines does not seem to hamper Chinese companies' enthusiasm for using domestic products in wind power generators. This is partly due to protectionism…. Wind power project applicants collaborate in their bids with state-owned wind power manufacturers. These manufacturers may not have better-quality, foreign equipment, but they are often closely linked with local governments.[25]

Indeed a range of Government regulations have given an advantage to domestic over foreign wind turbine manufacturers.[26] Mathews and Tan recognise the 'developmental' nature of the Government's strategy in wind power, but describe any protectionism as 'aimed at rapidly building the capabilities of China's renewable power sectors ... before reducing the protections and subsidies and allowing the full force of international competition to prevail'.[27] However, the problem with this is that what appears to be happening is that the system has become woefully short of competition – domestic or international – and that whilst it may grow in volumetric terms it is not growing in terms of efficiency.

All that having been said, it is also the case that the Chinese windfarms are generating rapidly increasing proportions of electricity supply, and these increases surpass those of the nuclear power industry. This can be seen in Figure 6.1.

Certainly China generates more electricity from wind power compared to any other country. However, the evidence here is that if China wants to export substantial numbers of wind turbines abroad it has to improve, and also to find means of clearly demonstrating, the perceived and actual performance of its wind turbines. Introducing better competition at home is the likely way of doing this, along with standardised performance evaluation processes for wind turbines. Targets for renewable energy should be expressed in terms of electricity generated rather than capacity installed. Even if the system of assessing officials for promotion on the basis of industrial achievement continues, then it is important to assess claims for wind power deployment on the basis of actual wind power output rather than mere capacity installed.

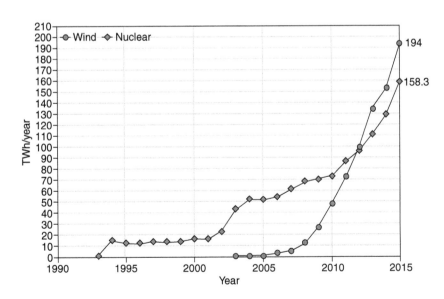

Figure 6.1 Wind and nuclear electricity production in China compared to 2015.

Source: Bernard Chabot, Renewables International, 15 March, 2016, http://cf01.erneuerbareenergien. schluetersche.de/files/smfiledata/5/5/8/4/6/2/141WindNucBICS2015.pdf.

Of course, ultimately the test for windfarm performance should be on financial performance, which, as it were, cuts out the vagaries of administrative politics. This demands a more market-oriented set of incentive structures, or, at least, that the premium price system that already exists for promoting renewable energy should be the sole financial driver of the renewable energy programme, which it does not appear to be at the moment. This is as opposed to Western wind power development which responds solely to financial incentives and seeking good returns. There is a system of 'feed-in tariffs' in China (a system devised originally in Denmark and Germany) whereby wind power (and also solar pv farm) operators are paid a guaranteed payment for each unit of electricity they generate for a number of years. However, whilst this is influential as an incentive, it is questionable whether it is as important as the bureaucratic imperative to build more renewable energy.

In the USA, wind power deployment (which is encouraged by federal tax incentives for investment) is less in volume terms compared to that of China, but the competition in US wind markets is helping reduce capital costs and improve the efficiency of the wind power installations themselves, hence leading to lower prices paid for electricity generated by windfarms.[28]

Of course, we do not want to see a drift towards a position in some EU countries such as the UK and Poland, where premium price contracts are being abolished, or severely limited for renewable energy. This is being done in the name of reducing costs, but under close inspection can actually result in a policy that is simply biased against renewable energy. In the UK, for example, the Government announced in 2015 that onshore wind power developers and solar farm developers will no longer have access to contracts with guaranteed future prices for electricity production. Yet such payments are being offered for nuclear power, and fossil fuel generators are paid incentives called 'capacity payments' which are not payable to wind and solar sources. In Germany, contracts to supply renewable energy are now being rationed much more severely than was the case a few years ago. In Poland, wind power development has effectively been more or less banned under laws introduced in 2016. Nevertheless, wind power capacity is still expanding significantly in many EU countries. In Germany total wind capacity now (at the time of writing) exceeds 45 GWe, mainly onshore, and it is still growing.

China's land area is 27 times that of Germany, and 27 times 45 GWe of current German wind power capacity comes to around 1200 GWe if the same amount of wind power was built per given land area as in Germany. This would represent approaching half of China's electricity consumption or 20 per cent of China's total primary energy. Yet Germany's population density is substantially higher than China, and moreover, in China, the rural population is relatively much poorer. This means that there is likely to be not only much greater relative space for wind turbines compared to Germany, but much less opposition to them, given that opposition is very often based on perceived effects on property prices. Rather, poorer areas may welcome wind turbines because of the development that goes with the windfarms. In short, the potential for wind power providing a very large share of Chinese energy requirements is immense. The Chinese planning system needs to give more opportunity to local people to have a say about developments, including windfarms, although, as in Spain where there is a relatively poor rural population co-existing with extensive windfarm developments, local people have often successfully pressed for local areas to receive more economic benefits from the windfarm development.

In fact the total economically attractive Chinese wind resource (mainly onshore, with some offshore) is estimated by the Chinese National Centre for Renewable Energy is estimated to be 'more than 3.0 TW'.[29] This would generate rather more than the entire current level of Chinese electricity consumption.

By comparison, in the USA, the policies favouring wind power are moderately good in some states, and incentives at a Federal level are secured for a limited period. However, many US states have structures which effectively prevent developers of wind or solar farms from being offered the plausible long term 'power purchase agreements' (PPAs) which are needed to ensure the developers can sell their electricity at a high enough price to achieve a reasonable return on investments. This is worst in various south eastern states where the electricity system is effectively controlled by private monopolies. Companies in states such as South Carolina, Georgia and Florida are allowed to raise money in advance from electricity consumers for building nuclear power stations which may or may not be constructed sometime in the future. They have been very resistant in the past (and to a great extent still are) to giving PPAs to solar and wind developers, and they seem to prioritise conventional fossil and nuclear generation over renewable energy, despite the increasing cost-effectiveness of renewable compared to traditional power plant. Hence, the criticisms of Chinese wind power policies need to be put into perspective. One problem that besets renewable energy developers in the USA and Europe is that they have to compete with existing large conventional plant whose construction costs have already been paid – and so their electricity may appear to be more expensive when in fact it may not be. In China there is much the same problem – although this is partially overcome by the state injunction on the major electricity generation companies to meet increasing targets for renewable energy deployment. Nevertheless, if the Chinese wind power industry was driven by competitive pressures then the price of electricity from wind power, which has been tumbling around the world in recent times, would go down even faster and China could be a world leader in manufacturing wind turbines.

A further aspect of the lack of competition in the electricity system in general is the tendency for a lack of joined-up thinking when it comes to connecting renewable energy to the grid and absorbing the maximum of electricity from the renewable energy system into the grid. One result of the lack of market integration is that there are often long gaps between wind turbines being installed and wind turbines being connected to the grid. Chen reports that '[a]ccording to the State Electricity Regulatory Commission, at the end of 2010, among 44.7 GW of total 201 installed wind power capacity, only 31.07 GW of wind energy was connected to the power grid'.[30] Grid reinforcement was not coordinated with wind farm development.

As a regular reader of *Wind Power Monthly*'s account of the upward trends of Chinese wind power deployment I have been puzzled by the notion that developers would install windfarms without being connected to the electricity distribution system, thus depriving them of any immediate certainty of them producing electricity, and therefore an income stream to give a return on investment. People would lose money hand over fist, I thought. But the answer to this conundrum is that the Chinese electricity system may not be as closely associated with quality (in this case high electricity production) as opposed to quantity (installing generation capacity) as it should be. As discussed, the system was, and still is, largely driven by encouraging bureaucrats in state-owned sectors.

The efficiency of the wind turbine fleet was reduced further by the fact that coal-fired power stations received priority of despatch, which, in layman's terms means that if demand for electricity was relatively low, it was the wind turbines that got shut down, not the coal-fired power stations. These problems may abate if the Government implements a system where wind is given despatch priority ahead of coal, but at the time of writing this is yet to materialise. This problem of despatch priority is a strategic problem that is much bigger even than the problem of the difficulty of connecting windfarms to the grid.

Hitherto, the 'big five' electricity generators who dominate the Chinese electricity market have been focussed on developing conventional, usually coal-fired, power stations, with renewable energy seen mainly as a side-line. But this is now changing, and not only are the dominant electricity generators having to plan for more of a renewable future, but the six grid systems that exist across China are having to think more in terms of how they can integrate renewables and assure transfers of energy from where renewable energy is produced to where the electricity is to be consumed. This involves building transmission lines involving voltages so high that they would be unheard of in countries like the UK. Often this involves building transmission lines to transfer energy from the north and west, where renewable energy in all of its forms has most production, to the east and the coast where there is the most demand for electricity. However, so far, new transmission lines have not been built fast enough.

According to an account by a government development agency, the largest wind resources are 'along the grassland and Gobi Desert of China's northern, northeast and northwest regions, Tibet and the southeast coastal regions'.[31] So far the biggest development of wind power has been in Northern provinces, Xinjiang, Inner Mongolia and Gansu. Yet much of this power needs to be exported to the Eastern seaboard where there is more demand. A consequence has been that the Government has suspended planning approvals from windfarms in the northern provinces, effectively forcing developing to look for developments further south.[32] Nevertheless orders for some transmission lines with massive capacity are on the way to take the power to where it is needed. For example ABB, the Swiss based engineering company, has won an order to build a world record-breaking 10 GW transformer with a 1,600 km long 800 Kv transmission line to take power to the east of the country.[33]

Nevertheless, appallingly large amounts of wind energy production are 'constrained' or left idle. This amounted to some 34 TWh in 2015 – by comparison this is equivalent to 10 per cent of all UK energy consumption. It amounts to around 15 per cent of total available production from China's wind power capacity in that year.[34,35] It is not just the lack of transmission capacity that is the problem, but a system where coal-fired power stations will often be given priority to carry on production over windfarms. Given the fact that wind production is zero cost whilst the coal-fired capacity burns coal which costs money, this hardly makes sense in economic terms never mind ecological ones. But the Chinese system is heavily reliant on a matrix of agreements and understandings between power companies and electricity distributors that defies market logic. This is another example of how the electricity system is lacks arrangements that maximise competition.

Despite the fact that, by 2015, wind turbine capacity was nearly twice as big in China as installed in USA, the amount of electricity generated by the wind power was actually very slightly higher in the USA than in China. In 2016, China seemed to be on course to overtake USA production, but this is a milestone that, in view of relative capacity deployed, should have been achieved several years ago. The USA's system has focused on competitive efficiency (generally speaking), but not so much on increasing the volume of renewable energy as in China. China needs to combine both these objectives – of volume growth and efficiency, the latter being achieved by making the electricity system work on more competitive lines.

Some analysts of China's electricity future imply that the problem of absorbing high penetrations of renewable energy into the grid represents a barrier to its large scale adoption.[36] However, given that the proportion of penetration of fluctuating renewable energy is already a lot higher in European countries like Germany Spain Denmark and the UK, without experiencing anything like the wastage of renewable experienced in China, it is plausible to assume the problem lies with the way that the Chinese grid is managed at the moment.

Solar photovoltaics (pv)

Here I am talking about solar pv, or solar electric production rather than solar thermal. Solar hot water systems are, nevertheless, widely deployed in China and they are being spread further. However, the potential for use of solar pv is likely to be much wider as their usage is not restricted to part of particular buildings heating requirements, but can be fed into the grid. Moreover solar pv farms are built independently of the existence of buildings. Altogether the potential of solar power is stupendous compared to the total energy needs of China. The Chinese National Centre for Renewable Energy argues that if deployed aggressively, solar power could generate 4,800 TWh by 2050,[37] which is over 85 per cent of current Chinese electricity consumption.

Deployment of solar pv in China is rapidly increasing, but when China's solar pv industry built up, it was mostly for export. China now easily leads the world in the production of renewable energy equipment for the two leading 'new' renewable energy sources, wind power and solar photovoltaics (pv). China beats everyone in the world when it comes to production of solar pv, boasting production of around 70 per cent of the 43 GW solar pv panels capacity sold in the world in 2015.[38] Half of this (15 GW) was installed in China, but that still means that one in every two solar panels installed outside China was manufactured by Chinese companies. In 2015, China overtook Germany as the country with the largest amount of solar pv installed. There is a good argument that Germany with its feed-in tariff system paved the way for the rapid increase in solar pv deployment accompanied by its rapid reduction in cost, with costs tumbling by around 80 per cent in the period 2010 to 2015.[39] Initially, German companies manufacturing solar pv were at the forefront of this progress, but increasingly China has taken over. However, German interest in supporting solar pv deployment has declined. Germany, along with other EU states, has become increasingly concerned with reducing costs rather than increasing rates of installation of renewable energy and solar pv in particular. Ironically this has happened just as the cost of solar pv has fallen greatly. Manufacturing possibilities for solar pv in Germany have thus been undermined.

According to Li Hejun, the Chairman of the leading thin-film solar manufacturing company Han energy,

> China's PV industry developed mainly because of the spill-over effect from the new energy revolution promoted by foreign governments, and European governments in particular … particularly the German Government…. The PV products and manufacturing from China were very competitive in European markets because they were cheap and manufacturing in China is inexpensive.[40]

It is hardly surprising, then, that six out of the ten largest solar pv manufacturing companies in the world are Chinese, Trina Solar and Yingli Green Energy being the biggest in 2014.[41] There is no shortage of complaints from the West about China allegedly 'dumping' cheap solar panels onto the world market. Indeed, first the USA and then the EU imposed punitive tariffs on imports of Chinese solar panels from 2012. China then retaliated by charging tariffs on exports of polysilicon, an ingredient of solar pv. All of this has increased the price of solar pv in the West.

Admittedly, you could say that like with many other Chinese state-owned enterprises, there is too much Government guaranteed credit being given to the biggest solar manufacturers, and there is the old adage about cheap Chinese labour, but this may be a one-sided caricature of Chinese success in this sector. Chinese wage costs have been increasing well above many developing countries, and if wage costs were a major factor in hi-tech engineering exports, then high-wage Germany would not be half as competitive as it is, given its strength in many engineering markets. If all it took was cheap labour and state guaranteed low interest loans then surely China would be dominating sales of wind power outside China, yet it is not. Western governments need to understand what is going on, not fool themselves with a few dismissive stereotypical comments, and in doing so give a false, self-serving justification for what seems, to many, to be protectionism against Chinese solar pv that increases the price of reducing carbon emissions.

In this case we need to look for the factors that have distinguished the wind power and solar pv industries in China. Indeed, a study written by researchers from the US National Renewable Energy Laboratory and Massachusetts Institute of Technology argued that, in comparing how it is that solar pv cells produced by China have undercut solar pv manufactured in the USA, 'the historical price advantage of a China-based factory relative to a U.S.-based factory is not driven by country-specific advantages, but instead by scale and supply-chain development'.[42] It is the Chinese ability to marshal economies of scale that has provided the dominant driver of their pre-eminence on international markets. In the case of solar pv, the Chinese have, in contrast to wind power, thrived in producing high quality product at cheap prices. A key difference is that in the case of solar pv, in contrast to wind power, the Chinese expanded their production on the basis of fiercely competitive international sales. The internal Chinese solar pv market has only arisen later, when it became apparent that without tapping the massive internal market Chinese solar expansion would be substantially limited. As late as 2010, 95 per cent of Chinese solar pv cells were exported.[43]

Indeed, solar pv is a prime example of where Chinese industry excels, that is when there is competition. This has to be based on technical expertise as well economies of scale, something that is vitally important in the case of solar pv since not only must the solar pv panels have to be cheaply mass produced, but they must also achieve as high efficiency as possible. Nevertheless, the emphasis in solar pv production has been on reducing manufacturing costs, with efficiency levels increasing as a secondary objective. The key milestone in achieving sales in the international market is the cost per kWh of the energy that is produced, and the assurance that the solar pv panels and associated equipment will carry on generating electricity in the long term.

There are arguments that, in China, a mixture of state and private ownership of solar pv firms, especially where the state ownership is local in nature, leads to a superior record of technical innovation.[44] That may be the case, but what the comparison between Chinese wind power and solar pv production suggests is that it is the extent of exposure to competition on price and quality that will be the factor that determines the success of international sales. The Chinese solar pv industry has grown up in competition with others on the international market, whilst Chinese wind power has not. Chinese production of solar pv was originally bound up with the export market, and not with the home market. It was not until around 2012 that the prices of solar pv declined to such an extent as to allow China to install solar pv at home. However, this decline in price, allied to the fact that trade sanctions in the USA and the EU were threatening export markets, meant that installation in China dramatically increased. Much of China's pv manufactured output is still exported, of course, and this keeps up the pressure on the Chinese solar pv industry to remain competitive with the rest of the world.

However, the solar pv industry has itself suffered from what Li Hejun describes as what government 'did too much of'.[45] He recounts problems with Suntech, one of the biggest solar pv manufacturers, which went bankrupt in 2013. The company was promoted from the start by the municipal authorities of Wuxi, a crucial role being for the local government being guaranteeing loans made to the company. 'Even after it (Suntech) became the largest solar power manufacturer in the world, the local government was still not satisfied with its size.'[46] This leads Hejun to argue that '[i]n microeconomics, companies should be managed independently, and take responsibility for their profit and loss'.[47] On the other hand, he argues there is an important role for central government to play in organising incentives to be available for particular technologies and in coordination the industry as a whole.[48] In many ways, Hejun (in effect) argues for a European style ecological modernisation approach where governments leave it up to decentralised, market arrangements, to decide what individual green energy companies should do, whilst promoting green technologies through 'smart' policy instruments and incentives.

Most of the Chinese output of solar pv is bound up with ground based solar farms, although there is now an increasing emphasis on integrating solar pv with new buildings. Solar pv is manufactured mainly in the east and the south of the country, although the most is installed in the western provinces of Qinghai and Xinjiang.[49] By 2016, Qinghai had the most solar pv of any province, and it has a target of generating all of its electricity from solar pv. By the beginning of 2016, it had 6 GW of solar pv installed, and planned to add another 7.1 GW in 2016. Delays in improving grid transmission are a problem for the province as it will often need to export its relative wealth of solar pv production, but the development possibilities (in a relatively poor region) are seen as being too great to delay installations.[50]

Solar resources are described as

> more abundant in the western and northern parts of China, such as Tibet, Qinghai, Xinjiang, Gansu, Ningxia and Inner Mongolia. Moreover, advantaged by its high elevation, the Qinghai Tibetan Plateau is particularly abundant in solar resources owing to having the longest sunshine duration.[51]

In future a challenge will be to install more in the south, and also to build enough transmission capacity to supply solar power to the south in the summer when air conditioning demand peaks. Linking energy efficient air conditioning with solar pv is the optimum path. Indeed China has been a leader in developing solar air conditioning systems. Development of such technologies, along with reducing costs of battery storage, will make solar pv a dominant form of energy in the coming decades.

Much attention is focused on the limitations of solar – that is, its obvious dependence on sunshine for production – and not enough on how it is the most advanced energy source in terms of flexibility of where it can be deployed. The biggest barrier to realising the potential of solar power has been its high cost. However, that is now being overcome and the lengthening production lines, technological fine tuning and supply chain cost efficiencies forged by the solar industry, led currently by Chinese companies, are opening up an ever-increasing market for solar pv. Electricity systems are themselves being made to be more flexible, and part of this development is allied to the great reductions in cost of electricity storage technology that is driven by the need to have as lightweight as possible battery systems for computers and electric cars. Indeed, the development of electric cars and solar power march hand in hand through the development of cheaper and more effective storage systems. The costs of storage have not yet fallen fast enough to replace conventional power stations, but the costs are falling fast.[52]

The costs of solar pv are proving to be competitive with fossil fuel plant in an increasing number of countries, and it has been estimated that costs have fallen by around a quarter every time the global installed capacity has doubled.[53] Within ten or 20 years this rate of progress may see solar power, alongside wind power, as the cheapest choice for energy supply technologies regardless of other factors. Moreover, the electricity system is being made more flexible by the increased use of motor vehicles, which can themselves be used as a store for energy when the sun is not shining or the wind is not blowing.

Elon Musk, the US entrepreneur who helped found PayPal before going into producing electric cars (the Tesla) and Space X, is a big proponent of the link between storage and solar pv. He says 'China can "easily" support all its power demand using home-grown solar power'.[54]

Indeed, looking at the figures generated by the plan produced by the China National Renewable Energy Centre, which goes up to 2050, in their 'high penetration' scenario they see solar as potentially providing an electricity output that is equivalent to the large bulk of current levels of electricity consumption in China and over 40 per cent of China's total current primary energy requirements. Given the decline in solar pv prices, and the continuing potential for economies of scale in the mass production of solar pv, as well as scope for technical optimisation (including efficiency gains in absorbing sunlight) the cost of solar pv could fall to very low levels making it the cheapest energy source in 2050. Certainly, the supreme advantage of solar pv in terms of its ability to be installed in all shapes and sizes and the propensity for reductions in cost mean that in future the ultimate barrier to solar's growth may be the ability of the electricity system to usefully absorb all that is produced. However, that problem is amenable to incremental solutions, especially building up the ability of the system to store and release power through an expanding fleet of electric vehicles.

Solar pv is usually thought to be a 'clean' energy source, although in China there have been controversies surrounding pollution from solar pv factories. Indeed, one of Jinkosolar's plant was shut down for a time in the autumn of 2011 after pollution was said to be killing fish in a river next to the factory. There were strong local protests about the factory's environmental performance. Perhaps the problem in such cases is not so much with the technology itself as China's lax system of monitoring pollution, something that I commented upon in Chapter 5. Nevertheless the social and environmental controversies surrounding solar power in China are usually rather less than those associated with large hydroelectricity projects.

A contrast between wind power and solar pv in China

As can be seen from the foregoing discussion there are some strikingly different comparisons between China's success in exporting wind power and solar. In the case of solar pv the bulk of production of solar panels has, to date, been exported, although by 2015 around half of production was exported and half installed in China itself. However, in the case of wind power almost all of Chinese wind turbines are installed in China. Consequently China has controlled a much bigger share of the world market in solar pv panels compared to wind turbines.

What is an explanation for this difference? What we can say here is that there is a big difference in the amount of competition experienced by Chinese companies in both fields. Solar pv export orders are achieved in the context of intense competition to supply low cost products of good quality all around the world. On the other hand in China there is very little competition for its wind turbines from other countries. When the Chinese wind turbine industry grew up, unlike the case of solar pv, it was to supply the home market, and not for export.

An implicit preference in the electricity industry for domestically produced wind turbines combined with an emphasis on cost rather quality in procuring the turbines means that the domestic wind turbine manufactures have the market to themselves. They simply do not need to compete very much for the home market. This may have made a big contribution to the outcome where Chinese wind manufacturers have failed to capture a substantial part of the non-Chinese wind turbine manufacturing market. This difference (between outcomes in solar pv and wind power for China) may emphasise the importance of having a competitive environment for renewable energy if it is to reach its full potential. This is implicit in 'Eurocentric' ecological modernisation that I have discussed where it is assumed that whilst the state sets regulations, incentives and institutions that will favour appropriate technologies, it is left up to a competitive market to take decisions. This is in the expectation that such competition will optimise quality at a least cost for the consumer. It is also good for the green energy business.

However, some of the more general problems of a lack of competition and market integration in Chinese electricity systems will also affect solar pv, in so far as it also has to be integrated into the grid in China. It is just that because solar pv started as an industry that was sold pretty well solely abroad, then the solar panels themselves had to be highly competitive. But when it comes to them being used in China too much of solar pv is wasted in what is still an inefficiently organised electricity system. That inefficiency may be at least partly ascribed to the 'top-down' nature of the way that the industry is organised, and the lack of competitive pressures.

Hydroelectricity

Hydroelectricity is currently the second most important source of electricity after coal, and with local and climate pollution reduction as centrally important targets, hydroelectricity is certainly at the top of many central planners' choices for a solution. Indeed, hydroelectricity has been rapidly expanding in China. From 2010 to 2015 China's hydro capacity has been expanded by over 50 per cent to around 320 GWe producing almost 20 per cent of the nation's electricity. The Government's thirteenth Five Year Plan projects a further expansion, to 350 GWe by 2020, a notable facet of this expansion being that it is rather smaller than that which occurred in the 2010–2015 period under the previous Five Year Plan. Although it seems that this is likely to be achieved, with new schemes planned in the south-west of China where there are considerable untapped resources, perhaps the most rapid phase of expansion of Chinese hydro may have now passed.

There is a substantial initial capital cost in doing hydroelectric schemes, costs that can be more readily borne by a system which is mainly reliant on central decisions, and not so easily mobilised if decisions about what renewable fuels to deploy are left more to price mechanisms as expressed in competing for contracts for lowest prices. Hence as the system moves in China away from such as centrally planned mechanism as reforms take hold, then hydroelectric schemes may seem less compelling.

However, an even more important pressure for a slowdown in the hydro building programme may be the social and economic fallout from such schemes. The massive, 22 GWe Three Gorges Dam was intensely controversial even during the (now passing) core developmental phase of Chinese economic expansion, but in future the opposition to such schemes can only increase. There are different figures bandied around for how many people were told to move to make way for the Three Gorges project, but the number is over one million. The mass movement of people may have been a feature of centralised planning in China for various purposes, but its reputation and political support has waned.

There are also considerable ecological criticisms on hydro developments. Some argue that the dams being built in areas like Tibet will be vulnerable to earthquakes in a seismically active zone.[55] The still nature of the waters in hydro-reservoirs is said to harm wildlife, and rivers downstream may dry out. Nevertheless, it might be safe to assume some considerable continued expansion for the next decade, but perhaps opposition and dwindling resources will prevent further development of large schemes after then.

Alongside the hydropower developments, technically speaking, are pumped storage schemes, which help the electricity system respond to shortages of energy. The sort of system flexibility provided by pumped storage is certainly helpful to using variable supplies of wind power and solar pv. Pumped storage uses reservoirs (which can be existing ones) to store water, perhaps excess renewable energy production, which then can be used when renewable supplies are low. There are 70 GWe of pumped storage planned for 2020.

However, ordinary hydro power stations can also be used to act as balancing devices, with the hydro-turbines being wound down when there is say, a lot of wind power, and then the stored water used as energy supply when there is less wind power on the system. The difference between this operation and dedicated pumped storage facilities is that the latter are primed to be an especially rapid response. But the fact that China does have large quantities of hydro facilities could make the system very flexible and fits in well with a build-up of variable renewable energy sources.

Nuclear power

Expansion of nuclear power is currently a cornerstone of China's energy plans. In fact, China has come relatively late to being a major investor in nuclear power. It is planned to expand nuclear power capacity from 25 GWe in 2015 to 58 GWe in 2020. This would provide roughly 8 per cent of China's electricity supply. The Government, as part of the drive to secure 20 per cent of primary energy (note: energy, not electricity) from non-fossil sources by 2030, aims for 120–150 GWe of nuclear power to be installed by 2030.[56]

The nuclear construction programme, which aims also to sell reactors to other parts of the world, stalled in the wake of a corruption scandal in 2009, and then following the Fukushima accident in 2011. But now it has gained momentum once again. However, this is happening at the same time as concern about China's industrial safety record in general has risen (for instance, in the wake of the Tianjin accident), and green politics, also on the rise in China, is naturally suspicious of nuclear power for its safety record and problems with radioactive contamination. But the problem for the Chinese nuclear industry is that concern seems to be rather wider than the usual green suspects.

'The Chinese are beginning to wrestle with the same issues that Western countries were dealing with, concerning fear of the technology, transparency in decision making and trust of the authorities,' said Mark Hibbs, a Carnegie Peace Endowment Researcher.[57]

That, in a nutshell is the problem, with the fear, as far as the nuclear industry is concerned that there will be a nuclear slowdown in building new schemes similar to what has happened in the West. There, strict regulatory conditions have provided the context to great difficulties in keeping costs down. Meeting increasingly tough safety standards seems to lead to increasing costs. Practically no nuclear power stations have been completed in the last decade in the West and the few that have started being built in the USA, Finland and France (since the year 2000) have experienced long construction overruns in time and cost.

The earliest Chinese nuclear power plants have been installed on the coast, and new plans have been made for inland plant. But these seem to be attracting greater opposition. Safety is a key concern, but so are other impacts including nuclear power's voracious demand for water abstraction. There does not seem to be any reluctance on the part of Chinese activists and even scientists to criticise the Government's nuclear power policy. One veteran scientist, He Zuoxiu, in the past heavily associated with establishment projects commented: 'There were internal discussions on upgrading (nuclear power) standards in the past four years, but doing so would require a lot more investment which would affect the competitiveness and profitability of nuclear power.' He also said, 'Nuclear energy costs are cheap because we lower our standards'.[58] China is bringing online the latest Generation III reactors, which may also carry with them the added burden of increased complexity. That having been said, at the time of writing, sufficient nuclear construction is going ahead that will bring nuclear capacity up to at least around 50 GWe of capacity. On top of those up to around 50 GWe are 'firmly' planned, and proposals for others are being put together.

However, in the nuclear power business, 'planned' power stations do not at all necessarily equal plant that is actually going to be built to completion.[59] The extent to which future power stations will be up and running will depend on the success of the industry in overcoming the opposition to nuclear power that has increased in recent years, and, of crucial (and often poorly understood) importance, whether the nuclear industry can resist its costs being increased through stricter regulations governing safety requirements. If it can succeed in keep such regulatory costs down, then it will be going against a world trend. However, given that in many other respects, including environmental policy, China is tending to converge with the West, that may be a heroic assumption.[60] A problem for nuclear power is that while there is at least a strong threat of upwards pressure on its costs, the costs of key (wind and solar) competitors to fill the needed increase in non-fossil capacity are coming down.

China hopes to emulate its success in exporting solar pv through exporting its own designs for nuclear power. However, such efforts have got off to a slow start. Its involvement in what has been hoped to be a revival of the British nuclear power sector has been marked by delays in the Chinese attempt to build a power plant in the UK (Hinkley C) in collaboration with the French state-owned company EDF. In return for investing in Hinkley C, Chinese nuclear developers are being given the possibility by the UK Government of building one or more nuclear power plants in the UK. Whether other countries can be persuaded to accept the nuclear standards and thus lower costs associated with Chinese plant remains to be seen. Certainly, the initial agreement, reached in 2014, with the China General Nuclear Power Corporation, was to build a nuclear power plant of Chinese design in Bradwell, in Essex in the UK. However, it could be argued that this agreement relied not so much on a British appreciation of Chinese nuclear engineering, but rather at least as much to the fact that the Hinkley C main developers, EDF, were struggling to find anybody else to invest in Hinkley C itself. As discussed, it remains to be seen for how long Chinese regulators will uphold its current approach to regulating the safety of nuclear reactor designs in China itself.

Electric cars and storage

I am writing about electric cars and electricity storage in the same section for one very good reason – the progress of each is intimately related to the other. Electricity storage has received a tremendous boost through the market niche provided by lap tops and smart phones where there is a need to store as much power as possible in as small a space as possible (and recharge the batteries as soon as possible). But now an increasing portion of the technology push for optimising electricity storage is coming from the growth in the electric car market. The market for new electric cars is, like a lot of other things, now biggest in China. So is the production of electric batteries. Lithium batteries are the mainstay of the battery industry as the moment, although other battery technologies wait in the wings. These will further increase the all-important power density per weight ratio that will allow electric cars to become ever more lightweight and thus require less power to drive them further.

The term electric vehicles should also include electric bikes, in which China is the unquestioned leader. Over 200 million electric bicycles are owned in China, with no other nation boasting more than a couple of hundreds of thousands.[61] The authorities frown on their use – it is claimed they can cause accidents too often – but that has not curbed their popularity.

Electric vehicles (EVs) are also strategically important as a way of extending the reach of non-fossil fuels in general, and renewable energy in particular, through to new sectors previously the preserve of other forms of final energy consumption, in this case mostly petroleum based. The proportion of new cars which are electric cars or 'plug-in' hybrid electric is rapidly growing. These proportions are particularly high in Norway, for example, which has set regulations and incentives to encourage them. They are growing as a consumer luxury item, via, for instance purchases of the Tesla, in the USA, and they are also growing in China where there are various regulations and incentives that encourage them. The number of EVs in the world doubled in 2015.[62]

The Chinese based BYD company is the largest electric vehicle maker in China and also the world. One Chinese purchaser of a car made by BYD is quoted as saying: 'I always thought I would own a car when I was a kid, but I didn't think about having an electric car because I didn't know the technology would move so fast'.[63] In China, some 188,000 electric cars were sold in 2015, and that number is set to greatly increase in 2016. This compares to around 116,000 electric cars sold in the USA in 2015.[64] The size of the sales in China is surprising given that electric cars are still expensive compared to standard petroleum power vehicles. However, because of the drive to cut air pollution in cities, the national and local governments are piling up incentives and rules to encourage people to buy electric cars.

Currently (in 2016) the impact of each extra electric vehicle on the carbon footprint of China is broadly neutral compared to a conventionally fuelled road vehicle. Whilst electric cars are much more (just over three times) efficient in terms of turning energy input (electricity compared to gasoline/petrol/diesel) into the movement of the vehicle, around three-quarters of the fuel for electricity production comes from coal. This means that there will be roughly the same carbon emissions per mile driven by an average conventionally fuelled vehicle compared to an EV in 2016.[65] However, things are changing, and the proportion of non-fossil fuel used by the electricity system in China is increasing quickly. This means as time goes on, and as the proportion of hydro, nuclear, and new renewable energy input goes up, the advantage of electric vehicles over conventionally fuelled vehicles will grow. So EVs are a good medium term and an excellent long term bet for reducing carbon emissions from China.

There are generous subsidies being offered by the Chinese Government for EV purchases. The cities have set rules limiting the number of days conventionally powered vehicles can run, whereas EVs do not have such limitations. On top of this, EVs can often use bus lanes and also while there is a long waiting list for an ordinary car, a registration for an EV can be secured quickly. So-called 'low speed electric vehicles' (LEVs) have proved especially popular in China. They are small cars that are cheap to buy and handy for getting around urban areas.

However, the Government is concerned to ensure that the heavier end of the road transport market is covered by EVs. Now the Government is to invest in companies to produce EVs for the taxi and bus market.[66] This will reduce the use of diesel, which has increasingly been implicated in the production of high levels of health-damaging particulate pollutants. Indeed, this focus on reducing pollution from diesel vehicles, which is implicated in leading to many deaths, seems to be growing in many countries, perhaps leading to an earlier than expected paradigm shift towards electric powered solutions. For example, BYD is marketing an electric goods van which has a range of 100+ miles, a top speed of 65 miles an hour and a '"Vehicle-to-Grid" system that allows the truck to deliver power back to the grid, to a load, or to another vehicle'.[67] This sort of development is likely to be a key theme of the future as the battery power of electric vehicles is linked to the electricity grid.

The costs of batteries alongside issues such as the availability of charging sites for EVs, the speed with which the EV batteries can be recharged and the range of the EVs are all key factors determining the rate of increase of EV sales. Yet the indices of all these factors are rapidly improving in favour of electric vehicles. Battery technology is being rapidly enhanced and production lines for the batteries are growing longer, as are the supply-chain economics of scale, thus reducing the costs of the electric batteries – indeed, such cost reductions mirror the cost reductions in solar pv that have occurred. Indeed, the growth in demand for batteries and the array of technological advances that will make them lighter and cheaper to deliver given amounts of power suggests that electric battery technology will have a profound impact on energy and society in the not very distant future.

A study written by Nykvist and Nilsson said, of the cost of batteries 'that industry-wide cost estimates declined by approximately 14% annually between 2007 and 2014'.[68] At those rates of decline, electric cars would cease becoming a 'niche' market by 2025 and become mainstream. This may usher in a 'paradigm shift' in car use.[69]

According to Bloomberg, reporting in early 2016,

> Battery prices fell 35 percent and are on a trajectory to make unsubsidized electric vehicles as affordable as their gasoline counterparts in the next six years.... Electric cars will reduce the cost of battery storage and help store intermittent sun and wind power. In the move toward a cleaner grid, electric vehicles and renewable power create a mutually beneficial circle of demand.

The Bloomberg analysis insists that supplies of lithium needed for the current generation of batteries 'is not an issue'.[70]

As I have noted earlier, the Chinese economy is especially good at capturing economies of scale through big production lines and well organised supply chains. This implies that China is now well placed to drive down the cost of electric batteries and electric cars much in the same way as it did in the case of solar pv. Chinese manufacturers such as BYD are in a fierce competitive battle with people like Elon Musk and his Tesla operation to further this aim. The Chinese car manufacturers are somewhere in between the export oriented Chinese solar pv industry and the introverted, less world competitive, Chinese wind industry. China is exporting substantial numbers of EVs, but its non-Chinese share is still fairly modest.

Electric cars are important for Chinese public policy for four vital reasons. First, because of the need to reduce the various noxious emissions from motor vehicles – nitrogen oxides, such as volatile organic compounds, and sulphur oxides, and second, because of the need to restrain the import bill arising from China's increasing oil deficit. Two other collateral, and long term, advantages go alongside the increasing replacement of petroleum powered vehicles by EVs. One is that this substitution will be a way of reducing the carbon emissions from China. Another is that the advances and sheer volume of batteries that go along with the expansion of the EV market make a transition to deriving a high proportion of total Chinese energy from renewable energy sources more manageable. As Bloomberg points out, there is a 'virtuous circle' in an expanding market for batteries, thus reducing their costs, and also making the costs of storage that could help manage the variability of renewable energy sources.[71]

The increasing penetration of the EV into the road transportation market in China (as elsewhere) is likely to have the knock-on effect of encouraging production of much more fuel efficient vehicles powered by conventional petroleum fuels. This is in keeping with theory about what happens during the process of technological change, in that the threatened dominant technology tends to adopt, as a 'defence' strategy, technical changes that can enable the existing paradigm to remain in business.[72] In this case, given the advantage of lower fuel costs represented by EVs, this is likely to include reducing the costs of fuel consumption by improving fuel efficiency.

Of course, this strategy depends to some extent on ensuring that petroleum fuelled vehicles are not increased in attractiveness by lower oil prices. Taxation on motor vehicle fuels needs to be increased. In turn this will make electric cars a more attractive option for consumers sooner than will otherwise occur.

The deployment of EVs as a means of balancing variable output from renewable energy sources is, as David McKay has argued, likely to make a dramatic difference to the balancing capabilities of the electricity system.[73] A comprehensive way of utilising EVs as part of an electricity storage-and-use system will make it much easier to control an electricity system dominated by renewables. If, for example, the Chinese system controllers could induce through charging pricing incentives, 500 million Chinese EVs to take on 2 kW of power each, that would absorb power equivalent to about 80 per cent of the total peak generating capacity in the whole of China. That would help solve the problem of too much power being generated by wind and/or solar plant that can be absorbed by the system – thus avoiding its wastage. Alternatively, of course, the cars could be induced to use their stored power rather than recharging, thus helping the system continue providing full services when there were not enough solar or wind power being generated.

Of course, car batteries are by no means the only means of battery use in the electricity system. Positioning batteries in the local electricity distribution system will also be important as a means of balancing fluctuating output from renewables. These batteries, which are already being deployed in various situations around the world, allow distribution systems at the most local level to become quasi-autonomous. Excess power from renewables can be stored and then released when there is less variable renewable power available. They have wider system benefits of reducing spending on transformers and supplying expensive peak demand.

Such changes could be effected by a pattern of reforms that meant that the Chinese electricity system became more flexible and where power markets respond to price signals. I will talk a little about some current discussions about reform of the regulation of the electricity system in China.

Governance and reform of the electricity system

As has been discussed in the cases of the wind and solar pv, the path to smoothing the way to a more efficient deployment of renewable energy is to move away from a system where choices about projects and decisions in and about supply chains is based essentially on patronage by government officials. Competition is already part of the system in manufacturing solar pv given its international market, but the same is not the case in wind power where there is a lack of competition in the domestic market. The system of different parts of the electricity industry having cosy deals with each other needs to change. Of course all of this needs to be run in parallel with a sea-change in attitudes to government control of maters such as electricity prices. These have remained under Government control, despite regular attempts to pilot possible changes.[74] Pricing reforms have been proposed again,[75] but it remains to be seen how thoroughgoing this will be and the extent to which it will increase competition.

A key issue is that, essentially, the major electricity generators must move from a system of seeing building and operating coal-fired power stations as their principal activity to one where the construction and operation of renewable energy is seen as their priority. Many, of course, would add nuclear power to this injunction, although there are also sceptics who argue that, in practice, the nuclear programme will fall well short of expectations. The most direct way of doing this within the terms of the present system is to make the power sector work to targets of renewable energy consumption, expressed as a proportion of total electricity delivered to consumers (rather than targets for capacity deployed). This will increase the incentive on all parties to increase the efficiency of the wind turbines and also the grid systems. In particular wind turbine manufacturers and windfarm developers will have to compete with each other to deliver the most renewable electricity. As a parallel measure the Government needs to establish a national monitoring and turbine registration centre to authorise independent, clear, assessments of the performance of different wind turbines. This will benefit their export potential.

Too often the focus, in Western commentaries, is on whether the companies are owned by the state or owned by private interests. Rather, in the case of renewable energy the emphasis ought to be on encouraging competition for the purpose of achieving the targets for sustainable energy that have been agreed by Government. There are various effective or actual monopolies in China's electricity and wind power sectors. But merely changing ownership may not solve this problem. As is the case in many states in the USA, private monopolies exist which can be as resistant to independent, alternative, energy initiatives as state owned monopolies. The only way to break open such monopolies is to set electricity companies' targets for renewable energy production, and to introduce incentives and penalties that make it profitable to meet those targets. That is true in the east, west, north or south of the planet, or anywhere in between. Competition is the key here.

Often the notion of 'free markets' is confused to imagine that there can be such a thing as perfect competition within electricity markets. All electricity markets have rules, liberalised electricity markets the most of all, even though the regulations do not set prices! But the rules themselves constrain activity, so the issue is not whether we have free markets but whether the rules that drive the electricity industry are suitable for achieving public policy objectives, in this case for sustainable energy. Competition is important in electricity, but it needs to be competition to secure environmental, social and technological objectives that are set by public policy.

Much of Chinese industry, as I have discussed, has been dominated by a productionist mentality which sees the quantity of products being the prime objective with the quality and environmental impact often being secondary considerations. In the wind power industry, of course, we are not as worried as too many wind turbines being produced. The problem is to make them more efficient. There is a pressing need for there to be competition, not cartels, between the existing companies. Hence the need to change the targets for the electricity industry to being in terms of the amount of energy generated rather than the capacity of machines deployed. The other reform, that is as important as providing competition, is to ensure that renewable energy has grid priority. This means that if there is too much power on the grid then it is the fossil fuel stations that are closed down, not windfarms or solar farms constrained, as has happened in the past in China to an excessive extent.

Some attempts are being made to open up the grid trading arrangements by 'opening power trading centres (first) in Beijing and Guangzhou, and there are also studies into setting up other provincial-level trading organisations,' according to an official of the powerful National Development Research Council (NDRC). The aim is to 'break the power sales monopoly held by the two state grid firms, the State Grid Corporation of China and the Southern Grid Corporation'.[76] Pilot projects are being developed in other provinces.

Joanna Lewis argues that '[w]hile advanced and "smarter" grid technologies may be able to help facilitate the integration of much larger amounts of wind power, political barriers to wind integration will require a different set of solutions'.[77] One problem that she sees as difficult to solve is that posed by the existence of large amounts of coal-fired combined heat and power plant in some of the best wind resource areas in the north which feed into the north and Mongolian grids. '[T]hey (the combined heat and power plant) must be kept running in order to produce heat in the cold winter'.[78]

Kaare Sandholt, one of a team of Danish advisers to the Chinese Government, says that:

> Agreements between the distribution authorities and coal power plant operators to guarantee them a certain numbers of hours of production a year need to be somehow circumvented to ensure that renewables have despatch priority. Just announcing that renewable energy will have grid despatch priority is not enough.

He also argues, among other recommendations, that transmission interconnectors need to be extended and made flexible.

> A power trading market operating on a nationwide basis needs to be implemented. Indeed much better interconnection needs to be completed in order to solve the power imbalance with the south of the country experiencing

power shortages. Solar production during the summer could help solve the power shortages caused by air conditioning demands (as well as installing much more efficient air conditioners).

Sandholt also argues for development of other means of achieving system flexibility including management of demand. Combined heat and power plant, for example, should include large heat stores so that 'renewable energy can be used to turn electricity into heat during times when there was too much renewable energy on the electricity system'.[79]

Certainly, the argument about who should get grid priority is moving away from the interests of the coal industry and its power plants. According to the Paulson Institute in April of 2016 the National Development Reform Commission report backed policies which require

> coal plant owners to pay wind or solar plant owners whose energy is curtailed.... China has more wind and solar capacity than any other country, but it also has the highest rates of curtailment: 15% of the energy from wind and 12% of the energy from solar is wasted as of 2015. The biggest reason: economic incentives currently favor using energy from coal plants, even when low-cost wind or solar is available.[80]

A central problem is that the initial assumption (made by the Government), namely that electricity demand would grow quickly, allowing continued growth of capacity in both thermal (coal-fired) and renewable energy generating capacity, has proved wrong. The programme of building of coal-fired power stations has continued unabated leading to a situation where a lot more coal-fired capacity is trying to supply what is now (because of increased non-fossil generation) a declining amount of electricity required from coal-fired power plant. The result is that even though solar and wind plant are being constrained very often, coal plant are now being utilised for little more than half the time – in 2015 the average 'capacity factor' of coal plant, a measure of how much the power plant is used compared to its production if it was running all the time, fell to 57 per cent.[81]

Hence an urgent reform is to retire older power plant, although this will lead to pressures from the power plant operators for compensation. However, other than curtailing renewable energy generation still further and/or reducing targets for development of non-fossil fuels, there seems no other option.

Despite these caveats there is little doubt that many in China, including key officials, have grand plans for the renewable energy future. The State Grid Company of China (SGCC), for example has unveiled plans at the World Economic Forum for what would amount to a global grid system called the Global Energy Interconnection (GEI) system. 'China hopes to connect wind farms in the Arctic Circle with solar farms located on the Equator, in a system that will transcend national boundaries and provide clean energy everywhere'. Liu Zhenya, the SGCC chairman argues that the GEI is the best option if renewable sources of energy, like solar and wind, are ever going to become a practical alternative to burning dirty fossil fuels. According to the SGCC, if renewable energy generation is increased at an annual rate of 12.4% worldwide each year, then by 2050 renewable energy could account for 80% of the world's total energy consumption.[82]

These are just some initial reforms – as implied in the earlier section on electric cars, there will have to be some radical changes to ensure that electric vehicle (EV) storage can usefully complement the integration of fluctuating renewable energy sources. Of course, the emphasis here needs to be on achieving competition to achieve an ecologically sustainable energy system. As part of this, wind and solar systems can be utilised with much greater efficiency. The amount of energy generated from a given amount of capacity should, after effective reforms to the electricity system, be considerably increased over and above what it is at the moment. This includes ensuring that renewable energy projects are connected to the grid at the same time as they are built, that they have grid priority and also that the system has means of ensuring the use of the renewable energy when there is otherwise insufficient demand on the system. Various means of doing this have been discussed.

Projecting the future

Having come so far in this book to discuss the drivers of, and pressures on, the energy industry in China, it may be reasonable to look into the future and conclude by looking at what might be a plausible outcome. That is, if China follows what is implied in this book, namely a determined implementation of a sustainable energy strategy; sustainable in terms of reducing both local and global pollution and also in reducing reliance on oil imports. A key argument in this book is that China's pattern of energy growth is slowing and that energy consumption is likely, in the long term, to be no more than what it is at its present level. As argued earlier, the shift to a lower growth, service-oriented economy will cut projections of energy growth, and the fact that services consume only a small fraction of the manufacturing output that they are replacing will reduce any tendency towards energy growth even further. Even at present, energy growth is small compared to trends since the 1980s, and whilst, at present, the Chinese Government has been induced by political pressure to keep afloat much of its now excess capacity heavy industry (of which steel is a prime example), over time this tendency will be reduced, and energy growth rates will decline. Meanwhile, of course, as discussed in this chapter, there will be substantial and continuing fuel switching to non-fossil sources which will steadily act not only to meet the supreme political target of lowering local air pollution, but also of achieving goals of reducing carbon emissions.

The China National Renewable Energy Centre (CNREC) has drawn up a projection based on its 'high' projection for renewable energy to be met by 2050. It seems, by today's standards at least, to be optimistic in its assessment of how far growth in energy consumption can be restrained. It projects that energy growth will cease by 2025, and then decline so that by 2050 total Chinese energy consumption will be slightly less than it was in 2015.[83] In 2015, energy consumption was 1.5 per cent higher than it was in 2014.[84] Since China's population growth is likely to cease in the next ten years, and, as has happened already in Japan, population may decline thereafter, this is one downward pressure on energy growth that will be added to others. These include the reduction in the considerable energy inefficiencies in the Chinese energy economy and also less strong economic growth as the Chinese economy matures and shifts away from its over-productionist past. An implicit condition of the stabilisation of energy consumption has, of course, to be the strengthening of EM trends in China, including the transition to a much more service-based economy, the energy economy becoming more competitive and an increase in the ability of local people to ensure that local developments are more energy efficient.

The CNREC put forward detailed projections for the expansion of renewable energy, which it projects as constituting 60 per cent of total energy production/ consumption in China in 2050.[85] Under the CNREC projection, electricity usage expands as a proportion of the energy economy with electricity production accounting for around two-thirds of primary energy production in 2050. There are reasons to see these trends as being plausible, although whether they are as strong as the CNREC suggests is to be seen in the future. Certainly electricity usage will expand to include much of the transportation sector since much of this will be powered by electricity through EVs. Additionally, a lot more heat may be delivered through heat pumps which work on electricity. They will supply this heat through industrial sized district heating systems and also homes. There will be a growth in services which will consume a higher proportion of electricity than what has been consumed previously.

Having stabilised energy consumption, carbon emissions can then be steadily reduced, mainly by switching to low carbon fuels. China National Renewable Energy Centre (CNREC) projects there will be around 100 GWe of nuclear power and 550 GWe of hydropower in place by 2050. However, much larger amounts of renewable energy, that is solar power and wind power, are seen as being deployed by 2050. Between them solar power and wind power are projected to generate over 60 per cent of Chinese electricity by 2050, with the rest being mainly divided up between hydro, nuclear, biomass, gas and a residual contribution from coal. Altogether, 91 per cent of electricity is projected to come from non-fossil fuels.[86] Under this scenario wind power alone will generate a roughly equivalent amount of electricity to that consumed in China in 2015. In order to achieve this level, deployment of wind power and solar power speeds up rapidly from 2025 onwards. That seems likely to fit in with the reductions in costs associated with wind power and solar power that have been gathering pace in recent years.

I have calculated the reductions in carbon emissions that would be associated with the CNREC's projections, and the reduction would be of the order of 75 per cent assuming that the biomass sources included came from sustainable sources. The reduction in carbon emissions would be around two-thirds even if the 'biomass' was substituted by fossil fuels.

In fact, management of the quantity of the mainly variable renewable energy projected for 2050 will be less difficult than may be assumed. For a start there will be substantial hydro and nuclear sources available, and given appropriate market reforms and electricity charging systems, storage through EVs, and storage embedded in distribution systems there will be much system flexibility. At the end of the day the glut of coal-fired power stations in the Chinese system today will mean that there will still be a lot ready to generate for short periods as required if some balancing from them is still required.

Of course, reduction in carbon emissions will continue after 2050 because transportation will increasingly be powered by electricity, and the electricity sources will come from renewable energy. EVs will take over most of the road transportation market, and by 2050 it is also likely that some aircraft will be powered by electricity using rapidly advancing battery technology. China is already taking a lead in producing light aircraft powered by batteries.[87]

Conclusion

In this chapter I have looked at how, and in what conditions, China could engage in fuel switching to dramatically reduce China's carbon emissions. A large part of this effort will be concerned with constraining energy consumption itself. That having been said, another large part will be building up non-fossil fuels, and the plausibility of this has been the focus in this chapter. Indeed, a dramatic reduction of China's carbon emissions by 2050 can be seen as very plausible. Deployment of wind power and solar pv are key elements of the fuel switching strategy, as is the proliferation of electric vehicles (EVs). EVS will play a substantial role in both reducing emissions compared to vehicles powered by petroleum based fuels and also in helping to manage variable renewable energy.

Among the lessons from this coverage of supply-side technologies is that outcomes are much more effective under conditions of competition. The contrast between the Chinese solar pv and wind power industries bear this out. The Chinese wind industry looks relatively inefficient compared to Chinese solar. In the wind industry, while the output is massive, it sells to a captive and clientelist system where networks and links between local governments and different companies seem to matter at least as much, if not more than competition based on quality and output. Innovations have been developed which suit a captive market rather than a competitive one, often paying insufficient regard to the uniqueness of patents in the international market, which comes back to haunt wind companies when they try to export product.

By contrast, the solar pv system has excelled in both innovation in its technology and also the ability to develop supply chain efficiencies and economies of scale in manufacturing. Western detractors may harp about the soft loans available for solar pv manufacturers, but this ignores the point that in the solar pv sector Chinese companies have simply gone out into the international market place and out-competed with the West.

Paradoxically, in terms of lessons for the relation of government, industry and markets, renewable energy has more lessons for China than the rest of the world. Certainly, soft loans have helped the nascent Chinese solar pv industry to develop. However, if that was all that provided international success then the Chinese wind industry would also most likely have been successful on the international market as well. The point is that the Chinese solar pv industry was strengthened and nourished by the competition that was available on the international market, not its home market. The home market, still rigged for developmental purposes, is not sufficiently competitive, as can be seen in the case of China's wind power industry. It will only be when the Chinese wind industry is put under more competitive pressures that outcomes will match the efficiencies currently enjoyed in Western nations. This also has to be extended to the electricity industry as a whole, where deals between different companies seem to drag progress back from where it should be if there were more competitive markets.

In theoretical terms, it can be seen that whilst the deployment of renewable energy would seem to be pointing in the direction of technological outcomes associated with ecological modernisation, the economic governance arrangements may not. There is, at present, insufficient competition in Chinese domestic electricity arrangements in general, including renewable energy. Moreover, special interests of the coal lobby appear to be resisting necessary reforms to the electricity market to make it more flexible to accommodate high penetrations of renewable energy.

I argue here (and the NDRC also argues) that declining costs of wind power and solar pv in particular will speed up development of new renewable energy sources.[88] However, in contrast to the Chinese Government, I would argue that environmental and safety issues surrounding hydro developments and nuclear power will reduce the rate of development of these latter fuel sources.

Like the Chinese Government explains through its NDRC report on renewable energy, I would expect the deployment of renewable energy speed up from the 2020s. It is probable that energy consumption is likely to be a lot lower than that which is projected by the Chinese Government. This will especially be the case if, or probably when, economic growth in the medium term is reduced by the need to clear bad debts that have built up in the Chinese economy. Of course a given quantity of non-fossil deployment will have a greater impact in reducing carbon emissions in a lower energy scenario rather than a high energy scenario.

Altogether, this means that it is possible to see that China's carbon emissions could be reduced by two-thirds or more by 2050 compared to emissions in 2015. This would fulfil China's contribution to meeting the minimum target set by the Paris Agreement of keeping post-industrial increases in temperature to 2 degrees.

Of course, the energy establishment may scoff at my low projections for energy growth, but perhaps the arguments (and experience of exaggerated projections of energy growth in various instances in the past) should make them be a little more thoughtful on this issue.

However, a more plausible argument for scepticism as to whether China will indeed cut its carbon emissions by so radical amounts is that the political will may not exist to overcome institutional obstacles to the integration and efficient deployment of renewable energy and associated measures. On the other hand, I take note, as discussed earlier in the book, that bottom-up pressures for ecological reform and pollution abatement are very strong. That, allied to the declining costs of renewable energy and calls for the economy to be modernised in a more competitive fashion, seems to have a good chance of prevailing in the coming years.

Notes

1 Smith, M. (2016) 'While fossils crashed in 2015, clean energy soared', *Clean Energy Canada*, 29 February, available online at http://cleanenergycanada.org/while-fossils-crashed-in-2015-clean-energy-soared/
2 Ng Wei, A. and Gaventa, J. (2016) 'China plans to dominate clean tech race', E3G, 17 March, available online at www.e3g.org/library/china-accelerates-while-europe-deliberates-on-the-clean-energy-transition
3 Frankfurt School-UNEP Collaborating Centre (2016) 'Global; Trends in Renewable Energy Investment', *UNEP-Bloomberg New Energy Finance*, available online at http://fs-unep-centre.org/sites/default/files/publications/globaltrendsinrenewableenergy investment2016lowres_0.pdf?utm_content=buffera0c81&utm_medium=social&utm_ source=twitter.com&utm_campaign=buffer
4 Ng, S., Mabey, N. and Gaventa, J. (2016) 'Pulling Ahead On Clean Technology China's 13th Five Year Plan Challenges Europe's Low Carbon Competitiveness, E3G, available online at www.e3g.org/docs/E3G_Report_on_Chinas_13th_5_Year_ Plan.pdf
5 Ibid., p. 7
6 Mathews, J. and Tan, H. (2015) *China's Renewable Energy Revolution*, Houndsmill, Basingstoke: Palgrave, p. 145
7 Dai, H., Xie, X, Xie., Y., Liu, J. and Masui, T. (2016) 'Green growth: The economic impacts of large-scale renewable energy development in China', *Applied Energy*, vol. 162, 435–449
8 Toke, D. (2011) *Ecological Modernisation and Renewable Energy*, London: Palgrave
9 Howe, M. (2015) 'Non-Fossil Sources provide 25% of China's Electricity', *Cleantechnica*, 11 March, available online at http://cleantechnica.com/2015/03/11/non-fossil-fuel-sources-provide-25-chinas-electricity/
10 Ibid.
11 Ibid.
12 International Hydropower Association (2016) *China*, available online at www.hydro-power.org/country-profiles/china
13 Unsigned (2016) 'China's electricity mix: changing so fast that CO_2 emissions may have peaked', *Energy Post*, 1 March, available online at www.energypost.eu/chinas-electricity-mix-changing-fast-co2-emissions-may-peaked/
14 Ibid.
15 McCrone, A. (ed.) (2016) 'Global Trends in Renewable Energy Investment 2016', *UNEP/Bloomberg New Energy Finance*, available online at http://fs-unep-centre.org/ sites/default/files/publications/globaltrendsinrenewableenergyinvestment-2016lowres_0.pdf, see pp. 31–32 in particular

16 Child, B. (2016) 'Leonardo DiCaprio says China can be climate change "hero"', *Guardian*, 21 March, available online at www.theguardian.com/film/2016/mar/21/leonardo-dicaprio-says-china-can-be-climate-change-hero

17 IEA statistics on electricity consumption for China (2016) *World Bank Data*, available online at http://data.worldbank.org/indicator/EG.USE.ELEC.KH.PC?locations=CN

18 Figures for USA extrapolated from data in Mooney, C. (2015) 'Here's how much faster wind and solar are growing than fossil fuels', *Washington Post*, 9 March, available online at www.washingtonpost.com/news/energy-environment/wp/2015/03/09/heres-how-much-faster-wind-and-solar-are-growing-than-fossil-fuels/

19 CNREC (2015) 'China 2050 High Renewable Energy Penetration Scenario and Roadmap Study', 26 May, China National Renewable Energy Centre, available online at www.cnrec.org.cn/english/result/2015-05-26-474.html

20 Cusick, D. (2016) 'Chinese wind turbine maker is now world's largest', *Scientific American*, 23 March, available online at www.scientificAmerican.com/article/chinese-wind-turbine-maker-is-now-world-s-largest/

21 Tyler, L. (2016) 'Vestas Edges Out Goldwind For Wind Turbine Market Share', *North American Wind Power*, 31 March, available online at http://nawindpower.com/vestas-edges-out-goldwind-for-wind-turbine-market-share

22 Chen (2015) op. cit., p. 160

23 Gosens, J. and Lu, Y. (2014) 'Prospects for global market expansion of China's wind turbine manufacturing industry', *Energy Policy*, vol. 67, 301–318, p. 307

24 Andrews-Speed, P. (2012) *The Governance of Energy in China*, London: Palgrave, pp. 111–116

25 Chen (2015) op. cit., pp. 204–205, citing McDowall, W., Ekins, P., Radošević, S. and Zhang, L. (2013) 'The development of wind power in China, Europe and the USA: how have policies and innovation system activities co-evolved?' *Technology Analysis & Strategic Management*, vol. 25, no. 2, 163–185

26 Mathews, J. and Tan, H. (2015) *China's Renewable Energy Revolution*, London: Palgrave, pp. 119–120

27 Ibid., p. 120

28 Milborrow, D. (2016) 'Global Costs Analysis – the year offshore wind power costs fell', *WindPower Monthly*, 29 January, available online at www.windpowermonthly.com/article/1380738/global-costs-analysis-year-offshore-wind-costs-fell

29 CNREC (2015) op. cit., p. 3

30 Chen, C-F. (2015) 'The Politics Of Renewable Energy In China: Towards A New Model Of Environmental Governance?' PhD, University of Bath, available online at http://opus.bath.ac.uk/46738, pp. 200–201

31 TEDA Wind (2008) 'Key Industries Brief', *Tianjin Economic Development Agency*, available online at http://en1.investteda.org/aboutteda/keyindustriesbrief/wind/default.htm

32 Liu, C. (2016) 'Facing Grid Constraints, China Puts a Chill on New Wind Energy Projects', *Inside Climate News*, 28 March, available online at http://insideclimatenews.org/news/28032016/china-wind-energy-projects-suspends-clean-energy-climate-change

33 ABB press release (2016) 'ABB wins orders over $300 million to strengthen China's power grid and lower environmental impact', *ABB Media Department*, 18 April, available online at www.abb.com/cawp/seitp202/3833cb3f8e91f260c1257f990025d34f.aspx

34 Bloomberg News (unsigned) (2016) 'China's Idled Wind Farms May Spell Trouble for Renewable Energy', *Bloomberg News*, 29 July, available online at www.bloomberg.com/news/articles/2016-06-28/trouble-in-renewable-energy-spotted-in-china-s-idled-wind-farms

35 Shepard, C. and Hornby, L. (2016) 'China's Wind Energy Groups Cry Foul Over

Grid Curbs', *Financial Times*, 31 March, available online at https://next.ft.com/content/1743dfb8-f729-11e5-803c-d27c7117d132

36 Wang, Z., Zhu, Y., Zhu, Y. and Shi, Y. (2016) 'Energy structure change and carbon emission trends in China', *Energy*, vol. 115, 369–377, p. 376

37 Ibid., p. 12

38 Lindon, H. (2016) 'China's National Energy Administration: Plan Is To Triple Solar PV Capacity By 2020', *Sustainnovate*, 26 March, available online at http://sustain novate.ae/en/industry-news/detail/chinas-national-energy-administration-plan-is-to-triple-solar-pv-capacity-b

39 Morris, C. (2016) 'How Germany helped bring down the cost of PV', *The Energy Transition*, 20 January, available online at http://energytransition.de/2016/01/how-germany-helped-bring-down-the-cost-of-pv/?platform=hootsuite

40 Li, H. (2015) *China's New Energy Revolution*, New York: McGraw Education, pp. 214–215

41 Wang, U. (2014) 'Guess Who Are The Top 10 Solar Panel Makers In the World?' *Forbes*, 3 December, available online at www.forbes.com/sites/uciliawang/2014/12/03/guess-who-are-the-top-10-solar-panel-makers-in-the-world/#76b0bcf92812

42 Goodrich, A. C., Powell, D. M., James, T. L., Woodhouse, M. and Buonassisi, T. (2013) 'Assessing the drivers of regional trends in solar photovoltaic manufacturing', *Energy and Environmental Science*, vol. 6, 2811–2821, available online at http://pubs.rsc.org/en/Content/ArticleLanding/2013/EE/C3EE40701b#!divAbstract

43 Goodrich, A., James, T. and Woodhouse, M. (2011) 'Solar PV Manufacturing Cost Analysis: U.S. Competitiveness in a Global Industry', *Presentation by NREL*, 11 October, available online at www.nrel.gov/docs/fy12osti/53938.pdf

44 Tylecote, R. (2015) 'Ownership and Innovation in Chinese solar photovoltaic firms: an analysis of the effects of state, private, and foreign shareholding on patenting performance', PhD thesis, Imperial College, London, available online at https://spiral.imperial.ac.uk/handle/10044/1/26286

45 Li, H. (2015) op. cit., p. 210

46 Ibid., p. 214

47 Ibid., p. 214

48 Ibid., p. 214

49 Target Map (2016) 'Solar pv map of China', available online at www.targetmap.com/viewer.aspx?reportId=46583

50 Shaw, V. (2016) 'China: Qinghai targets additional 7.1 GW of renewables in 2016', *PV Magazine*, 4 January, available online at www.pv-magazine.com/news/details/beitrag/china-qinghai-targets-additional-71-gw-of-renewables-in-2016_100022603/#ixzz46G79mCsb

51 CENSERE Market Intelligence (2012) 'Solar Photovoltaic Energy Study 2012', *CENSERE*, available online at www.censere.com/index.php/en/component/hikashop/product/5-solar-pv-energy-study-3q2012/lang-en-GB

52 Malik, M. (2015) 'Lower-Cost Wind and Solar Will Drive Energy Storage Technology', *Bloomberg Technology*, lower-cost-wind-and-solar-will-drive-energy-storage-technology

53 Randall, R. (2016) 'We've almost reached peak fossil fuels for electricity', *Bloomberg New Energy Finance*, 13 June, available online at www.bloomberg.com/news/articles/2016-06-13/we-ve-almost-reached-peak-fossil-fuels-for-electricity, available online at https://thinkprogress.org/youll-never-believe-how-cheap-new-solar-power-is-7c17051c1152#.v3ayycr58

54 Soo, Z. (2016) 'China can "easily" support all its energy demand using homegrown solar power, says Tesla's Musk in Hong Kong', *South China Morning Post*, 26 January, available online at www.scmp.com/tech/innovation/article/1905467/china-can-easily-support-all-its-energy-demand-using-homegrown-solar

55 Mukerjee, M. (2015) 'The Impending Dam Disaster in the Himalayas', *Scientific*

American, 1 August, available online at www.scientificAmerican.com/article/the-impending-dam-disaster-in-the-himalayas/

56 World Nuclear Association (2016) 'Nuclear Power in China', *World Nuclear Association*, available online at www.world-nuclear.org/information-library/country-profiles/countries-a-f/china-nuclear-power.aspx

57 Buckley, C. (2015) 'China's nuclear vision collides with villagers' fears', *New York Times*, 21 November, available online at www.nytimes.com/2015/11/22/world/asia/chinas-nuclear-vision-collides-with-villagers-fears.html?_r=2

58 Graham-Harrison, E. (2015) 'China warned over 'insane' plans for new nuclear power plants', *Guardian*, 25 May, available online at www.theguardian.com/world/2015/may/25/china-nuclear-power-plants-expansion-he-zuoxiu?CMP=share_btn_tw

59 Schneider, M. and Froggatt, A. (2015) 'The World Nuclear Industry Status Report', *Mycle Schneider Consulting*, p. 34, available online at www.worldnuclearreport.org/IMG/pdf/20151023MSC-WNISR2015-V4-LR.pdf

60 World Nuclear Association (2016) op. cit., available online at http://world-nuclear.org/information-library/country-profiles/countries-a-f/china-nuclear-power.aspx

61 Timmons, H. (2013) 'Consider the e-bike: Can 200 million Chinese be wrong?' *Quartz*, 22 February, available online at http://qz.com/137518/consumers-the-world-over-love-electric-bikes-so-why-do-us-lawmakers-hate-them/

62 Pressman, M. (2016) 'Number of electric cars world wide climbs to1.3 million', *Vannex*, 1 March, available online at http://evannex.com/blogs/news/77801925-number-of-electric-cars-worldwide-climbs-to-1-3-million-tesla-model-s-takes-top-spot-among-new-ev-registrations

63 Le Beau, P. (2016) 'China's BYD looks to double electric vehicle sales', *CNBC*, 28 April, available online at www.cnbc.com/2016/04/28/chinas-byd-looks-to-double-electric-vehicle-sales.html

64 Ibid.

65 In fact, an EV will have a slightly lower carbon emission per km driven assuming average fuel economy of 7.33l/100 km and the decline of coal's share of electricity production in 2015 to 73 per cent, the rest being non-fossil fuel. See Yang, Z. (2015) 'China still lagging on fuel consumption in 2014', *International Council for Clean Transportation*, 18 September, available online at www.theicct.org/blogs/staff/china-still-lagging-fuel-consumption-2014

66 Shepherd, C. (2016) 'China shifts gear to drive electric car development', *Financial Times*, 25 February, available online at www.ft.com/cms/s/0/a55e7d36-db8a-11e5-a72f-1e7744c66818.html#axzz47DkUlxYl

67 Field, K. (2015) 'While Tesla tackles cars BYD attacks diesel emissions with new truck line', *Cleantechnica*, 3 May, available online at http://cleantechnica.com/2016/05/03/tesla-cars-byd-electric-trucks/

68 Nykvist, B. and Nilsson, M. (2015) 'Rapidly falling costs of battery packs for electric vehicles', *Nature Climate Change*, vol. 5, 329–332, p. 329

69 Nykvist, B. and Nilsson, M. (2015) op. cit.

70 Randall, T. (2016) 'Here's how electric cars will cause the next oil crisis', *Bloomberg*, 25 February, available online at www.bloomberg.com/features/2016-ev-oil-crisis/?cmpid=yhoo.headline

71 Ibid.

72 Geels, F. (2002) 'Technological transitions as evolutionary reconfiguration processes: a multi-level perspective and a case-study', *Research Policy*, vol. 31, 1257–1274, see p. 1270

73 McKay, D. (2009) *Sustainable Energy – Without the Hot Air*', Cambridge: UIT, pp. 194–195, also accessible at available online at www.withouthotair.com/c26/page_194.shtml

74 Andrews-Speed, P. (2012) op. cit.

75 Bo, A., Weibin, L., Aiming, Z. and Wei, Z. (2015) 'China's Market-Oriented Reforms in the Energy and Environmental Sectors', *Pacific Energy Summit, National Bureau of Asian Research*, available online at http://nbr.org/downloads/pdfs/ETA/PES_2015_workingpaper_AnBo_et_al.pdf

76 Unsigned (2015) 'China plans power trading exchanges to free up electricity prices', *Thomson-Reuters*, 12 November, available online at http://uk.reuters.com/article/china-power-reform-idUKL3N1372RG20151112

77 Lewis, J. (2013) *Green Innovation in China*, New York: Columbia Press, p. 141

78 Ibid., p. 141

79 Interview with Kaare Sandholt, 21 July, 2015 and email exchange with author 8 September, 2016

80 Hove, A. (2016) 'A new opening for clean energy in China', *Paulson Institute*, 22 April, available online at www.paulsoninstitute.org/paulson-blog/2016/04/22/a-new-opening-for-clean-energy-in-china/

81 Overton, T. (2016) 'Despite Policy Shifts, China Faces Huge Coal-Fired Overcapacity', *Power*, 3 August, available online at www.powermag.com/despite-policy-shifts-china-faces-huge-coal-fired-overcapacity/?mypower

82 Wang, S. (2016) 'China hopes to build a $50 trillion global wind and solar power grid by 2050', *Shanghaiist Daily*, 17 July, available online at http://shanghaiist.com/2016/07/17/global_energy_grid.php?utm_content=bufferfdea7&utm_medium=social&utm_source=twitter.com&utm_campaign=buffer

83 CNREC (2015) '2050 High Renewable Penetration Scenario and Roadmap Study', *National Development and Reform Commission*, p. 13, available online at www.efchina.org/Attachments/Report/report-20150420/China-2050-High-Renewable-Energy-Penetration-Scenario-and-Roadmap-Study-Executive-Summary.pdf

84 BP (2015) *Statistical Review of World Energy*, available online at www.bp.com/en/global/corporate/energy-economics/statistical-review-of-world-energy.html

85 CNREC (2015) op. cit., p. 7

86 CNREC (2015) op. cit., pp. 5–8

87 Unsigned (2015) 'China's first battery powered plane cleared for production', *Sputnik International*, 15 November, available online at http://sputniknews.com/asia/2015 1205/1031279735/china-battery-powered-plane.html

88 CNREC (2015) op. cit.

7   Conclusion

China, with a fifth of the world's population, and a still developing economy, is key to the extent to which what has been called 'dangerous climate change' can be averted. The aims of the Paris Agreement may stand or fall with China, both for its own contribution and the example it will set the developing world. There is great potential for China to play its part well, although this conclusion is still dependent on China achieving, and moving beyond, the sort of environmental governance, regulation and market efficiency that has already been achieved in Europe. That conclusion arises after we consider the economics, politics, consumption patterns and energy supply possibilities. China suffers from high pollution levels at present, but the growing middle classes are putting increasing pressure on the Government to deal with this. In addition to this, China has, for economic reasons, to shift away from its present over-productionist industrialist path. Either the Government achieves this or it will be forced into doing so. Dire warnings have emerged about China's increasing bad debt crisis, and dealing with this in itself seems likely to reduce economic growth, and with it constrain any growth in energy consumption, and with it carbon emissions.

I argued in Chapter 2 that our measure of whether China is in a position to achieve radical reductions in carbon emissions must begin with an assessment of whether China achieves what I set out as minimum conditions for European-style ecological modernisation (EM). In as much as China's policies and practices are different from this 'Eurocentric' EM, I discuss the relative effectiveness of Chinese practice compared to this EM in encouraging activities associated with reducing carbon emissions. This includes renewable energy and actions to lower energy consumption.

EM's core notion of the simultaneous achievement of ecological protection and continued rates of economic development may be closer to the horizon in China than has been recognised in the past. This is partly because of the fact that China is on a transition to a much less polluting, much more service-based economy. Service dominated economies have much lower rates of economic growth than developmentalist economies. Crucially, in addition to this, services themselves use several times less energy than manufacturing. This more mature economic pathway may be redolent of what has happened in the EU, and structural aspects of Chinese (relatively dense) urban environment may mimic European conditions, more than that of the USA.

Currently per capita carbon emissions for China are much the same as for the EU. Put simply, there is no particular reason to assume that they will rise beyond this given that the developmentalist phase of Chinese economic expansion is ending. As was discussed in Chapter 4, urban density and patterns of settlement are much more like Europe than the USA's much more dispersed patterns of settlement and large floor space per person. Public policy is tending towards entrenching urban density as a means of reducing environmental impact.

On the other hand there is substantial activity, and there are considerable pressures, to build renewable energy supplies. The Chinese Government, impelled by a need to cut air pollution and protect energy security, is investing heavily in non-fossil energy sources, especially wind power and solar power. The costs of these resources are steadily declining to such an extent that soon they will be the first choices for installation on grounds of cost, let alone pollution reduction. China has vast resources for renewable energy. With the prospect of a stabilisation of energy consumption fuel, switching to lower carbon fuels will steadily reduce China's carbon footprint. Combining these perspectives produces a conclusion that China may be set to reduce its energy related carbon emissions by over half, perhaps two-thirds of 2015 levels of carbon emissions by 2050. More radical reductions are envisaged in projections issued by the China National Centre for Renewable Energy.

However, such a prospect is dependent on the recent increase in deployment of renewable energy being maintained and increased. The Government needs to see this, or be induced to see this by pressure from below, as being an end itself rather than an accidental policy pursued because the Government expected and/or hoped electricity demand would increase faster than it has or is likely to.

There has been some discussion over the extent of recent change – whether carbon emissions have substantially dropped, or merely stalled in the 2014 and 2015 period. But either conclusion is highly significant. The question emerged of whether this was some sort of blip after which there would be back to business as usual and strong economic growth and surging energy consumption. Alternatively it could represent a long term trend, and that is the conclusion supported in this book.

However, changes in governance are still needed if China is to achieve the 'core' conditions of ecological modernisation (EM) that are a prerequisite for radical cuts in carbon emissions. This is the conclusion that we come to by comparing the core conditions of EM with what exists in China today. These core conditions include: modest economic growth levels in a service-oriented economy; mobilising green technologies to tackle environmental problems; environmental governance and agreement about technological means; 'smart' market based means of promoting green technological solutions pursued in a competitive economic environment.

Modest economic growth levels in a service-oriented economy

I argue that the lower rates of growth of energy consumption are a long term trend, with the probability that rates of growth will become lower rather than higher. This has been a feature of conditions in Europe in recent years, and China's transition into a less developmentalist economy is likely to parallel European patterns of lower pressure for energy growth. This allows greater possibilities for ecological protection to be reconciled with economic development, the classic condition of EM – especially as large scale deployment of renewable energy substitutes for coal in particular.

China's technique of building infrastructure and selling cheap manufactured products worked until the early years of this century to the extent that such investment reaped returns that repaid the initial investments, at least in additional economic activity that was generated. However, as discussed in Chapter 3, this strategy has become unsustainable in different ways. Increasingly the Government's continued emphasis on spending on infrastructure has yielded only short terms gains in employment whilst building up debts for the longer term. It has produced vast volumes of pollution. Large debts have accumulated. The cost advantages enjoyed by China in its erstwhile effort to be the manufacturing centre of the world have declined.

Moreover, study of other developmentalist economies suggests that this outcome is to be expected, and that as part of a solution the economy will turn much more towards services as economic activities. This, in turn, means lower economic growth. An economy that consists of a much higher proportion of services is bound to use much less energy than before since services consume much smaller quantities of energy compared to manufacturing. A second effect is that an economy that is dominated by services is likely to have much lower rates of economic growth, and lower rates of economic growth mean less energy is consumed. However, this shift is being slowed because the Government feels it is constrained by interests associated with energy-intensive industries. Many of these are state-owned which are being kept afloat through government backed loans and contracts. Nevertheless, a trajectory towards lower growth rates and more service-led development seems inevitable, whether planned by government policy or resolved as a result of an economic recession triggered by the country's accumulating debt crisis.

Mobilising green technologies to tackle environmental problems

The rapid deployment of renewable energy in China does much to demonstrate that the country is taking its ecological responsibilities seriously and this strategy certainly fits in well with the demands of an ecological modernisation approach. New renewable energy sources, wind and solar, as well as rapidly improving electric vehicles and batteries are now key centres of attention in the Chinese energy industries. They are set to dominate the delivery of China's energy requirements. China is a centre for innovation in the solar pv and also the electric vehicle market, and they are very competitive in international markets, dominating the solar pv market in particular. China also manufactures the largest amount of wind power in the world, although almost exclusively for the Chinese market.

China's National Renewable Energy Centre has suggested that there are immense, economically practicable, renewable energy resources, mainly in the form of solar pv and wind power. Indeed, such resources would be enough to power the whole of China's energy consumption – that is not just electricity. However, the electrification of the economy is likely to continue. China is taking a lead in developing electric motor vehicle technology and seems poised to repeat the mass production and economies of scale techniques that it has used to such powerful effect in the case of solar pv to build a battery market and, linked with it, a dominant electric vehicles market in China. This seems likely to be in place by 2050, which will transform the way energy is used and distributed.

The projections made by China's National Renewable Energy Centre, discussed in Chapter 6, assume that energy consumption will stabilise, but that non-fossil energy sources (mainly solar pv and wind power) will provide over two-thirds of China's energy by 2050. Overall, China's carbon emissions will be reduced by at least two-thirds under such a scenario. The transition, of course, does not end there. It is perhaps a little too far away to make too many predictions about post 2050 outcomes, but within China itself, as well as in the West, there are technological breakthroughs happening that can lead to even air travel being powered by renewable energy, with the Chinese already taking a lead in battery powered flight.

However, as a caveat to all of this, China's recent growth rates in renewable energy still need to be increased to achieve the scenarios described by the CNREC, and if cost declines in the technologies are to help to increase the technology deployment, then the energy markets need to be competitive and be bounded by the right institutions to enable this. Moreover, there must be a concern that recent rapid deployment of renewable energy is predicated on governmental projections for much higher growth in energy consumption, projections which would themselves, if realised, mean than radical carbon reduction targets could not be met.

Environmental governance and agreement about technological means

The Chinese Government has immense pressure on it to ensure that radical targets for pollution reduction are achieved. Combating pollution has sharply risen up the political agenda in recent years as the middle classes have expanded and demanded a clean environment. In fact, the structures of the Chinese state, which are oriented and incentivised towards increasing production as their prime objective, seem ill-suited to achieve these wishes. But change must come in order to satisfy the demands of the Chinese people for all reasonable progress being made to reduce air pollution.

Certainly, the sort of environmental governance that is in evidence in Europe has not (yet) been achieved in the case of China. Its authoritarianism may involve 'consultation', but industry and commerce will only become more responsive to environmentalist demands from civil society if local officials are made accountable for their actions. That is a fundamental part of European style ecological modernisation that has not yet been met. Moreover, the injunction on local officials that their careers depend on demonstrating how they have expanded the local economy (rather than respond to local people's wishes) sets up an inbuilt bias towards development at the expense of environmental protection. There are some bright areas of good practice in some cities, but at the moment they are too rare, and often 'pilot' projects of various sorts are rolled out to improve the environment, without them being translated effectively to policy covering the country as a whole.

This pattern of development needs to be fully abandoned. The role of the local state needs to be changed. It needs to become more accountable to local people in order that its responsibilities for reducing pollution (and improving energy efficiency) are clear and not made ambivalent by links with local industry. Top-down, so called 'environmentalism authoritarianism' may be a good description of the Chinese system, but the evidence in this book suggests that it is a greatly inferior way to improve the environment compared to the 'Eurocentric' ecological modernisation analysed in this book.

This brings us to another aspect of EM. This is one of involving competition to produce efficient and innovative outcomes. The state's role should be that of setting the right regulations, incentives and institutional conditions to promote ecological technologies rather than the state taking decisions to favour this or that company.

'Smart' market based means of promoting green technological solutions pursued in a competitive economic environment

This links with another aspect of European style EM that has not yet been met in China, that of dealing with economic governance. It is true that China has become a much more capitalist country, but the comparison I have drawn between solar pv and wind power in China illustrates that the search for profits in China does not always equal achievement of a competitive and thus more efficient economy. The system of giving local government officials the task of promoting development has run its course, and the system of networks by which business is done needs to be replaced by a competitive energy economy, as I have discussed in Chapter 6. Wind power in China, which relies almost solely on a domestic wind manufacturing sector, appears protected from competition both within China and from outside. The industry is held back by this lack of competition and reliance on doing business through networks of interest. Some would call this 'cronyism'. Hence Chinese wind power has not been competitive outside of China and Chinese wind manufacturers have had little success in selling abroad. But China's solar pv industry, which initially had little in the way of home markets, had to be competitive in order to sell abroad with the consequence that its products are seen as high quality and low cost in the international market.

In addition, China's energy, and particularly electricity, sector needs to become much more based on flexible and competitive mechanisms in order to help to efficiently absorb increasing amounts of fluctuating renewable energy supplies. Much renewable energy is being wasted because coal-fired power plants are still, in effect, being given priority of despatch. A system based on competitive markets could overcome this problem, but a system which runs on the basis of decisions made through established networks of interest cannot.

European style EM involves Government setting the right 'macro' institutional conditions through regulations and incentives to drive the economy in a green direction. But competitive pressures need to be allowed to complete the task. That is one of the clear lessons which emerge out of a study of Chinese renewable energy. The state's role remains very important, but it must focus on setting the right macro conditions, to encourage renewable energy and energy efficiency.

Policies designed to encourage energy efficiency and also more sustainable urban planning are being proposed, although their implementation is as yet patchy. There is a long way to go here, of course, and reforming the courts to ensure they can really crack down on pollution and reforming the way the local state is run to ensure that local people make planning decisions are important. Top-down methods have succeeded in promoting renewable energy development, but as several Western European countries have demonstrated, rapid build-up of renewable energy can be achieved through 'smart' policies of regulations and incentives to meet national targets. This is rather than the Chinese method of local governments promoting their own company favourites to meet national renewable energy goals. The Chinese method has achieved results, but often on the basis of a lack of competition and inefficient results.

The implications of the scenarios discussed in this book are immense. It means the more modest target of containing temperature rises to 2 degrees as set by the Paris Agreement may be possible to achieve. If China, representing a major part of the developing world, and the leader of much of that world, can achieve such levels of carbon reductions, then other states will follow. They will follow partly because of the adoption of the technologies that simultaneously become available, but also because, politically, governments will be unable to refuse the demands of civil society pressure for reduction in air pollution through burning of fossil fuels.

This book has primarily focussed on energy and carbon reduction, although, as discussed in Chapter 2, we have to consider the context of how the Chinese people have put environmental issues, and the fight against pollution, at the top of the political agenda. Many issues need to be faced to protect the Chinese environment – water pollution and shortages, biodiversity challenges, toxic discharges and industrial safety, polluted farmlands and food, to name but some of the most serious. Indeed, the struggle against some of these may prove even more difficult than the task of reducing air pollution from energy sources. Yet if China can make the progress in reducing carbon emissions outlined in this book then there is a better prospect for the building of the practical means to abate these other problems.

So, in final summative conclusion, in terms of scoring China on its achievement of the four ecological modernisation criteria that I have outlined, we can say that it has so far achieved a score of around two out of four. It has started a transition towards a more modest pattern of economic growth with services taking up a larger part of the economy; the Government has done well to engineer a rapid increase in the amounts of non-fossil fuels being installed. On the other hand, two criteria remain largely unfulfilled. In terms of environmental governance there continues to be a conflict between local officials' responsibility for combating pollution and their role, upon which their career progression depends, in fostering economic development. In terms of economic governance, there is too much emphasis on the top-down management of the award of contracts to specific companies, as opposed to letting the market be guided by the 'smart' policy instruments within which competition can produce more efficient outcomes.

Bibliography

ABB press release (2016) 'ABB wins orders over $300 million to strengthen China's power grid and lower environmental impact', *ABB Media Department*, 18 April, available online at www.abb.com/cawp/seitp202/3833cb3f8e91f260c1257f990025d34f.aspx

Agence-France Presse (2015) 'China encourages environmental groups to sue polluters', *Guardian*, 7 January, available online at www.theguardian.com/environment/2015/jan/07/china-encourages-environmental-groups-to-sue-polluters

Agency Reporter (2015) 'China's middle class overtakes US as largest in world', *The Telegraph*, 14 October, available online at www.telegraph.co.uk/finance/china-business/11929794/Chinas-middle-class-overtakes-US-as-largest-in-the-world.html

Andrews-Speed, P. (2012) *The Governance of Energy in China*, Houndmills, Basingstoke: Palgrave

Ansar, A., Flyvbjerg, B., Budzier A. and Lunn, D. (2016) 'Does infrastructure investment lead to economic growth or economic fragility? Evidence from China', *Oxford Review of Economic Policy*, vol. 32, no. 3, 360–390, available online at http://oxrep.oxford journals.org/content/32/3/360.short

Arlidge, J. (2016) 'What's happened to the Great Malls of China?', *Sunday Times Style Magazine*, 24 January

Asafu-Adjeye, et al. (2015) *An eco-modernist manifesto*, – A Manifesto To Use Humanity's Extraordinary Powers In Service Of Creating A Good Anthropocene, available online at www.ecomodernism.org/

Associated Press (unsigned) (2016) 'Four-fifths of China's water from wells 'unsafe because of pollution', *Guardian*, 12 April, available online at www.theguardian.com/environment/2016/apr/12/four-fifths-of-chinas-water-from-wells-unsafe-because-of-pollution

Bäckstrand, K., Elgström, O. (2013) 'The EU's role in climate change negotiations: from leader to "leadiator"', *Journal of European Public Policy*, vol. 20, no. 10, 1369–1386

Barro, R. (2016) Economic Growth and Convergence, Applied Especially to China, *NBER Working Paper No. 21872*, Cambridge, MA: National Bureau of Economic Research, available online at www.nber.org/papers/w21872

Barton, D., Chen, Y. and Chun, A. (2013) 'Mapping China's middle class' *McKinsey Quarterly*, June, available online at www.mckinsey.com/insights/consumer_and_retail/mapping_chinas_middle_class

BBC (unsigned) (2006) Booming nations 'threaten Earth', *BBC News*, 12 January, available online at http://news.bbc.co.uk/1/hi/sci/tech/4604556.stm

BBC (unsigned) (2015) 'China smog: Beijing residents buy fresh air from Canada', *BBC online*, 21 December, available online at www.bbc.co.uk/news/world-asia-35155357

Beeson, M. (2010) 'The coming of environmental authoritarianism', *Environmental Politics*, vol. 19, no. 2, 276–294

Bell, D. (2015) *Political Meritocracy and the Limits of Democracy*, New Jersey: Princeton

Bernardini, O. and Galli, R. (1993) 'Dematerialization: long term trends in the intensity of use of materials and energy', *Futures*, 25

Bin, Z. (2016) 'Easing China's transition to a services economy', *Paulson Policy Memorandum*, London: Paulson Institute, available online at www.paulsoninstitute.org/wp-content/uploads/2016/04/PPM_Services_Zhang-Bin_English.pdf

Bloomberg News (unsigned) (2016a) 'China plans to tear down walls of gated condos and let public in', *Bloomberg*, 11 April, available online at www.bloomberg.com/news/articles/2016-04-11/china-plans-to-tear-down-walls-of-gated-condos-and-let-public-in

Bloomberg News (unsigned) (2016b) 'China's Idled Wind Farms May Spell Trouble for Renewable Energy', *Bloomberg News*, 29 July, available online at www.bloomberg.com/news/articles/2016-06-28/trouble-in-renewable-energy-spotted-in-china-s-idled-wind-farms

Blühdorn, I. (2000) 'Ecological Modernisation and Post-Ecologist Politics', in Spaargaren, G., Mol, A. and Buttel, F., *Environment and Global Modernity*, London: Sage, pp. 216–225

Bo, A., Weibin, L., Aiming, Z. and Wei, Z. (2015) 'China's Market-Oriented Reforms in the Energy and Environmental Sectors', *Pacific Energy Summit, National Bureau of Asian Research*, available online at http://nbr.org/downloads/pdfs/ETA/PES_2015_workingpaper_AnBo_et_al.pdf

BP (2015) *Statistical Review of World Energy*, available online at www.bp.com/en/global/corporate/energy-economics/statistical-review-of-world-energy.html

BP (2016) *Statistical Review of World Energy*, June, available online at www.bp.com/content/dam/bp/pdf/energy-economics/statistical-review-2016/bp-statistical-review-of-world-energy-2016-full-report.pdf

Brautigam, D. (2011) *The Dragon's Gift – The real story of China in Africa*, Oxford: Oxford University Press

Buckley, C. (2015) 'China's nuclear vision collides with villagers' fears', *New York Times*, 21 November, available online at www.nytimes.com/2015/11/22/world/asia/chinas-nuclear-vision-collides-with-villagers-fears.html?_r=2

Carter, N. (2001) *The Politics of the Environment*, Cambridge: Cambridge University Press

Carter, N. and Mol, P. (2007) 'China and the Environment: Domestic and transnational Dynamics of a Future Hegemon', in Carter, N. and Mol, P., *Environmental Governance in China*, London: Routledge

Carter, N. and Mol, P. (2007) *Environmental Governance in China*, London: Routledge

CENSERE Market Intelligence (2012) 'Solar Photovoltaic Energy Study 2012', *CENSERE*, available online at www.censere.com/index.php/en/component/hikashop/product/5-solar-pv-energy-study-3q2012/lang-en-GB

Center for Legal Assistance to Pollution Victims (2015) 'Chinese environmental lawyer takes on the powerful to give voice to vulnerable pollution victims', 22 March, available online at www.clapv.org/english_lvshi/meitibaodao_content.asp?id=59&title=Media&titlecontent=meitibaodao_list&lei1=107

Chen, C.-F. (2015) The Politics Of Renewable Energy In China: Towards A New Model Of Environmental Governance?, PhD, Bath: University of Bath, available online at http://opus.bath.ac.uk/46738/

Chen, C.-F., Noesselt, N. and Witt, L. (2016) 'Environmentalism without Democracy? Green Urbanization in China', *Paper to 2016 Political Studies Association (UK)*,

Brighton, 21–23 March, available online at www.psa.ac.uk/sites/default/files/conference/papers/2016/Conference%20Paper_PSA2016_3.pdf

Chen, K. and Chen, A. (2016) 'China faces massive closures of small thermal power plants', *Bloomberg Business News*, 29 August, available online at www.reuters.com/article/us-china-power-idUSKCN114103

Chew, J. (2015) 'Chinese Officials Admit They Faked Economic Figures, *Fortune*, 14 December, available online at http://fortune.com/2015/12/14/china-fake-economic-data/

Child, B. (2016) 'Leonardo DiCaprio says China can be climate change "hero"', *Guardian*, 21 March, available online at www.theguardian.com/film/2016/mar/21/leonardo-dicaprio-says-china-can-be-climate-change-hero

China Daily (unsigned) (2007) 'Local Officials Need Oversight', *China Daily*, 24 January, available online at www.chinadaily.com.cn/cndy/2007-01/24/content_790745.htm

China Digital Times (unsigned) (2012) 'Dirty Air and Succession Jitters in Beijing', *China Digital Times*, 12 August, available online at http://chinadigitaltimes.net/2012/06/dirty-air-and-succession-jitters-cloud-beijings-judgment/

China Digital Times (unsigned) (2015) 'Study: China's Air Pollution Kills 1.6 Million a Year', *China Digital Times*, available online at http://chinadigitaltimes.net/2015/08/study-chinas-air-pollution-kills-1-6-million-a-year/

Christoff, P. (1996) 'Ecological Modernisation, Ecological Modernities', *Environmental Politics*, vol. 5, no. 3, 476–500

Chu, B. (2013) *Chinese Whispers*, London: Phoenix,

Chun, Z. (2015) 'Residents of SW China City protest against foul air', *China Dialogue*, 15 April, available online at www.chinadialogue.net/blog/7844-Residents-of-SW-China-city-protest-against-foul-air/en

Clark, D. and Kiln (2013) 'Which fossil fuel companies are most responsible for climate change?', *Guardian*, 20 November, available online at www.theguardian.com/environment/interactive/2013/nov/20/which-fossil-fuel-companies-responsible-climate-change-interactive?CMP=twt_gu

Climate Action (unsigned) (2016) 'Beijing will close 2,500 polluting firms in 2016', 11 January, *Climate Action*, available online at www.climateactionprogramme.org/news/beijing_will_close_2500_polluting_firms_in_2016

Climate Action Tracker (unsigned) (2016) *Climate Action Tracker*, 'China', available online at http://climateactiontracker.org/countries/china.html

CNREC (2015) '2050 High Renewable Penetration Scenario and Roadmap Study', *National Development and Reform Commission*, p. 13, available online at www.efchina.org/Attachments/Report/report-20150420/China-2050-High-Renewable-Energy-Penetration-Scenario-and-Roadmap-Study-Executive-Summary.pdf

CNREC (2015) 'China 2050 High Renewable Energy Penetration Scenario and Roadmap Study', 26 May, China National Renewable Energy Centre, available online at www.cnrec.org.cn/english/result/2015-05-26-474.html

Cox, W. (2012) 'World Urban Areas Population Density – a 2012 update', *New Geography*, 3 May, available online at www.newgeography.com/content/002808-world-urban-areas-population-and-density-a-2012-update

Curran, E. (2015) 'State Companies: Back on China's To-Do List', *Bloomberg*, 30 July, available online at www.bloomberg.com/news/articles/2015-07-30/china-s-state-owned-companies-may-face-reform

Cusick, D. (2016) 'Chinese wind turbine maker is now world's largest', *Scientific American*, 23 March, available online at www.scientificAmerican.com/article/chinese-wind-turbine-maker-is-now-world-s-largest/

Dahlgreen, W. (2016) 'Global survey: Britain among least concerned in the world about climate change', *YouGov*, 29 January, available online at https://yougov.co.uk/news/2016/01/29/global-issues/

Dai, H., Xie, X., Xie, Y., Liu, J. and Masui, T. (2016) 'Green growth: The economic impacts of large-scale renewable energy development in China', *Applied Energy*, vol. 162, 435–449

Davies Boren, Z. (2016a) 'China stops building new coal-fired power plants', *Greenpeace Energydesk*, 24 March, available online at http://energydesk.greenpeace.org/2016/03/24/china-crackdown-new-coal-power-plants/

Davies Boren, Z. (2016b) 'Global coal bubble: Power plants in the pipeline to cost $1 trillion', *Greenpeace Energy Desk*, 30 March, available online at http://energydesk.greenpeace.org/2016/03/30/global-coal-boom-bust/

Delbeke, J. and Vis, P. (2015) *EU Climate Policy Explained*, London: Routledge

Department of Energy/Energy Information Administration (1993) *Annual Energy Outlook 1993*, Washington DC: Energy Information Service

Department of Environment Food and Rural Affairs (UK) (2016) 'Official Statistics – UK's Carbon Footprint', available online at www.gov.uk/government/statistics/uks-carbon-footprint

Duckett, J., Wang, H. (2013) 'Extending political participation in China: new opportunities for citizens in the policy process', *Journal of Asian Public Policy*, vol. 6, no. 3, 263–276

Duggan J. (2015) 'Welcome to Baoding, China's most polluted city', *Guardian*, 22 May, available online at www.theguardian.com/cities/2015/may/22/baoding-china-most-polluted-city-air-pollution-beijing-hebei

E3G (unsigned) (2015) 'Europe's Declining Gas Demand', *E3G*, 15 June, available online at www.e3g.org/news/media-room/europes-declining-gas-demand

Economist (unsigned) (2008) 'A lot to be angry about', *Economist*, 1 May, available online at www.economist.com/node/11293734

Economist (unsigned) (2010) 'Budding Greens', *Economist*, 15 June, available online at www.economist.com/node/16592268

Economist (unsigned) (2013) 'China bans new government buildings in corruption curb', *Economist*, 23 July

Economist (unsigned) (2014) 'Counting Ghosts', *Economist*, 4 January, available online at www.economist.com/news/china/21592628-china-opens-books-its-big-spending-local-governments-counting-ghosts

Economist (unsigned) (2015a) 'Deleveraging delayed, credit growth is still outstripping economic growth', *Economist*, 22 October, available online at www.economist.com/news/finance-and-economics/21676837-credit-growth-still-outstripping-economic-growth-deleveraging-delayed

Economist (unsigned) (2015b) 'China plans power trading exchanges to free up electricity prices', *Thomson-Reuters*, 12 November, available online at http://uk.reuters.com/article/china-power-reform-idUKL3N1372RG20151112

Elliott, D. (1978) *The Politics of Nuclear Power*, London: Pluto Press

Energy Information Administration (2015) 'Coal Use in China is Slowing', 17 September, available online at www.eia.gov/todayinenergy/detail.cfm?id=22972

Energy Post (unsigned) (2016) 'China's electricity mix: changing so fast that CO_2 emissions may have peaked', *Energy Post*, 1 March, available online at www.energypost.eu/chinas-electricity-mix-changing-fast-co2-emissions-may-peaked/

European Environment Agency (2015) 'Trends and projections in Europe 2015 Tracking progress towards Europe's climate and energy targets', Copenhagen: *European*

Environment Agency file:///C:/Users/Toke/Downloads/Trends%20and%20projections% 20in %20Europe%202015.pdf.pdf

Evans, S. (2015) 'Climate pledge puts China on course to peak emissions as early as 2027', *Carbon Brief*, 1 July, available online at www.carbonbrief.org/climate-pledge-puts-china-on-course-to-peak-emissions-as-early-as-2027

Evans-Pritchard, A. (2016) 'Fitch reveals the $2 trillion black hole in China's economy that heralds a lost decade', *Daily Telegraph*, 22 September, available online at www. telegraph.co.uk/business/2016/09/22/fitch-warns-bad-debts-in-china-are-ten-times-official-claims-sta/

Fei, M. (2012) Are Chinese Banks Hiding 'The Mother of All Debt Bombs'?, *The Diplomat*, 10 September, available online at http://thediplomat.com/2012/09/are-chinese-banks-hiding-the-mother-of-all-debt-bombs/

Fenby, J. (2014) *Will China Dominate the 21st Century?*, Cambridge: Polity Press

Field, K. (2015) 'While Tesla tackles cars BYD attacks diesel emissions with new truck line', *Cleantechnica*, 3 May, available online at http://cleantechnica.com/2016/05/03/ tesla-cars-byd-electric-trucks/

Fong, M. (2016) *One Child*, New York: Houghton Mifflin Harcourt

Frankfurt School-UNEP Collaborating Centre (2016) 'Global; Trends in Renewable Energy Investment', *UNEP-Bloomberg New Energy Finance*, available online at http:// fs-unep-centre.org/sites/default/files/publications/globaltrendsinrenewableenergy investment2016lowres_0.pdf?utm_content=buffera0c81&utm_medium=social&utm_ source=twitter.com&utm_campaign=buffer

Fulin, C. (ed.) 'Decisive Role of the Market – China Reform Research Report', *China Institute for Reform and Development*, Haikou, Hainan: China Intercontinental Press

Geal, S. and Hilton, I. (2014) 'China's Environmental Governance Challenge', in *Governing for Sustainability*, Worldwatch Institute, Washington: Island Press, pp. 129–137

Geels, F. (2002) 'Technological transitions as evolutionary reconfiguration processes: a multi-level perspective and a case-study', *Research Policy*, vol. 31, 1257–1274

Ghemawat, P. (2013) 'Why China's middle class will solve its air pollution problems', *Fortune*, 7 November, available online at http://fortune.com/2013/11/07/why-chinas-middle-class-will-solve-its-air-pollution-problems/

Gilley, B. (2012) 'Authoritarian environmentalism and China's response to climate change', *Environmental Politics*, vol. 21, no. 2, 287–307

Goldenburg, S. (2015) 'Obama's carbon reduction plan under attack from 24 states and Republicans', *Guardian*, 23 October, available online at www.theguardian.com/us-news/2015/oct/23/obama-carbon-coal-power-plant-epa-lawsuit-republicans

Goodrich, A. C., Powell, D. M., James, T. L., Woodhouse, M. and Buonassisi, T. (2013) 'Assessing the drivers of regional trends in solar photovoltaic manufacturing'. *Energy and Environmental Science*, vol. 6, 2811–2821, available online at http://pubs.rsc.org/ en/Content/ArticleLanding/2013/EE/C3EE40701b#!divAbstract

Goodrich, A., James, T. and Woodhouse, M. (2011) 'Solar PV Manufacturing Cost Analysis: U.S. Competitiveness in a Global Industry', *Presentation by NREL*, 11 October, available online at www.nrel.gov/docs/fy12osti/53938.pdf

Gosens, J. and Lu, Y. (2014) 'Prospects for global market expansion of China's wind turbine manufacturing industry', *Energy Policy*, vol. 67, pp. 301–318

Graham-Harrison, E. (2015) 'China warned over 'insane' plans for new nuclear power plants', *Guardian*, 25 May, available online at www.theguardian.com/world/2015/ may/25/china-nuclear-power-plants-expansion-he-zuoxiu?CMP=share_btn_tw

Grantham Research Institute (unsigned) (2016) 'China's 2030 peak-emissions target likely to be met within the next 10 years', *Grantham Research Institute*, 7 March, available online at www.lse.ac.uk/GranthamInstitute/news/chinese-emissions-may-already-have-peaked/

Green, F. and Stern, N., 'China's "new normal": structural change, better growth and peak emissions' *Grantham Institute on Climate Change and the Environment/ Centre for Climate Change and Economics Policy*, available online at www.lse.ac.uk/Grantham Institute/wp-content/uploads/2015/06/China_new_normal_web1.pdf

Greenpeace (2015) 'Laggards and leaders: the energy transition in BRICS countries', Hamburg, Germany: *Greenpeace International* available online at www.greenpeace.org/international/Global/international/briefings/climate/COP21/Greenpeace_BRICS_factsheets.pdf

Grubb, M., Sha, F., Spencer, T., Hughes, N., Zhang Z. and Agnolucci P. (2015) 'A review of Chinese CO2 emission projections to 2030: the role of economic structure and policy', *Climate Policy*, vol. 15, sup. 1, s7–s39

Guildford, G. (2013) 'Half of the Rice in Guangzhou Is Polluted', *The Atlantic*, 21 May, available online at www.theatlantic.com/china/archive/2013/05/half-of-the-rice-in-guangzhou-is-polluted/276098/

Guizhen, H., Mol, A. and Yonglong, L. (2016) 'Wasted Cities in China', *Environmental Development*', vol. 18, 2–13

Guoqing, W., Nadin, R. and Opitz-Stapleton, S. (2016) 'A balancing act: China's water resources and climate change', p. 104, in Nadin, R., Opitz-Stapleton, S. and Yinlong, X., *Climate Risk and Resilience in China*, London: Routledge pp. 96–128

Guorui, L. and Hanfu, H. (2012) 'Long struggle for a cleaner Lake Tai', *China Dialogue*, 14 February, available online at www.chinadialogue.net/article/4767-Long-struggle-for-a-cleaner-Lake-Tai-

Hager, M. (2014) 'China's Wu Hong continues to speak out on pollution in Lake Tai', available online at www.planetexperts.com/chinas-wu-lihong-continues-speak-pollution-lake-tai/

Hajer, M. (1995) *The Politics of Environmental Discourse*, Oxford: Oxford University Press

Herrendorf, B., Rogerson, R. and Valentinyi, A. (2013) *Growth and Structural Transformation*, NBER Working Paper No. 18996, Cambridge MA: National Bureau of Economic Research, available online at www.nber.org/papers/w18996

Hoffamn, S. and Sullivan, J. (2015) 'Environmental Protests Expose Weakness In China's Leadership', *Forbes Magazine*, 22 June, available online at www.forbes.com/sites/forbesasia/2015/06/22/environmental-protests-expose-weakness-in-chinas-leadership/

Hornby, L. and Lin, L. (2016) 'China Protest Against Nuclear Waste Plan', *Financial Times*, 7 August, available online at www.ft.com/content/dacb775a-5c7f-11e6-bb77-a121aa8abd95

Hove, A. (2016) 'A new opening for clean energy in China', *Paulson Institute*, 22 April, available online at www.paulsoninstitute.org/paulson-blog/2016/04/22/a-new-opening-for-clean-energy-in-china/

Howe, M. (2015) 'Non-Fossil Sources provide 25% of China's Electricity', *Cleantechnica*, 11 March, available online at http://cleantechnica.com/2015/03/11/non-fossil-fuel-sources-provide-25-chinas-electricity/

IEA statistics on electricity consumption for China (2016) *World Bank Data*, available online at http://data.worldbank.org/indicator/EG.USE.ELEC.KH.PC?locations=CN

Intergovernmental Panel on Climate Change Synthesis Report (2014) *Climate Change Synthesis Report – Summary for Policymakers*', p. 9, available online at www.ipcc.ch/pdf/assessment-report/ar5/syr/AR5_SYR_FINAL_SPM.pdf

International Hydropower Association (2016) *China*, available online at www.hydropower.org/country-profiles/china

IPE (2015) Institute of Public and Environmental Affairs, available online at www.ipe.org.cn/index.aspx

Inside Climate News (unsigned) (2016) 28 March, available online at http://insideclimatenews.org/news/28032016/china-wind-energy-projects-suspends-clean-energy-climate-change

Janicke, M. (2008) 'Ecological modernisation: new perspectives', *Journal of Cleaner Production*, vol. 16, 557–565, p. 563

Janicke, M. (2009) 'On Ecological and Political Modernisation' in Mol, A., Sonnenfield, D. and Spaargaren, G. (eds) *The Ecological Modernisation Reader*, London: Routledge, 28–41, p. 35

Jänicke, M. and Lindemann, S. (2010) 'Governing environmental innovations', *Environmental Politics*, vol. 19, no. 1, 127–141

Janicke, M., Monch, H., Rannenberg, T. and Simonis, U. (1989) 'Structural Change and Environmental Impact, *Environmental Monitoring and Assessment*, vol. 1, no. 2 99–114

Jingrong, L. (2012) 'Beijing releases PM10 density figures', *China.org.cn*, 12 January, available online at www.china.org.cn/environment/2012–01/12/content_24390197.htm

Jingxi, X. (2015) 'Blast in Fujian plant blamed on poor equipment', *China Daily*, 22 April, available online at www.chinadaily.com.cn/china/2015-04/22/content_20508516.htm

Johnson, A. (2016) 'China Grants Courts Greater Autonomy on Limited Matters', *New York Times*, 2 January, available online at www.nytimes.com/2016/01/03/world/asia/china-grants-courts-greater-autonomy-on-limited-matters.html?_r=0

Johnson, C. (2001) 'Japanese Capitalism Revisited', *Japanese Policy Research Institute*, available online at www.jpri.org/publications/occasionalpapers/op22.html

Johnson, T. (2016) 'Regulatory dynamism of environmental mobilization in urban China', *Regulation & Governance*, vol. 10, 14–28

Jordan, W. (2015) 'Global survey: Chinese most in favour of action on climate change', *YouGov*, 10 June, available online at https://yougov.co.uk/news/2015/06/07/Global-survey-

Kahya, D. (2015) *Greenpeace Energy Desk Dispatch*, 6 August, available online at http://energydesk.greenpeace.org/2015/08/06/daily-dispatch-china-media-monitoring-uk-oil-nuclear-world-wind/

Kaiman, J. (2014) 'China's eco-cities: empty of hospitals, shopping centres and people', *Guardian*, 14 April, available online at www.theguardian.com/cities/2014/apr/14/china-tianjin-eco-city-empty-hospitals-people

Klimont, Z., Smith, S. and Cofala, J. (2013) 'The last decade of global anthropogenic sulfur dioxide: 2000–2011 emissions', *Environmental Research Letters*, vol. 8, no. 1, available online at http://iopscience.iop.org/article/10.1088/1748–9326/8/1/014003/meta

Knutsen, H. and Ou, X. (2015) 'Ecological Modernisation and Dilemmas of Sustainable development in China', in Hansel, A. and Wethel, U. (eds), *Emerging economies and challenges to sustainability: Theories, strategies, local realities*, London: Routledge, pp. 65–78

Koehn, P. (2015) *China Confronts Climate Change*, London: Routledge

Korsbakken, J. and Peters G. (2016) 'China CO_2 emissions growth slowed in 2014 & 2015. May be down in 2015, but too close to call', supplemental to Korsbakken, *et al.*, available online at https://twitter.com/jikorsbakken

Korsbakken, J., Peters, G. and Andrew, R. (2016) 'Uncertainties around reductions in China's coal use and CO_2 emissions', *Nature Climate Change*, 28 March, available online at www.nature.com/nclimate/journal/vaop/ncurrent/full/nclimate2963.html

Kramer, J. (2015) 'Economic Insight: China: Zombification instead of a crash', *Commerzbank*, available online at https://research.commerzbank.com/delegate/publication?params=0%2B6I0ndQR829Lw8lNu54JbF9l3Hf2b6yTTLDsi%2BvIrG9dLM6sGJ1smz5YSY6etBo

Kyo, L. (2015) 'A contentious chemical plant in China has exploded for the second time in two years', *Quartz*, 7 April, available online at http://qz.com/377929/a-contentious-chemical-plant-in-china-has-exploded-for-the-second-time-in-two-years/

Lai, K., Wong, C. and Cheng, T. (2012) 'Ecological modernisation of Chinese export manufacturing via green logistics management and its regional implications', *Technological Forecasting and Social Change*, vol. 79, 766–770

Langhelle, O. (2000) 'Why ecological modernization and sustainable development should not be conflated', *Journal of Environmental Policy and Planning*, vol. 2 no. 4, 303–322

Langhelle, O. (2009) 'Why Ecological Modernisation and Sustainable Development should not be conflated', in Mol, A., Sonnenfield, D. and Spaargaren, G. (eds), *The Ecological Modernisation Reader*, London: Routledge, pp. 391–417

Larson, C. (2012) 'China's Ma Jun on the fight to clean up Beijing's dirty air', *Yale Environment 360*, available online at http://e360.yale.edu/feature/chinas_ma_jun_on_the_fight_to_clean_up_beijings_dirty_air/2515/

Larson, C. (2015) 'China gets a little more fresh air', *Bloomberg Business Week*, 16 August, available online at www.bloomberg.com/news/articles/2015-08-06/pollution-china-gets-a-little-more-fresh-air

Larson, E. (2014) 'China's Growing Coal Use Is World's Growing Problem', 27 January, available online at www.climatecentral.org/blogs/chinas-growing-coal-use-is-worlds-growing-problem-16999

Le Beau, P. (2016) 'China's BYD looks to double electric vehicle sales', *CNBC*, 28 April, available online at www.cnbc.com/2016/04/28/chinas-byd-looks-to-double-electric-vehicle-sales.html

Lee, I., M. Syed and Xueyan, L. (2013) 'China's Path to Consumer-Based Growth: Reorienting Investment and Enhancing Efficiency,' IMF *Working Paper 13/83*, Washington: International Monetary Fund

Levitt, T. (2015) 'Ma Jun: China has reached its environmental tipping point', *Guardian*, May 19, available online at www.theguardian.com/sustainable-business/2015/may/19/ma-jun-china-has-reached-its-environmental-tipping-point?utm_medium=twitter&utm_source=dlvr.it

Lewis, J. (2013) *Green Innovation in China*, New York: Columbia Press, p. 141

Li, H. (2015) *China's New Energy Revolution*, New York: McGraw Education

Lindon, H. (2016) 'China's National Energy Administration: Plan Is To Triple Solar PV Capacity By 2020', *Sustainnovate*, 26 March, available online at http://sustainnovate.ae/en/industry-news/detail/chinas-national-energy-administration-plan-is-to-triple-solar-pv-capacity-b

Liu, C. (2011) 'China Tackles Energy-Wasting Buildings', *Scientific American*, 27 July, available online at www.scientificAmerican.com/article/china-tackles-energy-wasting-buildings/

Liu, C. (2016) 'Facing Grid Constraints, China Puts a Chill on New Wind Energy Projects', 28 March, available online at https://insideclimatenews.org/news/28032016/china-wind-energy-projects-suspends-clean-energy-climate-change

Liu, W., Zhang, J., Bluemling, B., Mol, A. and Wan, C. (2015) Public participation in energy saving retrofitting of residential buildings in China, *Applied Energy*, vol. 147, 287–296

Lo, K. (2015) 'How authoritarian is the environmental governance of China?', *Environment Science & Policy*, vol. 54, 152–159

Ma, J. (2004 – English edition) *China's Water Crisis*, Norwalk, CT: EastBridge

Ma, W. (2014) 'Meet the Biggest Polluter in China's Most Polluted City', *Wall Street Journal*, 16 September, available online at www.wsj.com/articles/economics-versus-pollution-in-chinas-dirtiest-city-1410901992

Malik, M. (2015) 'Lower-Cost Wind and Solar Will Drive Energy Storage Technology', *Bloomberg Technology*, available online at www.bloomberg.com/news/articles/2015-11-17/lower-cost-wind-and-solar-will-drive-energy-storage-technology

Martens, S. (2007) 'Public Participation with Chinese Characteristics: Citizen Consumers in China's Environmental Management', p. 66, in Carter, N. and Mol, P., 'China and the Environment: Domestic and transnational Dynamics of a Future Hegemon', in Carter, N. and Mol, P., *Environmental Governance in China*, London: Routledge, pp. 63–82

Mathews, J. and Tan, H. (2015) *China's Renewable Energy Revolution*, Houndsmill Basingstoke: Palgrave

Maughan, T. (2015) 'The dystopian lake filled by the world's tech lust', *BBC*, 2 April, available online at www.bbc.com/future/story/20150402-the-worst-place-on-earth

McCrone, A. (ed.) (2016) 'Global Trends in Renewable Energy Investment 2016', *UNEP/Bloomberg New Energy Finance*, available online at http://fs-unep-centre.org/sites/default/files/publications/globaltrendsinrenewableenergyinvestment2016lowres_0.pdf, see pp. 31–32 in particular

McDonald, I. (2015) 'Hang in There Australia, Your Exports to China Will Double', *Bloomberg Business*, 19 October, available online at www.bloomberg.com/news/articles/2015-10-19/hang-in-there-australia-your-exports-to-china-will-double

McKay, D. (2009) 'Sustainable Energy – Without the Hot Air', Cambridge: UIT, pp. 194–195, available online at www.withouthotair.com/c26/page_194.shtml

McKinsey Quarterly (2015) 'China's rising internet wave', January, available online at www.mckinsey.com/insights/high_tech_telecoms_internet/chinas_rising_internet_wave_wired_companies

Meadows, Donella H., *et al.* (1972) *The Limits to Growth*, New York: Universe Books

Milborrow, D. (2016) 'Global Costs Analysis – the year offshore wind power costs fell', *WindPower Monthly*, 29 January, available online at www.windpowermonthly.com/article/1380738/global-costs-analysis-year-offshore-wind-costs-fell

Mol, A. (1995) *The Refinement of Production – Ecological Modernisation Theory and the Chemical Industry*, Utrecht: Van Arkel

Mol, A. (2006) 'Environment and Modernity in transitional China: Frontiers of Ecological Modernisation', *Development and Change*, vol. 37 no. 1, 29–56, pp. 32–33

Mol, A., Sonnenfield, D. and Spaargaren, G. (eds) (2009) *The Ecological Modernisation Reader*, London: Routledge

Mol, A., Spargaaren, G. and Sonnenfeld, D. (2009) 'Ecological Modernisation: Three Decades of Policy Practice and Theoretical Reflection' in Mol, A., Sonnenfield, D. and Spaargaren, G., *The Ecological Modernisation Reader*, London: Routledge, pp. 3–16

Moody, A. (2015) 'Dissecting China's five year plan', *Daily Telegraph*, 23 November, available online at www.telegraph.co.uk/sponsored/china-watch/politics/12006280/china-five-year-plan.html

Mooney, C. (2015) 'Here's how much faster wind and solar are growing than fossil fuels',

Washington Post, 9 March, available online at www.washingtonpost.com/news/energy-environment/wp/2015/03/09/heres-how-much-faster-wind-and-solar-are-growing-than-fossil-fuels/

Morris, C. (2016) 'How Germany helped bring down the cost of PV', *The Energy Transition*, 20 January, available online at http://energytransition.de/2016/01/how-germany-helped-bring-down-the-cost-of-pv/

Mukerjee, M. (2015) 'The Impending Dam Disaster in the Himalayas', *Scientific American*, 1 August, available online at www.scientificAmerican.com/article/the-impending-dam-disaster-in-the-himalayas/

Munro, N. (2014) 'Profiling the Victims: public awareness of pollution-related harm in China', *Journal of Contemporary China*, vol. 23, no. 86, 314–329

Myllyvyrta, L. (2015) 'China coal use falls: CO_2 reduction this year could equal UK total emissions over same period', *Greenpeace Energy Desk*, 14 May, available online at http://energydesk.greenpeace.org/2015/05/14/china-coal-consumption-drops-further-carbon-emissions-set-to-fall-by-equivalent-of-uk-total-in-one-year/

Nadin, R., Opitz-Stapleton, S. and Yinlong, X. (2016) *Climate Risk and Resilience in China*, London: Routledge

National Bureau of Statistics of China (2014) 'Total Consumption of Energy and its Composition', available online at www.stats.gov.cn/tjsj/ndsj/2014/indexeh.htm

National Energy Administration (2016) 国家能源局发布2015年全社会用电量, 15 January, available online at www.nea.gov.cn/2016-01/15/c_135013789.htm

Naughton, B. (2007) *The Chinese Economy*, Cambridge, MA: MIT Press

Ng, E. (2016) 'China Shenhua delays coal power plant construction on orders from Beijing', *South China Morning Post*, 29 March, available online at www.scmp.com/business/companies/article/1931597/china-shenhua-delays-coal-power-plant-construction-orders-beijing

Ng, S., Mabey, N. and Gaventa, J. (2016) 'Pulling Ahead On Clean Technology China's 13th Five Year Plan Challenges Europe's Low Carbon Competitiveness, E3G, available online at www.e3g.org/docs/E3G_Report_on_Chinas_13th_5_Year_Plan.pdf

Ng Wei, A. and Gaventa, J. (2016) 'China plans to dominate clean tech race', E3G, 17 March, available online at www.e3g.org/library/china-accelerates-while-europe-deliberates-on-the-clean-energy-transition

Nykvist, B. and Nilsson, M. (2015) 'Rapidly falling costs of battery packs for electric vehicles', *Nature Climate Change*, vol. 5, 329–332, p. 329

Nylander, J. (2015) 'Sweden's Top Economist Puts China's GDP Growth At 3%, But Others Are Even Less Optimistic', *Forbes Magazine*, 23 September, available online at www.forbes.com/sites/jnylander/2015/09/23/swedens-top-economist-puts-chinas-gdp-growth-at-3-others-are-less-optimistic/#1a0a30c62243

Overton, T. (2016) 'Despite Policy Shifts, China Faces Huge Coal-Fired Overcapacity', *Power*, 3 August, available online at www.powermag.com/despite-policy-shifts-china-faces-huge-coal-fired-overcapacity/?mypower

Pei, M. (2015) 'China's war on corruption could hasten Communist Party's decline', *Nikkei Asian Review*, 19 May, available online at http://asia.nikkei.com/Viewpoints/Perspectives/China-s-war-on-corruption-could-hasten-communist-party-s-decline?page=2

Pettis, M. (2013) *Avoiding the Fall: China's Economic Restructuring*, Washington: Carnegie Endowment for International Peace

Pressman, M. (2016) 'Number of electric cars world wide climbs to1.3 million', *Vannex*, 1 March, available online at http://evannex.com/blogs/news/77801925-number-of-electric-cars-worldwide-climbs-to-1-3-million-tesla-model-s-takes-top-spot-among-new-ev-registrations

Price, L., Levine, M., Zhou, N., Fridley, D., Aden, N., Lu, H., McNeil, M., Zheng, N., Qin, Y. and Yowargana, P. (2011) 'Assessment of China's energy-saving and emission-reduction accomplishments and opportunities during the 11th Five Year Plan', *Energy Policy*, vol. 39, 2165–2178, p. 2165

Qin, L. (2014) 'China's pollution protests could be slowed by stronger rule of law', *China Dialogue*, 12 November, available online at www.chinadialogue.net/article/show/single/en/7483-China-s-pollution-protests-could-be-slowed-by-stronger-rule-of-law

Randall, R. (2016) 'We've almost reached peak fossil fuels for electricity', *Bloomberg New Energy Finance*, 13 June, available online at www.bloomberg.com/news/articles/2016-06-13/we-ve-almost-reached-peak-fossil-fuels-for-electricity

Randall, T. (2016) 'Here's how electric cars will cause the next oil crisis', *Bloomberg*, 25 February, available online at www.bloomberg.com/features/2016-ev-oil-crisis/?cmpid=yhoo.headline

Roach, S. (2015) 'China's services sector is growing, but far too few Chinese are spending', *South China Morning Post*, 27 November, available online at www.scmp.com/comment/insight-opinion/article/1884050/chinas-services-sector-growing-far-too-few-chinese-are

Russell Jones, R. (2015) 'To destroy human civilisation we just need to continue with business as usual', *Guardian*, letter, 10 December

Sanderson, H. and Forsyth, M. (2013) *China's Superbank*, Hoboken, New Jersey: Wiley

Schlosberg, D. and Ronfret, S. (2008) 'Ecological modernisation, American style', *Environmental Politics*, vol. 17, no. 2, 254–275

Schneider, F. (2013) 'The Crisis of China's Environmental Pollution: What does it Take to Clean Up the PRC?' *Politics East Asia*, available online at www.politicseastasia.com/studying/chinas-environmental-pollution/

Schneider, M. and Froggatt, A. (2015) 'The World Nuclear Industry Status Report', *Mycle Schneider Consulting*, p. 34, available online at www.worldnuclearreport.org/IMG/pdf/20151023MSC-WNISR2015-V4-LR.pdf

Schreurs, M. (2013) 'Climate Change in an Authoritarian State: The Ambivalent Case of China', p. 459, in Dryzek, J., Norgaard, R. and Schlosberg D., *The Oxford Handbook of Climate Change and Society*, Oxford: Oxford University Press, 449–463

Shabecoff, P. (2000) *Earth Rising – American Environmentalism in the 21st century*, Washington DC: Island Press

Shapiro, J. (2016) *China's Environmental Challenges*, Cambridge: Polity Press

Shaw, V. (2016) 'China: Qinghai targets additional 7.1 GW of renewables in 2016', *PV Magazine*, 4 January, available online at www.pv-magazine.com/news/details/beitrag/china-qinghai-targets-additional-71-gw-of-renewables-in-2016_100022603/#ixzz46G79mCsb

Shepard, C. and Hornby, L. (2016) 'China's Wind Energy Groups Cry Foul Over Grid Curbs', *Financial Times*, 31 March, available online at https://next.ft.com/content/1743dfb8-f729-11e5-803c-d27c7117d132

Shepherd, C. (2016) 'China shifts gear to drive electric car development', *Financial Times*, 25 February, available online at www.ft.com/cms/s/0/a55e7d36-db8a-11e5-a72f-1e7744c66818.html#axzz47DkUlxYl

Shepherd, W. (2015) 'After "Under the Dome": Can China solve its air pollution crisis?', *City Metrics*, 25 March, available online at www.citymetric.com/horizons/after-under-dome-can-china-solve-its-air-pollution-crisis-877

Shi, H. and Zhang, L. (2007) 'China's Environmental Governance of Rapid Industrialisation', pp. 132–133 in Carter, N. and Mol, P., 'China and the Environment: Domestic and transnational Dynamics of a Future Hegemon', in Carter, N. and Mol, P., *Environmental Governance in China*, London: Routledge, pp. 123–144

Shoemaker, B. (2014) 'China Pollution – Blue Skies over Beijing', *The Diplomat*, 10 November, available online at http://thediplomat.com/2014/11/china-pollution-blue-skies-over-beijing/

Smith, M. (2016) 'While fossils crashed in 2015, clean energy soared', *Clean Energy Canada*, 29 February, available online at http://cleanenergycanada.org/while-fossils-crashed-in-2015-clean-energy-soared/

Smith, N. (2015) 'China's economy is worse than you think', *Bloomberg View*, 3 November, available online at www.bloombergview.com/articles/2015-11-03/china-s-slump-might-be-much-worse-than-we-thought

Sonnenfield, D. (2009) 'Contradictions of Ecological Modernisation: Pulp and Paper Manufacturing in South East Asia', in Mol, A., Sonnenfield, D. and Spaargaren, G., *The Ecological Modernisation Reader*, London: Routledge, 372–390,

Sonnenfield, D. and Rock M. (2009) 'Ecological Modernisation in Asian and other Emerging Economies', in Sonnenfield, D. (2009) 'Contradictions of Ecological Modernisation: Pulp and Paper Manufacturing in South East Asia', in Mol, A., Sonnenfield, D. and Spaargaren, G., *The Ecological Modernisation Reader*, London: Routledge, 359–371

Soo, Z. (2016) 'China can "easily" support all its energy demand using homegrown solar power, says Tesla's Musk in Hong Kong', *South China Morning Post*, 26 January, available online at www.scmp.com/tech/innovation/article/1905467/china-can-easily-support-all-its-energy-demand-using-homegrown-solar

Spargaaren, G. (2009) 'Sustainable Consumption: A Theoretical and Environmental Policy Perspective', in Mol, A., Sonnenfield, D. and Spaargaren, G. (eds) *The Ecological Modernisation Reader*, London: Routledge, pp. 318–333

Spegele, B. (2016) 'China Looks to Placate Nuclear-Project Protesters', *Wall Street Journal*, available online at www.wsj.com/articles/china-cracks-down-on-nuclear-project-protests-1470734568

Sputnik International (unsigned) (2015) 'China's first battery powered plane cleared for production', *Sputnik International*, 15 November, available online at http://sputnik news.com/asia/20151205/1031279735/china-battery-powered-plane.html

Stanway, D. and Chen. K. (2016) 'False emissions reporting undermines China's pollution fight', *Reuters*, 17 January, available online at http://uk.reuters.com/article/us-china-power-emissions-idUKKCN0UV0XS

Stanway, S. (2015) 'China risks social conflict if war on pollution lags – govt researchers', *Reuters*, 10 April, available online at www.reuters.com/article/us-china-environment-idUSKBN0N10N220150410

State of Green (2015) 'District Heating In The Chinese City Anshan', *Danfoss*, available online at https://stateofgreen.com/en/profiles/danfoss/solutions/district-heating-in-the-chinese-city-anshan

Stern, D. (2004) 'The Rise and Fall of the Environmental Kuznets Curve', *World Development*, vol. 32, no. 8, pp. 1419–1439

Stringer, D. (2014) 'China's rare earth toxic time bomb to spur mining boom', *Bloomberg Business*, 4 July, available online at www.bloomberg.com/news/articles/2014-06-03/china-s-rare-earth-toxic-time-bomb-to-spur-12-billion-of-mines

Szarka, J. (2012) 'Climate challenges, ecological modernization and technological forcing: policy lessons from a comparative US-EU analysis', *Global Environmental Politics*, vol. 12, no. 2, 87–109

Target Map (2016) *Solar pv Map of China*, available online at www.targetmap.com/viewer.aspx?reportId=46583

TEDA Wind (2008) 'Key Industries Brief', *Tianjin Economic Development Agency*, available online at http://en1.investteda.org/aboutteda/keyindustriesbrief/wind/default.htm

Teets, J. (2014) *Civil Society under Authoritarianism: the China Model*, Cambridge: Cambridge University Press

The World Bank/Development Centre for Research of the State Council of the People's Republic of China (2014) *Urban China*, Washington, DC: World Bank Group, available online at www.worldbank.org/content/dam/Worldbank/document/EAP/China/WEB-Urban-China.pdf

Timmons, H. (2013) 'Consider the e-bike: Can 200 million Chinese be wrong?' *Quartz*, 22 February, available online at http://qz.com/137518/consumers-the-world-over-love-electric-bikes-so-why-do-us-lawmakers-hate-them/

Toke, D. (2011) *Ecological Modernisation and Renewable Energy*, London: Palgrave

Trading Economics (2016) *Indicators*, available online at www.tradingeconomics.com/

Tylecote, R. (2015) 'Ownership and Innovation in Chinese solar photovoltaic firms: an analysis of the effects of state, private, and foreign shareholding on patenting performance', PhD thesis, Imperial College, London, available online at https://spiral.imperial.ac.uk/handle/10044/1/26286

Tyler, L. (2016) 'Vestas Edges Out Goldwind For Wind Turbine Market Share', *North American Wind Power*, 31 March, available online at http://nawindpower.com/vestas-edges-out-goldwind-for-wind-turbine-market-share

US Environmental Protection Agency (2015) *Global Greenhouse Gas Emissions Data*, www3.epa.gov/climatechange/ghgemissions/global.html

US Energy Information Service (2016) *International Energy Outlook 2016*, available online at www.eia.gov/forecasts/ieo/pdf/emissions.pdf

Wall Street Journal Staff (2013) 'Loans to Steel traders Pose Risk', *Wall Street Journal*, 4 February, available online at http://blogs.wsj.com/deals/2013/02/04/loans-to-steel-traders-in-china-pose-risk/

Wang S., Li, Q. and Zhou, C. (2016) 'The relationship between economic growth, energy consumption, and CO_2 emissions: Empirical evidence from China', *Science of the Total Environment*, vol. 542, Part A, 360–371

Wang, G. and Zheng, Y. (eds) (2013) *China: Development and Governance*, Singapore: World Scientific

Wang, S. (2016) 'China hopes to build a $50 trillion global wind and solar power grid by 2050', *Shanghaiist Daily*, 17 July, available online at http://shanghaiist.com/2016/07/17/global_energy_grid.php?utm_content=bufferfdea7&utm_medium=social&utm_source=twitter.com&utm_campaign=buffer

Wang, U. (2014) 'Guess Who Are The Top 10 Solar Panel Makers In the World?', *Forbes*, 3 December, available online at www.forbes.com/sites/uciliawang/2014/12/03/guess-who-are-the-top-10-solar-panel-makers-in-the-world/#76b0bcf92812

Wang, Z., Zhu, Y., Zhu, Y. and Shi, Y. (2016) 'Energy structure change and carbon emission trends in China', *Energy*, vol. 115, 369–377, p. 376

Watkins, E. (1954) 'Air pollution aspects of the London fog of December 1952', *Quarterly Journal of the Royal Meteorological Society*, vol. 80, no. 344, 267–271

Watts, J. (2010) *When a Billion Chinese Jump*, London: Faber and Faber

Weale, A. (1992) *The New Politics of Pollution*, Manchester: Manchester University Press

Whiting, S. (2001) *Power and Wealth in Rural China*, Cambridge: Cambridge University Press

Wildau, G. (2015) 'Growth data buoy China at "pivotal moment" in economic rebalancing', *Financial Times*, 19 October, available online at www.ft.com/cms/s/2/df727b0c-763c-11e5-8564-b4bb9a521c63.html#axzz3vWZVxZY5

Wildau, G. and Hornby, L. (2016) 'China GDP grows 6.7 per cent in second quarter on boost from infrastructure', *Financial Times*, 15 June, available online at www.ft.com/content/103712f6-4979-11e6-8d68-72e9211e86ab

Wilson, L. (2014) 'How big is a house', *Shrink That Footprint*, available online at http://shrinkthatfootprint.com/how-big-is-a-house

Woetzel, J. and Seong, J. (2015) 'What You Need to Know About China's Surprising Strengths in Innovation', *Huffington Post*, available online at www.huffingtonpost.com/jonathan-woetzel/china-strength-innovation_b_8359026.html

World Bank (2011) 'CO2 emissions per capita in metric tons', available online at http://data.worldbank.org/indicator/EN.ATM.CO2E.PC

World Bank (2015) *Per Capita Economic Growth Data*, available online at http://data.worldbank.org/indicator/NY.GDP.PCAP.KD.ZG

World Bank (2015) *Population Growth Data*, available online at http://data.worldbank.org/indicator/SP.POP.GROW

World Bank (2016) *Carbon Emissions*, available online at http://data.worldbank.org/indicator/EN.ATM.CO2E.PC

World Energy Council (2015) 'Energy Efficiency Indicators', available online at www.wec-indicators.enerdata.eu/

World Health Organisation (2016) 'Ambient (outdoor) air pollution in cities database', *World Health Organisation*, available online at www.who.int/phe/health_topics/outdoorair/databases/cities/en/, see 'urban outdoor air pollution database, by country and city'

World Nuclear Association (2016) 'Nuclear Power in China', *World Nuclear Association*, available online at www.world-nuclear.org/information-library/country-profiles/countries-a-f/china-nuclear-power.aspx

World Steel Association (2016) *Top Steel Producing Companies*, available online at www.worldsteel.org/statistics/top-producers.html

Wu, Y. (2012) 'Energy intensity and its determinants in China's regional economies', *Energy Policy* 41, 703–711, p. 704

Xiaopo Lake Wetland Tourism Development Damage Case, available online at www.clapv.org/english_lvshi/ZhiChiAnJian_content.asp?id=70&title=Support%20cases&titlecontent=PD_zhichianjian

Yang, Z. (2015) 'China still lagging on fuel consumption in 2014', *International Council for Clean Transportation*, 18 September, available online at www.theicct.org/blogs/staff/china-still-lagging-fuel-consumption-2014

Yin, C. (2016) 'Failing eco-protection bureaus in the firing line', *China Daily*, 17 February, available online at http://europe.chinadaily.com.cn/china/2016-02/17/content_23515142.htm

York, R. and Rosa, E. (2003) 'Key Challenges to Ecological Modernization Theory – Institutional Efficacy, Case Study Evidence, Units of Analysis, and the Pace of Eco-Efficiency', *Organisation and the Environment*, vol. 16, no. 3, pp. 273–288

Yu, H., Tang, B., Yuan, X., Wang, S. and Wei, M. (2015) 'How do the appliance energy standards work in China? Evidence from room air conditioners', *Energy in Buildings*, vol. 86, 833–840

Yunfei, G. E. (2015) 'China will increase green buildings to 50% by 2020', CCTV, 10 December, available online at http://english.cntv.cn/2015/12/10/VIDE144972276 2008895.shtml

Zhang, B. and Cao, C. (2015) 'Policy: Four gaps in China's new environmental law', *Nature*, 517, 433–434, available online at www.nature.com/news/policy-four-gaps-in-china-s-new-environmental-law-1.16736

Zhang, B., Fei, H., He, P., Xu, Y., Zhanfeng, D. and Young, O. (2016) 'The indecisive role of the market in China's SO2 and COD emissions trading', *Environmental Politics*, vol. 25, no. 5, 875–898

Zhang, H. (2011) 'Green bounty hunters: engaging Chinese citizens in local environmental enforcement', *Woodrow Wilson Center for International Scholars – China Environment Series*, Issue 11, 2010–11, pp. 137–153, available online at www.wilsoncenter.org/sites/default/files/CES%2011%20%20Full%20Publication.pdf

Zhang, L., Mol, A. and Sonnenfeld, D. (2007) 'The interpretation of ecological modernisation in China', *Environmental Politics*, vol. 16, no. 4, 659–668, p. 665

Zhang, L., Gudmundsson, O., Thorsen,J., Lia, H. and Svendse, S. (2014) 'Optimization of China´s centralized domestic hot water system by applying Danish elements', *The 6th International Conference on Applied Energy – ICAE2014, Energy Procedia 61*, 2833–2840, p. 2835, available online at www.sciencedirect.com/science/article/pii/S1876610214033463

Zhou, Y. (2015) 'State power and environmental initiatives in China: Analyzing China's green building program through an ecological modernization', *Geoforum*, vol. 6, 1–12

Index

Page numbers in *italics* denote tables, those in **bold** denote figures.